Lecture Notes in Social Networks

More information about this series at http://www.springer.com/series/8768

Mehmet Kaya • Reda Alhajj

Editors

Influence and Behavior Analysis in Social Networks and Social Media

 Springer

Editors
Mehmet Kaya
Department of Computer Engineering
Firat University
Elazig, Turkey

Reda Alhajj
Department of Computer Science
University of Calgary
Calgary, AB, Canada

ISSN 2190-5428 ISSN 2190-5436 (electronic)
Lecture Notes in Social Networks
ISBN 978-3-030-02591-5 ISBN 978-3-030-02592-2 (eBook)
https://doi.org/10.1007/978-3-030-02592-2

Library of Congress Control Number: 2018913958

This Springer imprint is published by the registered company Springer Nature Switzerland AG
The registered company address is: Gewerbestrasse 11, 6330 Cham, Switzerland

Contents

Social Network to Improve the Educational Experience with the Deployment of Different Learning Models

Paúl Esteban Vintimilla-Tapia, Jack Fernando Bravo-Torres,
Pablo Leonidas Gallegos-Segovia, Esteban Fernando Ordóñez-Morales,
Martín López-Nores, and Yolanda Blanco-Fernández

1 Introduction

Until November 2017, Facebook recorded a 731.43% increase in the number of active users[1]; while YouTube, meanwhile, increased by 3000% its number of video hours uploaded[2] and Twitter 2000% its number of tweets published,[3] compared to 2009. This is evidence of the rapid growth of social networks (SNs) in recent years [1]. The pervasiveness of SNs empowers them to be present in every aspect of our lives: from comfort, security, entertainment, and e-commerce to political campaigns [2–4]. Education is not a process alien to this phenomenon, since the way in which students communicate, collaborate, and learn is being significantly modified [5]. In this sense, although SNs were initially designed solely to support interpersonal relationships, they can be used as valid tools for student-teacher purposes, particularly to innovate student/teacher relationships.

---

[1]https://www.socialbakers.com/statistics/facebook/.

[2]https://fortunelords.com/youtube-statistics/.

[3]https://www.omnicoreagency.com/twitter-statistics/.

P. E. Vintimilla-Tapia (✉) · J. F. Bravo-Torres · E. F. Ordóñez-Morales
Grupo de Investigación GITEL, Universidad Politécnica Salesiana, Cuenca, Ecuador
e-mail: pvintimilla@ups.edu.ec; jbravo@ups.edu.ec; eordonez@ups.edu.ec

P. L. Gallegos-Segovia
Grupo de Investigación GIHP4C, Universidad Politécnica Salesiana, Cuenca, Ecuador
e-mail: pgallegos@ups.edu.ec

M. López-Nores · Y. Blanco-Fernández
AtlantTIC Research Center, University of Vigo, Vigo, Spain
e-mail: mlnores@det.uvigo.es; yolanda@det.uvigo.es

© Springer Nature Switzerland AG 2019   1
M. Kaya, R. Alhajj (eds.), *Influence and Behavior Analysis in Social Networks
and Social Media*, Lecture Notes in Social Networks,
https://doi.org/10.1007/978-3-030-02592-2_1

On the one hand, they help to enhance the learning environment, achieving a greater commitment between the class and its participants, promoting a sense of belonging to a community of studies, which is of vital importance for the development of a correct educational process [6, 7]. They also facilitate outreach to experts in various fields, improving knowledge transfer [8]. On the other hand, from a technological point of view, today's mobile devices incorporate powerful electronic and telecommunications systems, which promote the use of different learning models through SNs [9]. This can be seen in the academic reasons why they are used. For example, when a wiki is consulted, a book or a scientific database is accessed, and self-learning has happened [10]; instead, when video material from any platform is viewed or an instant messaging service is used to specifically contact an individual, it initiates tutorial or peer learning, depending on whether the contact is with a teacher/expert or a classmate [11, 12]; and, finally, when a forum is used or virtual communities are created—whose members have common affinities—to resolve any concerns, collaborative learning is the key [13, 14]. In this way, the geo-temporal barriers of formal and teacher-centralized learning are broken down to encourage informal and student-centralized learning, giving the possibility of accessing and sharing knowledge when necessary [15].

Despite all the advantages offered by SNs in education, different studies have found serious difficulties that cannot be ignored [6, 16–18]. Firstly, their levels of security and privacy are not adequate, facilitating the possibility of tracking any user, whether students or teachers, and accessing their personal lives [16, 17]. They can also be used for nonacademic purposes, while a learning/teaching process is being carried out, which leads to a waste of time and, therefore, a decrease in the quality of study. Continuing with the same problem, since there are no records of the activities carried out by students, it is not possible to monitor their progress, preventing teachers from improving their teaching techniques [18]. In addition, students have a different view of the use of SNs, as they focus solely on using them for social purposes, which may result in a lack of motivation when it comes to using them as a means of learning [17]. Finally, there may be a process of information isolation or over-information, in which it is not possible to contact experts who manage each study topic in an optimal way, losing their valuable knowledge [19].

To solve the problems described, in this paper we broadened the concept of OPPIA (OPPortunistic Intelligent Ambient of learning), a social platform focused on developing different models of informal learning, according to the needs and preferences of each individual. It brings students closer to teachers or experts in different subjects, supporting better educational opportunities [20].

OPPIA is a platform that provides services with the necessary resources to strengthen and facilitate knowledge transfer among its users. Furthermore, the deployment of sporadic learning networks (SLNs)—a type of SNs that is created for a limited period of time—enables the formation of collaborative groups, which connects students with users who can resolve their concerns, regardless of whether or not prior contact has been established between them [20, 21]. In this way, the problem of information isolation is broken. It also incorporates different databases that store statistical information on the progress of its members.

This paper is organized as follows. Section 2 shows the theoretical development of SNs in education and how current technologies are being used by teachers and students. Section 3 presents the development of sporadic learning networks, which are one of OPPIA's most significant contributions. Section 4 describes OPPIA, its layer model, architecture, and main services. In Sect. 5, a first implementation of the platform is developed, and its acceptance by students is evaluated. Finally, Sect. 6 presents the main conclusions and future work.

2 Social Networks in Education

Social networks (SNs) are defined as *a group of Internet-based applications that builds on the ideological and technological foundations of Web 2.0 and that allows the creation and exchange of user-generated content* [22]. Thus, it is possible that they may be seen as a set of technological systems related to the collaboration and formation of communities for interpersonal purposes, being their most significant applications social platforms, wikis, blogs, and multimedia platforms [5].

Because of their ability to form communities, where students, teachers, and experts are grouped in the same virtual space, they can be considered educational tools [23]. However, for them to play this role, they must fulfill three conditions: boundary condition, heterogeneity condition, and responsibility condition [24, 25]. That is, they must have limits that allow common objectives to be achieved, must be conformed with heterogeneous groups of members that ensure a correct interaction, and must motivate a continuous socialization among their members [24].

The boundary condition defines the goals and rules about the behavior allowed for members of a community. On the other hand, the heterogeneity condition expresses that a community should be made up of members with different seniority (new-veterans), who have the capacity to resolve doubts (teachers-experts) and the predisposition to participate (students) in proposed activities. Finally, the responsibility condition establishes the characteristics that allow to describe each member according to the role that plays and the activities in which he/she participated.

When the conditions are analyzed, it is observed that they are present in most SNs because the majority of these have a usage policy that must be accepted by each user before registering as a participant (boundary condition). In addition, they allow the formation of self-organized communities, whose participants have the common goal of exchanging information (a condition of heterogeneity), and, through the implementation of a user profile, guarantee the temporary stay of each participant, giving access to their personal information (condition of responsibility) [24]. Thus, any SN can be seen as a valid learning tool and, according to its use, can be classified into three principal categories [26–28]:

- Horizontal social networks: They are aimed at a general public, without focusing on a specific topic. Among the most popular are Facebook, Twitter, and Google+.

- Professional social networks: Give sustenance to content related to work ambit. They allow stablish professional contacts, as well as the search for job opportunities. Among the most prominent is LinkedIn, Viadeo, and Xing.
- Social content networks: They form links between their participants through the generation and dissemination of content in different formats. Among the main ones are YouTube, Pinterest, Instagram, and SlideShare.

Of the before examples, Facebook, Twitter, and YouTube are the most widely used globally.[4] Students employ SNs for different purposes, including discussion of classes, out-of-school learning, and planning of educational collaborative activities [29]. However, the main reason students turn to its support is the exchange of information and knowledge [30]. In the remainder of this section, a review of these SNs is described.

2.1 Facebook

Facebook is currently the most used SN to establish interpersonal relationships at a global level. According to the statistics collected by the website *"We Are Social"*, until January 2017, it reached a total of 1871 million active users. Its main characteristic is to allow social interaction between its users. For this reason, it includes a set of technologies such as social groups, personal pages, instant messaging services, socialization of multimedia files, VoIP, and video calls. However, much of this interaction is achieved through the publication of content by each user [31].

Due to the characteristics presented and the welcome it has, Facebook can be used as a valid educational tool. As a result, several research studies have been carried out which focus on highlighting the benefits it offers. The authors of [32] assert that by providing different forms of communication, student/teacher relations have improved. To corroborate their hypothesis, they developed a research to analyze students' opinions regarding the use of Facebook as a study tool. Thus, 180 questionnaires were distributed to postgraduate and undergraduate students, from which they received 140 completed. These questionnaires were designed based on four variables: student perception, academic contribution, relationship with the student's faculty, and privacy and distraction concerns. The results show the students' willingness to use Facebook and SNs for educational purposes. Likewise, in [33], authors propose a study to explore the use of a Facebook page and group managed by teachers, with the aim of complementing and improving educational experiences. Through surveys, first- and second-year medical students at the university stated that they have found in this SN an effective form of communication with easy access to learning material.

---

[4]https://wearesocial.com/special-reports/digital-in-2017-global-overview.

implementation of SLNs, in the context of a learning network, is feasible. One can, at least to some extent, rely on the system to ensure that the characteristics of individuals are taken into account, that feedback is given and decisions are made.

(3) Social exchange theory: Group members negotiate through mutual interactions. They then receive personal rewards (education) while minimizing costs. People no longer fully control their results, and interdependencies are created: individual actions can influence the results and actions of all other individuals.

(4) States of expectation theory: It focuses on the cognitive processes that occur in each individual within the group. Newcomers make an impression and seek information about other members. Group members search their memories for stored information about the group and the tasks they face; take note of each other's actions and try to understand what caused each other's behaviors. Members with most status-winning features will rise to the top. The theory of the states of expectation, as well as the theory of social exchange, points to the importance of keeping a record of the various characteristics of SLN members. The value attached to the answer to a particular question that has been asked depends, for example, on the experience of the person providing the answer.

(5) Fast trust theory: If a community is to function, its participants must show a little trust in each other. Therefore, a specific form of trust known as "fast trust" can arise in temporary teams that form around a clear purpose and common task. These are precisely the conditions that apply to SLNs. According to the theory of rapid confidence, there is a willingness to suspend doubt about whether one can count on others, who are "strangers," to be able to work on the group's task. According to the theory of rapid confidence, SLNs will improve relatively quickly the social integration of learning network users.

In addition to the above, it is necessary to perform a more personalized filtering of the preferences of each user. So, personal and institutional relevant resources must be accessed, such as educational profile, experience, and learning interests. The target is to provide a smart and ubiquitous learning environment that encourages its users to collaborate with each other to achieve diverse goals in their educational processes. With this, the problems of information isolation and over-information, present in the SNs, are solved, since the students are put in contact with experts who can solve their academic doubts.

As can be observed in Fig. 1, SLNs base their structure and operation on relevant information extracted from formal information sources (*Institutional Learning Objects*) and informal sources of information (*Web Learning Objects*). This information is the starting point of the OPPIA platform for structuring of SLNs, since it allows to group users who have similar study preferences in the same virtual-temporal space. On the other hand, OPPIA has in mind the profiles, interests, and personalities of the users that are going to be grouped, which allows establishing cooperative education. Then, once a selected user agrees to join a SLN, OPPIA offers a range of learning resources and activities—both individual and group—

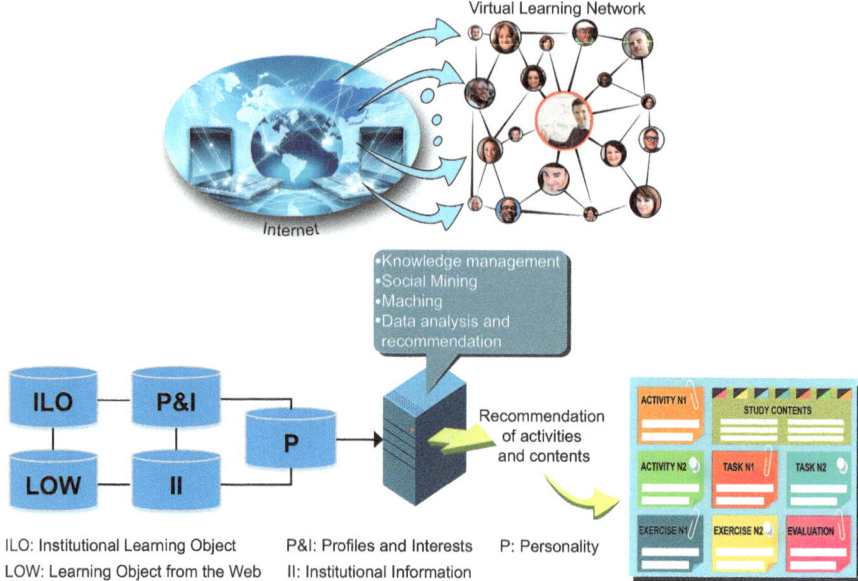

Fig. 1 Sporadic learning network: structure and operating

that needs to be developed over a given period of time. Three types of SLNs are possible [21]:

- Physical sporadic learning networks: In this type of network, thanks to geo-location, the system can determine a group of individuals close to each other, who may be potential members of a learning network. In this way, users who are selected according to their interests and profiles can configure a network in the same physical environment. The system will support the configuration of the network and the structure of the work to be developed.
- Virtual sporadic learning networks: In the case of a pure virtual network, potential candidates are physically distant from each other but connected to the system via the Internet. In this case, the interaction is carried out through intelligent tools and services provided by the platform. As in the previous case, the system will provide activities to be developed and learning resources.
- Hybrid sporadic learning networks: Hybrid networks, on the other hand, are a combination of the two previous ones. These networks make it possible to increase the possibility of interaction between students and to integrate experts or teachers geographically distant from the group and who, through their expertise, can enhance learning.

In the following section, the layer model, architecture, operating modes, and services offered by OPPIA are described.

4   OPPIA Platform

OPPIA (OPPortunistic Intelligent Ambient of learning) is an educational social platform that deploys different modes of informal learning, according to each student's needs. It helps to solve the difficulties of other SNs, as it focuses on providing opportunities for establishing interpersonal relationships, but from a more professional point of view. Thus, like any other Web 2.0 technology, it allows users to express their different opinions and personalities, with the difference that it has a more educational and private approach. In this way, it limits student/teacher relations to a field of study, in order to avoid compromising the private information of each user. This is achieved, to a large extent, by the simple fact that any user who accesses OPPIA's services is willing to learn or teach. In addition, the creation of sporadic learning networks (SLNs), one of its main characteristics, helps to undertake educational processes that connect students with experts in different subjects, improving the efficiency of knowledge transfer. On the other hand, it keeps a record of all the activities carried out, making it easier for teachers and educational institutions to monitor the progress of each student and thus improve academic quality. Finally, it deploys a recommendation system aimed at creating an environment that is attuned to unique preferences, creating a personalized and student-centered learning environment, with which you will feel comfortable while performing your academic activities.

In order to deploy all the features of OPPIA, it was necessary to use a number of technological tools. Therefore, the following subsections will describe its layer model, architecture, and operation.

4.1   Layer Model

The OPPIA platform relies on a fully interactive multilayer model organized in several layers and services. Conceptually, it has five layers (see Fig. 2) that will be described in the following subsections.

(1) Communication Layer This layer is responsible for providing the necessary mechanisms to establish connections proactively and transparently to users whenever deemed appropriate by the information from higher levels. So, the SLN relies firstly on ad hoc networks laid dynamically among mobile devices of the people (students, teacher, or experts), who happen to be close one to another at a given moment. Communications with network members in remote locations, with knowledge bases and learning services (upper layers), are done through links to hotspots or 3G/4G connections available. All protocols and mechanisms for establishing links and maintaining the necessary QoS levels are housed in this layer too.

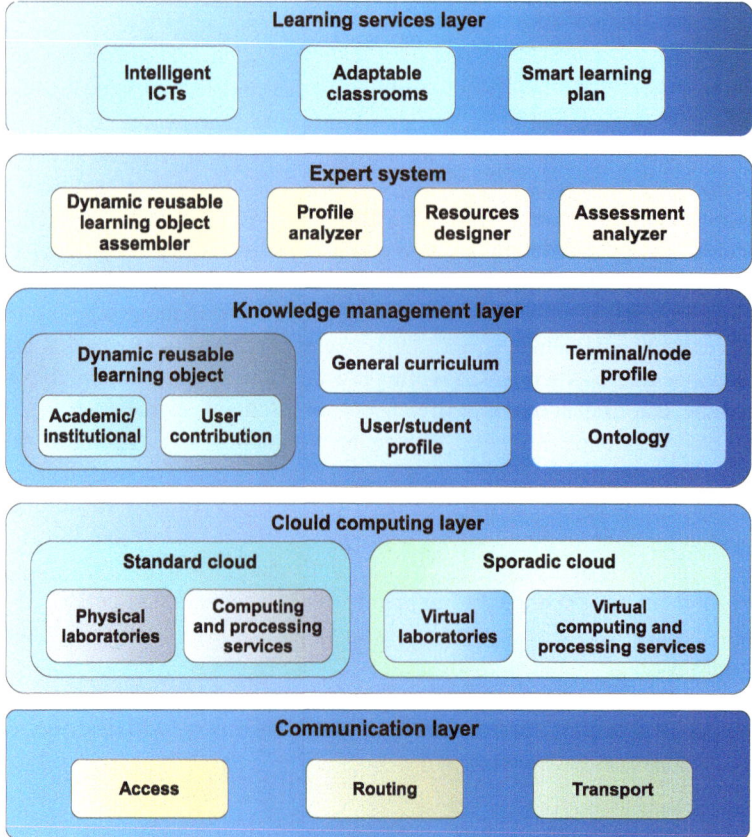

Fig. 2 The conceptual layers of the OPPIA platform

(2) Cloud Computing Layer The second layer aims to enable efficient sharing of resources available to each device within an SLN. The tandem between mobile devices and cloud computing works perfectly, due to handheld terminals that are constrained by their processing, battery life, and storage capabilities, whereas cloud computing provides the illusion of "infinite" computing resources [51, 52].

The extra resources required by the handheld devices can be provided either by (1) centralized servers in the cloud, depending on connectivity to the Internet; (2) cloudlets supported by fixed nodes at Internet edge; or (3) mobile terminals connected in the ad hoc network. With this in mind, OPPIA takes advantage of the concept of sporadic cloud computing (SCC) [53, 54], in which the devices of the user exploit both the resources available in the rest of terminals connected to the ad hoc network and those provided from external data centers. In this platform, SCC allows to generate virtual and distributed laboratories, conformed with existing resources in the devices of the different members of each SLN, who are physically close to each other. This avoids—as far as possible—dependence on access to the

Private Cloud

The private cloud is in charge of managing databases that provide information about users. It communicates with the public cloud through a connection tunnel, by means of which the identity parameters of each user are sent. These parameters go to the knowledge management instances (knowledge management) to work with the different databases. The private cloud is structured by two layers: knowledge management and database synchronization.

(5) Knowledge Management Layer Its purpose is to implement algorithms for classification, data mining, and machine learning, which allow us to work with the information provided by the different databases. This layer is responsible for providing the information required by the public cloud. A data mining algorithm is a set of heuristics and calculations that help create a model from each user's data. To create a model, the algorithm performs a trending analysis to determine optimal mine parameters. Thus, these parameters are applied throughout the initial data set to extract actionable patterns and detailed statistics. It should be emphasized that the databases that provide this information are hosted in the private cloud and are mined toward machine learning processes in the public cloud, generating results that are sent to the instances of the different layers, according to the needs that arise.

(6) Database Synchronization Layer Its main function is to make a middleware connection between the institutional learning object databases, the Web learning object databases, the institutional information databases, and the databases of each user's interest profiles. These databases are grouped in a cluster, which was divided into four different instances interconnected by virtual networks, forming high-performance clusters and high-availability clusters. High-performance, high-availability clusters enable better platform performance, while the client-server system minimizes resource consumption by users. It is necessary to implement an interpreter, since it works with heterogeneous databases. Additionally in this layer, a record of each service is generated, which feeds a relational database in MySQL, known as *OPPIA monitoring*. In this register, a tracking logbook and statistics of the activities are carried out by each user, as well as a databases monitoring.

4.3 OPPIA Operation

When a student registers his/her account, OPPIA immediately gets linked with the *academic monitoring* of the user and his/her different subjects, which is provided by an educational institution. In addition, an entry is created in the *OPPIA monitoring*, which allows to monitor and record all the activities developed. From this, OPPIA presents two modes of operation, the recommending mode and the voluntary mode, which depend on the predisposition of each student to initiate an educational process. In Fig. 4, the general operation of OPPIA can be observed.

In the recommend mode, OPPIA analyzes the performance of each student in a particular subject through his/her *academic monitoring*. If a user needs to reinforce

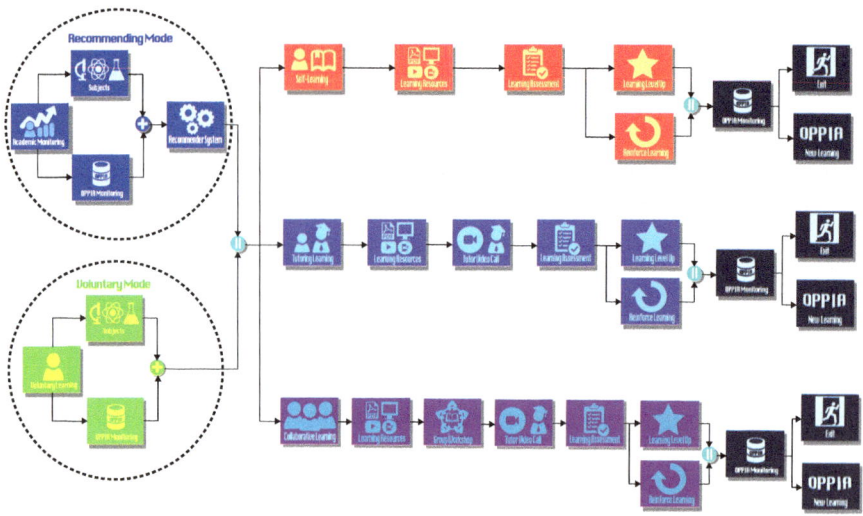

Fig. 4 OPPIA general operation. Recommender mode and volunteer mode

a topic, the platform's *recommender system* sends an e-mail notification to initiate a learning process. Whereas, in the voluntary mode, the student asks OPPIA to start a *voluntary learning* process in some subject area. In both modes, *OPPIA monitoring* is reviewed to determine the activities the student has already done, avoiding repeating them.

Whether in recommending mode or voluntary mode, OPPIA offers three educational models (self-learning, tutoring learning, and collaborative learning), which depend on the preferences of each student. Once a user initiates a learning process, OPPIA asks what educational model he/she wishes to pursue, analyzes the topics of each subject that need reinforcement or that student chose, and generates *learning resources*. To generate each *learning resource*, OPPIA uses a master database of subjects, known as *Subjects*, where all the knowledge that student must have to handle a certain subject is stored. The *learning resources* are generated according to the preferences of each student and can be readings in PDF format, video tutorials, instructional exercises, material on the Internet, and access to virtual machines.

According to the chosen educational model, OPPIA will implement the following actions:

- Self-learning model: When a student has developed the *learning resources* proposed, a *learning assessment* is generated which must be completed to guarantee the reinforcement of the user's knowledge. If said assessment is approved, the level will rise (*learning level up*); otherwise, the system will announce to continue to reinforce the knowledge (*reinforce learning*).
- Tutoring learning model: When a student has developed the *learning resources* that were settled, he/she is assigned to a specialist teacher in the subject that

has to be reinforced. Through a video call, the teacher will communicate with the student, and through a virtual whiteboard, he will explain any concerns he has (*tutor video call*). After this process, a *learning assessment* is generated that must be completed to guarantee the reinforcement of the knowledge. If the user approves it, the level will rise (*learning level up*); otherwise, the system will announce to continue to reinforce his/her knowledge (*reinforce learning*).

- Collaborative learning model: When a student has developed the *learning resources* that were proposed, he/she is added to a learning group made up of other students who share the need to acquire knowledge in the same subject of study. Once a team has been formed, a *group workshop* is presented which should be carried out through the socialization and collaboration of all its members. Afterward, the learning group is assigned to a teacher specialist in the subject that has to be reinforced. Through a video call, the teacher will communicate with the group, and through a virtual whiteboard, any concerns that a student has will be explained (*tutor video call*). After this process, an individual *learning assessment* is generated, which each student must complete to guarantee the reinforcement of their knowledge. If this assessment is approved, the level will rise (*learning level up*); otherwise, the system will announce to continue to reinforce the knowledge (*reinforce learning*).

If a student rises his/her level, OPPIA proposes to do another learning activity, where learning resources will be presented on other topics of study and an educational model can be chosen again. In the case the student should continue to reinforce his/her learning, OPPIA will present learning resources on the same subject of study and will allow the user to choose again which educational model he/she wishes to use (*new learning*). To finish the learning, the user just has to leave OPPIA (*Exit*). It is important to note that any activity performed by a student, whether to level up, reinforce their learning, or to leave, will be archived in *OPPIA monitoring*, following a process of control.

As for the teachers, they are chosen as volunteer collaborators who demonstrate expertise in an issue, which represent different educational institutions. However, any student who has completed a grade-level assessment may be selected as a teacher on the subject he/she has approved.

Finally, OPPIA bases its educational process on the Kolb learning cycle [57], so its operation can be understood in four stages. In the first stage or concrete experience, OPPIA analyzes the *academic monitoring* and the *OPPIA monitoring* to examine the current reality of the student. In the second stage or reflective observation, either the *recommender system* of OPPIA or the *voluntary learning* concludes that it is necessary for the student to follow a process of reinforcement of knowledge in some subject. In the third stage or abstract conceptualization, OPPIA presents *learning resources* that must be developed by the student, to deepen the study topic that must be reinforced. Finally, in the fourth stage or active experimentation, a *learning assessment* must be performed to check if he/she has acquired the necessary knowledge in the desired subject; the concrete experience changes too. The cycle is repeated as long as the student requires to learn.

In the following section, an implementation of OPPIA will be analyzed taking into consideration the reception it received based on responses to different questionnaires.

5 OPPIA Implementation

In this implementation, OPPIA was employed by a group of 45 students from the Universidad Politécnica Salesiana, Sede Cuenca, belonging to the subject of *mathematics 3*. The entrance to the platform was provided as support material to reinforce the classes taught in-person, and the contents of the course were grouped into different modules, providing a thread that facilitates navigation through the course. As part of the initial procedure, different profiles linked to the institutional e-mails of each student were created. In this way, the entire academic history became an input of the recommending system. It is important to note that OPPIA will always make recommendations for activities, regardless of whether it works on a voluntary or recommended mode. The only difference is that in the recommender mode, the student receives an e-mail to start a learning process; in the voluntary mode, he/she starts it on their own.

Depending on the chosen learning model, OPPIA may make the following activity recommendations:

- Self-learning: In this model, learning resources—readings, guides, presentations, and videos—were recommended, based on the ratings given to each item by similar users. A recommended study guide for a student is shown in Fig. 5a.
- Tutoring learning: In this case, two recommendations were generated. On the one hand, we looked for a teacher who dealt with the subject and had affinity— according to academic records— while on the other hand, we found an expert, who was rated in a positive way by other similar users. In the end, each student chose who they wanted to contact. Figure 5b shows the connection to a video call with an expert.
- Collaborative learning: In this model, it was recommended to join an SLN, whose members shared similar characteristics and preferences. The invitation to join an SLN is shown in Fig. 5c.

As an example, we will analyze OPPIA in the recommendation mode for a student. This student will be known as *student1* in this analysis. OPPIA agreed to his academic follow-up and determined the problems he had in *mathematics 3*. Then, OPPIA through its institutional e-mail notified that it could reinforce its knowledge by developing some learning activities. *Student1* decided to start learning with OPPIA and selected collaborative learning. It then became part of an SLN made up of students with similar preferences. To this team a group workshop was assigned, the tasks were developed by socialization among its members. At the end of the workshop, a teacher contacted the group by video call to answer each student's questions and explain any concerns through the use of electronic

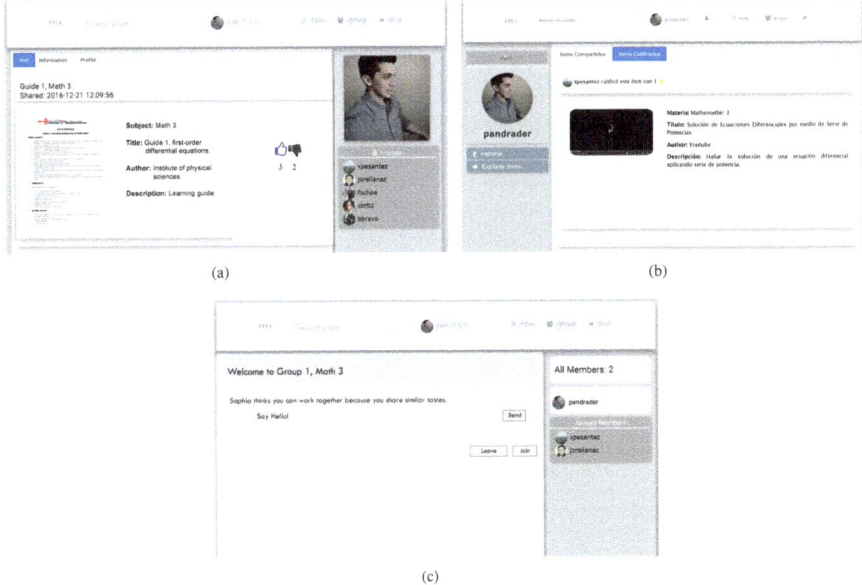

(a)   (b)

(c)

Fig. 5 Operation models of OPPIA

whiteboards. Ultimately, each student completed an individual assessment, which was approved by the *student1*. This means that he reinforced his/her knowledge of the proposed topics, so that his/her learning level went up, allowing him/her to access a new study module or complete his/her learning process. All activities developed by the *student1* were monitored and recorded by the OPPIA database.

Once students used the platform's services, they were asked to fill out two different questionnaires. The first served to measure the acceptance of OPPIA, while the second one helped to assess the impact of SLNs. Both handled acceptance scales, with the following options: Strongly Agree (SA), Agree (A), Disagree (D), and Strongly Disagree (SD); the questions asked were based on research conducted in [58].

On the one hand, Table 1 shows that students agree with most of the questions asked. However, when evaluating how easy it was to use the platform, it was found that 40% of the students had difficulty. This is mainly due to the lack of familiarity with OPPIA, since, being a first experiment in the subject of *mathematics 3*, there was no previous training. As a result, when analyzing if OPPIA met different academic needs, 38% of students also disagreed because they could not take full advantage of the platform's functions.

On the other hand, Table 2 shows how students experienced collaborative learning within an SLN. The vast majority agreed with the experience, assistance, and cooperation they found within the SLN. However, the biggest problem was communication, as 45% of the students had problems when contacting other

Table 1 Questionnaire on the use of OPPIA

	SA	A	D	SD
Did OPPIA stimulate the improvement of your learning?	47%	40%	9%	4%
Was the use of OPPIA fun?	49%	37%	11%	3%
Was the use of OPPIA easy?	23%	37%	27%	13%
Did OPPIA meet your personal requirements?	20%	42%	25%	13%
Did OPPIA help you to reinforce your knowledge?	58%	32%	7%	3%
Did OPPIA improve the efficiency of your learning?	68%	25%	5%	2%

Table 2 Questionnaire on the creation of SLNs

	SA	A	D	SD
Was the group experience better than the individual one?	52%	43%	3%	2%
The help I got from other users was useful?	65%	32%	3%	0%
Do you agree with the cooperation of members within the SLN?	46%	44%	6%	4%
Do you agree with the communication of members within the SLN?	28%	27%	25%	20%

members. This is reflected in the lack of experience when dealing with electronic boards, since there were cases in which the concepts or doubts discussed could not be explained by instant messaging or video calls.

6   Conclusions and Future Work

Two general conclusions can be drawn from the results obtained. OPPIA was widely accepted by students, fulfilling its main objective, to be a social tool to support learning and improve academic quality. Although there were some difficulties, especially due to lack of experience in handling the platform, the sensations it leaves behind are positive. On the other hand, with regard to SLNs, it can equally be said that they are a valuable resource for students, as they break away from the limitations of social circles and connect students with experts and teachers who are proficient in different subjects.

Furthermore, it is recommended to carry out prior training to gain experience and make the most of new educational resources. As future work, we will implement different recommendation algorithms to improve the efficiency of the suggestions made to students. Additionally, we will develop a social analysis based on Facebook and Twitter, to determine the personality of each user and to deploy a more specialized filtering and better cooperation within the SLNs.

Acknowledgements The authors would like to express their gratitude to Universidad Politécnica Salesiana, sede Cuenca, for the support provided for the development of this work.

References

1. A.M. Kaplan, M. Haenlein, Users of the world, unite! the challenges and opportunities of social media. Bus. Horiz. **53**(1), 59–68 (2010)
2. T. Correa, A.W. Hinsley, H.G. De Zuniga, Who interacts on the web?: The intersection of users' personality and social media use. Comput. Hum. Behav. **26**(2), 247–253 (2010)
3. M.N. Hajli, A study of the impact of social media on consumers. Int. J. Mark. Res. **56**(3), 387–404 (2014)
4. N. Spierings, K. Jacobs, Getting personal? the impact of social media on preferential voting. Polit. Behav. **36**(1), 215–234 (2014)
5. P.A. Tess, The role of social media in higher education classes (real and virtual)–a literature review. Comput. Hum. Behav. **29**(5), A60–A68 (2013)
6. A.E.E. Sobaih, M.A. Moustafa, P. Ghandforoush, M. Khan, To use or not to use? social media in higher education in developing countries. Comput. Hum. Behav. **58**, 296–305 (2016)
7. G. Townley, J. Katz, A. Wandersman, B. Skiles, M.J. Schillaci, B.E. Timmerman, T.A. Mousseau, Exploring the role of sense of community in the undergraduate transfer student experience. J. Commun. Psychol. **41**(3), 277–290 (2013)
8. F. Tiryakioglu, F. Erzurum, Use of social networks as an education tool. Contemp. Educ. Technol. **2**(2), 135–150 (2011)
9. J. Gikas, M.M. Grant, Mobile computing devices in higher education: Student perspectives on learning with cellphones, smartphones & social media. Internet High. Educ. **19**, 18–26 (2013)
10. V. Venkatesh, A.-M. Croteau, J. Rabah, Perceptions of effectiveness of instructional uses of technology in higher education in an era of web 2.0, in *2014 47th Hawaii International Conference on System Sciences (HICSS)* (IEEE, New York, 2014), pp. 110–119
11. C.B. Henriksen, H. Bregnhøj, S. Rosthøj, A. Ceballos, H. Kaas, I. Harker-Schuch, I. Andersen, S. Larsen, M. May, Technology enhanced peer learning and peer assessment. Tidsskriftet Læring og Medier (LOM) **9**(16) (2017)
12. S. Lauricella, R. Kay, Exploring the use of text and instant messaging in higher education classrooms. Res. Learn. Technol. **21**(1), 19061 (2013)
13. D. Coetzee, A. Fox, M.A. Hearst, B. Hartmann, Should your MOOC forum use a reputation system? in *Proceedings of the 17th ACM conference on Computer Supported Cooperative Work & Social Computing* (ACM, New York, 2014), pp. 1176–1187
14. M.-I. Dascalu, C.-N. Bodea, M. Lytras, P.O. De Pablos, A. Burlacu, Improving e-learning communities through optimal composition of multidisciplinary learning groups. Comput. Hum. Behav. **30**, 362–371 (2014)
15. A. Owusu-Ansah, P. Neill, M.K. Haralson, Distance education technology: higher education barriers during the first decade of the twenty-first century. Online J. Dist. Learn. Admin. **14**(2) (2011)
16. T. Kaya, H. Bicen, The effects of social media on students' behaviors; facebook as a case study. Comput. Hum. Behav. **59**, 374–379 (2016)
17. M. Au, J. Lam, Social media education: Barriers and critical issues, in *Technology in Education. Transforming Educational Practices with Technology* (Springer, Berlin, 2015), pp. 199–205
18. C.H. Davis III, R. Deil-Amen, C. Rios-Aguilar, M.S. Gonzalez Canche, Social media in higher education: a literature review and research directions. Report printed by the University of Arizona and Claremont Graduate University, vol. 8 (2012)
19. D.J. Kuss, M.D. Griffiths, Online social networking and addiction—a review of the psychological literature. Int. J. Environ. Res. Public Health **8**(9), 3528–3552 (2011)
20. J.F. Bravo-Torres, V.E. Robles-Bykaev, M.L. Nores, E.F. Ordóñez-Morales, Y. Blanco-Fernández, A. Gil-Solla, OPPIA: a context-aware ubiquitous learning platform to exploit short-lived student networks for collaborative learning, in *CSEDU 2016 - Proceedings of the 8th International Conference on Computer Supported Education*, Rome, April 21–23, 2016, vol. 1, pp. 494–498 [Online]. Available: https://doi.org/10.5220/0005903304940498

21. P.E. Vintimilla-Tapia, J.F. Bravo-Torres, P.L. Gallegos-Segovia, E.F. Ordónez-Morales, M. López-Nores, Y. Blanco-Fernández, Soppia: social opportunistic intelligent ambient of learning, in *Proceedings of the 2017 IEEE/ACM International Conference on Advances in Social Networks Analysis and Mining 2017, ASONAM '17* (ACM, New York, 2017), pp. 782–789
22. A.M. Kaplan, Social media, definition and history, in *Encyclopedia of Social Network Analysis and Mining* (Springer, New York, 2014), pp. 1825–1827
23. M. Castells, G. Cardoso, et al., *The Network Society: From Knowledge to Policy* (Johns Hopkins, Center for Transatlantic Relations, Washington, DC, 2006)
24. A.J. Berlanga, P.B. Sloep, L. Kester, F. Brouns, P. Rosmalen, R. Koper, Ad hoc transient communities: towards fostering knowledge sharing in learning networks. Int. J. Learn. Technol. **3**(4), 443–458 (2008)
25. L. Kester, P. Van Rosmalen, P. Sloep, F. Brouns, M. Brouwers, R. Koper, Matchmaking in learning networks: a system to support knowledge sharing (2006)
26. L. Russell, Strategic opportunities to increase the impact of science and technology in regional development: open innovation and the strategic value of horizontal social networks. Eur. Sci. J. **9**(10), 43–51 (2014)
27. S.R. Van Hook, Professional social networks (2012)
28. N.B. Ellison, et al., Social network sites: Definition, history, and scholarship. J. Comput.-Mediat. Commun. **13**(1), 210–230 (2007)
29. N.B. Ellison, C. Steinfield, C. Lampe, The benefits of facebook "friends:" social capital and college students' use of online social network sites. J. Comput.-Mediat. Commun. **12**(4), 1143–1168 (2007)
30. M. Gómez, El uso académico de las redes sociales en universitarios/the academic use of social networks among university students. Comunicar **19**(38), 131–138 (2012)
31. A. Da Silva, M.P. Barbosa, Facebook groups: the use of social network in the education, in *2015 International Symposium on Computers in Education (SIIE)* (IEEE, New York, 2015), pp. 185–188
32. I.A. Qureshi, H. Raza, M. Whitty, Facebook as e-learning tool for higher education institutes. Knowl. Manage. E-Learn. **6**(4), 440 (2014)
33. S. El Bialy, A. Jalali, A. Jaffar, Integrating facebook into basic sciences education: a comparison of a faculty-administered facebook page and group. Austin J. Anat. **1**(3), 1015 (2014)
34. H. Bicen, H. Uzunboylu, The use of social networking sites in education: a case study of facebook. J. UCS **19**(5), 658–671 (2013)
35. Y.M. Al-Dheleai, Z. Tasir, Facebook and education: students' privacy concerns. Int. Educ. Stud. **8**(13), 22 (2015)
36. S.B. Rinaldo, S. Tapp, D.A. Laverie, Learning by tweeting: using twitter as a pedagogical tool. J. Mark. Educ. (2011). https://doi.org/10.1177/0273475311410852
37. S.A. Paul, L. Hong, E.H. Chi, Is twitter a good place for asking questions? a characterization study, in *ICWSM* (2011)
38. E.M. Al-Mukhaini, W.S. Al-Qayoudhi, A.H. Al-Badi, Adoption of social networking in education: a study of the use of social networks by higher education students in oman. J. Int. Educ. Res. **10**(2), 143 (2014)
39. H. Kwak, C. Lee, H. Park, S. Moon, What is twitter, a social network or a news media? in *Proceedings of the 19th International Conference on World Wide Web* (ACM, New York, 2010), pp. 591–600
40. G. Veletsianos, Higher education scholars' participation and practices on twitter. J. Comput. Assist. Learn. **28**(4), 336–349 (2012)
41. H. Bicen, N. Cavus, Twitter usage habits of undergraduate students. Proc.-Soc. Behav. Sci. **46**, 335–339 (2012)
42. G. Tur, V.I. Marín, Enhancing learning with the social media: student teachers' perceptions on twitter in a debate activity. J. New Approaches Educ. Res. **4**(1), 46 (2015)

43. C. Evans, Twitter for teaching: can social media be used to enhance the process of learning? Br. J. Educ. Technol. **45**(5), 902–915 (2014)
44. R.D. Contreras-Chacón, J.F. Bravo-Torres, J.A. Yépez-Alulema, D.A. Cuji-Dután, P.E. Vintimilla-Tapia, Identification and recommendation of authorities on different topics based on twitter. Int. J. Pure Appl. Math. **114**(11), 117–126 (2017)
45. L. YouTube, "Youtube," Retrieved, vol. 27 (2011), p. 2011
46. A. Clifton, C. Mann, Can youtube enhance student nurse learning? Nurse Educ. Today **31**(4), 311–313 (2011)
47. A.A. Jaffar, Youtube: an emerging tool in anatomy education. Anat. Sci. Educ. **5**(3), 158–164 (2012)
48. M. Asselin, T. Dobson, E.M. Meyers, C. Teixiera, L. Ham, Learning from youtube: an analysis of information literacy in user discourse, in *Proceedings of the 2011 iConference* (ACM, New York, 2011), pp. 640–642
49. I. Duncan, L. Yarwood-Ross, C. Haigh, Youtube as a source of clinical skills education. Nurse Educ. today **33**(12), 1576–1580 (2013)
50. M. Knösel, K. Jung, A. Bleckmann, Youtube, dentistry, and dental education. J. Dental Educ. **75**(12), 1558–1568 (2011)
51. P. Mell, T. Grance, The NIST definition of cloud computing (2011)
52. S. Kim, S.-M. Song, Y.-I. Yoon, Smart learning services based on smart cloud computing. Sensors **11**(8), 7835 (2011)
53. E.F. Ordóñez-Morales, J.F. Bravo-Torres, J.V. Saiáns-Vázquez, Y. Blanco-Fernández, M. López-Nores, J. J. Pazos-Arias, Sporangium-validating the concept of sporadic social networks in pervasive applications, in *EUROCON 2015-International Conference on Computer as a Tool (EUROCON), IEEE* (IEEE, New York, 2015), pp. 1–6
54. E.F. Ordóñez-Morales, Y. Blanco-Fernández, M. López-Nores, J.F. Bravo-Torres, J.J. Pazos-Arias, M. Ramos-Cabrer, Sporangium: exploiting a virtualization layer to support the concept of sporadic cloud computing with users on the move, in *New Contributions in Information Systems and Technologies* (Springer, Basel, 2015), pp. 959–966
55. R.P. Valderrama, L.B. Ocaña, L.B. Sheremetov, Development of intelligent reusable learning objects for web-based education systems. Expert Syst. Appl. **28**(2), 273–283 (2005)
56. J.F. Bravo-Torres, P.E. Andrade-Rea, P.E. Vintimilla-Tapia, E.F. Ordoñez-Morales, M. López-Nores, Y. Blanco-Fernández, Leveraging short-lived learning networks to encourage collaborative peer learning, in *2017 Twelfth Latin American Conference on Learning Technologies (LACLO)*, October 2017, pp. 1–7
57. J.E. Stice, Using Kolb's learning cycle to improve student learning. Eng. Educ. **77**(5), 291–296 (1987)
58. S.R. Hiltz, Collaborative learning in a virtual classroom: highlights of findings, in *Proceedings of the 1988 ACM Conference on Computer-Supported Cooperative Work* (ACM, New York, 1988), pp. 282–290

Temporal Model of the Online Customer Review Helpfulness Prediction with Regression Methods

Shih-Hung Wu, Yi-Hsiang Hsieh, Liang-Pu Chen, Ping-Che Yang, and Liu Fanghuizhu

1 Introduction

Most online e-commerce platforms provide online review mechanism. On these platforms, people can read reviews and even comments on the reviews from other customers who bought the product in the past and knew the quality of the product. A customer's review often contains information related to the product itself and consumer preference. These information will affect the willingness to whether to buy the product or give similar reference in the future. Thus, retrieving information from helpful reviews has become an important issue. Some websites provide the helpfulness voting information for each review, which gives an objective reference for researchers on the helpfulness evaluation.

The prediction of the helpfulness of an online review is an interesting research topic. However, there is no publicly available online customer review corpus in Chinese, so we collect the online customer reviews from the Amazon.cn as the data set in our experiment. This online e-commerce platform provides commenting system, as shown in Fig. 1, which contains the opinion and the rating left by the customers who have bought the product item, and the helpfulness voting results from other customers who read this review. Previous works assumed that the voting result can be predicted by the text; however, we find that the voting result of an

S.-H. Wu (✉) · Y.-H. Hsieh
Department of Computer Science and Information Engineering, Chaoyang University of Technology, Taichung, Taiwan, Republic of China
e-mail: shwu@cyut.edu.tw

L.-P. Chen · P.-C. Yang
Institute for Information Industry, Taipei, Taiwan, Republic of China

L. Fanghuizhu
Shenyang Jianzhu University, Shenyang, China

© Springer Nature Switzerland AG 2019
M. Kaya, R. Alhajj (eds.), *Influence and Behavior Analysis in Social Networks and Social Media*, Lecture Notes in Social Networks,
https://doi.org/10.1007/978-3-030-02592-2_2

1. Helpful voting

35/36 人认为此评论有用

★★☆☆☆ 用过, 2014年12月30日

评论者 上官浩强 - 查看此用户发表的评论

已确认购买 (这是什么？)

评论的商品: Apple iPhone 6 Plus (64G) 4G智能手机(金色 公开版) (手机)

这个手机到货速度倒是挺快，就是回来以后手机用过，而且；里面的通话记录和电话本还都在…
也不是特别快。都想换货了。。。甚至怀疑是不是被换回来货。。

2. Review content

Fig. 1 Commenting system in Amazon.cn. Top box: 35 out of 36 customers think the review to be helpful. Bottom box: The review text

online review is not constant over time due to that time and people are required in voting. Previous works used the confidence index of voting result, the percentage of helpful vote, as the gold standard. We believe it is not suitable for a new review since it takes time to get votes. Therefore, in our experiment, we define new indexes other than the confidence. Product reviews in eight different product categories are collected as the review corpus, and we train the linear regression model to predict the usefulness index of a new review in each category.

In this paper, the temporal issue of voting result is tested by the linear regression of linguistic features in order to see whether a review is useful or not. In finding useful reviews, our system can even achieve higher accuracy without the help of voting system. An automatic assessment system can help people to find useful reviews on the websites that do not have a voting system.

The paper is organized as follows: Sect. 2 contains related work, Sect. 3 reports our method, Sect. 4 shows the experiments, and the final section is conclusion.

2   Related Works

In order to understand the quality of online customer review, recent researches provide various analyses. Mackiewicz proposed 11 characteristics of review quality [1]. Three of them are credibility, information content, and readability, but there is no conclusion on which characteristic can contribute more. Jun added the volume of sale as a weight to balance the influence between comments and product description [2], and found that reviews with the highest or lowest score are more arguable. Zhang proposed a method to reduce noisy reviews [3]. These researches aim to provide a better way to filter out the good reviews and reduce the bad ones.

In Chinese opinion mining literatures, Wang built a Chinese opinion system that could help farmers to find the customers in the e-commerce era [4]. Li proposed

	Sinica Treebank POS pattern rules
1	A-DE-Na
2	A-VH
3	Dfa-V_2-VH*
4	Dfa-(D)-(VA/VB/VI/VH*/VK)
5	Dfa-VH*-(VC)
6	Dfa-(VHC/VL)-(VH)
7	(D)-Dfa-(VA/VB/VC/VH*/VI/VJ/VK)
8	D-SHI-Dfa-VH*-(VC)
9	D-VH*-(VC)
10	VG-VH*
11	VH-DE-VH*
12	VJ-VH-(VC)

Table 1 Adopted rules of Chinese POS patterns [6]

a way to extract the opinion explanations from Chinese online reviews based on the lexicon learning method [5]. Peng used the combination of Chinese part-of-speech (POS) [6], shown in Table 1, to extract opinion terms. In order to extract the structure in Chinese review, Wei proposed a rule based on template matching method to improve the performance [7].

More and more companies are realizing the importance of online review. Zhang mentioned that online customer review can help a company to improve their products and to have a better understanding on what customers need [8]. Therefore, how to find the review with better quality is becoming a hot research topic.

Our experiment is conducted with R language [9]. Here we briefly list the formulas.

2.1 Linear Regression

Regression analysis can be divided into simple linear regression and multiple regression. Regression is used to study the relationship between a predictor variable and a response variable, and multiple regression is to explore several predictor variables and a response variable. The typical multiple linear regression formula:

$$y = \beta_0 + \beta_1 x_1 + \beta_2 x_2 + \cdots + \beta_n x_n + \varepsilon \tag{1}$$

where $\beta_0, \beta_1, \ldots, \beta_n$ are $n + 1$ parameters, y is the dependent variable, $x_1, x_2, \ldots, x_n$ are independent variable. The error ε is a random variable, assumed to be normally distributed. In our experiments, the y is the performance index, confidence, or DC, and x_i are the features.

2.2   The Coefficient of Determination

The coefficient of determination R^2 is the proportion of y variation that can be explained by the linear regression model. When $R^2 = 0$, it means y is not linear relationship to x_i. When $R^2 \neq 0$, it means the approximate linear relationship between y and x_i. The coefficient of determination R^2 is defined as:

$$R^2 = 1 - \frac{SSE}{SST} \qquad (2)$$

where total sum of squares: $SST = \sum (y_i - \overline{y})^2$; residual sum of squares: $SSE = \sum (y_i - \widehat{y_i})^2$.

Since the value of R^2 is sensitive to the sample size. In multiple regression, an adjusted R^2 is defined as:

$$\text{Adjusted } R^2 = 1 - \frac{\frac{SSE}{dfe}}{\frac{SST}{dft}} \qquad (3)$$

where dfe and dft are the degree of freedom for SSE and SST, respectively.

2.3   The Akaike Information Criterion

Akaike information criterion (AIC) is used for model selection. The AIC is a measure of the relative quality of statistical models for a given training set. AIC estimates the quality of a model relative to each of the other models.

$$AIC = n \, \ln \left(\frac{SSE}{n} \right) + 2k \qquad (4)$$

where n is the size of data and k is the number of parameter.

3   Method

The system flow is shown in Fig. 2. Our system collects the product reviews from Amazon.cn to build the Chinese review corpus. Since we believe that the confidence of voting result is not the best performance index, we define three more indexes in Sect. 3.5. Our system then uses the training data to build the regression model and test the model on a separated test data. The results will be discussed in Sect. 4.

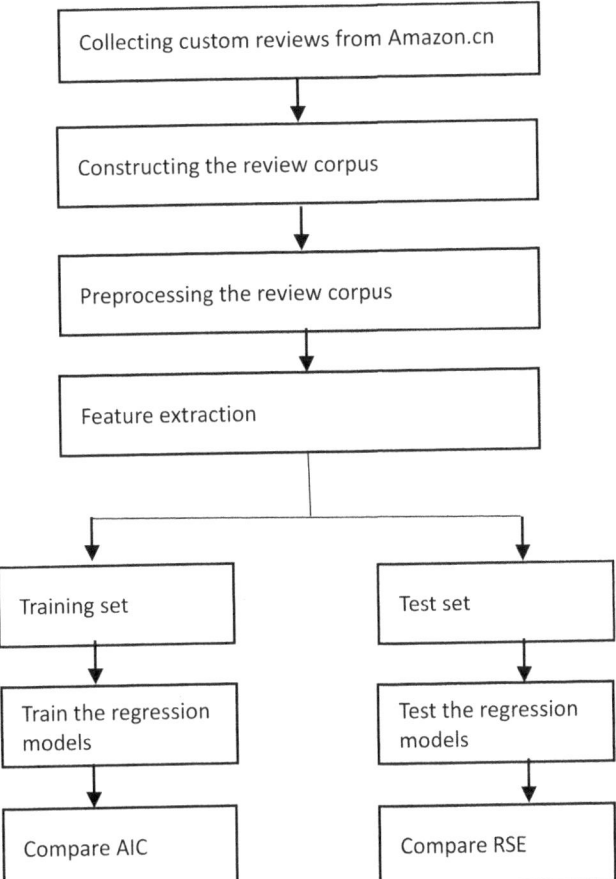

Fig. 2 System structure

3.1 Corpus Collection

On the corpus collection, we adapt the MetaSeeker V4.11 as the crawler, which is a freeware provided by GooSeeker [10]. Given a product category, our system collects the review content, the post date, the number of stars, and the voting result of each product review.

3.2 Morphological Preprocessing

For content morphological analysis, we use the online Chinese analysis system provided by Chinese knowledge information processing (CKIP) group [11]. This analysis system can parse Chinese text and give syntactic information. In our experiment, we use their parser and tokenization system to do the word segmentation and POS tagging. The POS tags are also used as the source of sentiment features.

3.3   Feature Set

To understand the quality of customer review, many features have been proposed. For example, Lu [12] provided several three classes of relevant features. We also implement some features including text-statistics features, syntactic features, sentiment features, and review's star. In the text-statistics, the statistical types of features include the number of words and the average length of sentences in a single review. In syntactic features, the percentage of speech type collects the results from CKIP analysis. The POS ratio is defined as the percentage of each POS, such as A, ADV, N, DET, M, P, Vi, and Tt, in one review to all reviews. Sentiment feature is a statistical review of the number of positive and negative words. Table 2 shows the feature set in our system. There are 14 features in total.

3.4   Sentiment Feature Selection

In order to find the sentiment in online reviews, we observe the result of CKIP word segmentation. Ku et al. mentioned that the morphological and syntactic structures can be used to identify opinion [13]. Hsieh et al. mentioned that the POS combination "ADV+vi" and "Vi" are more likely to be opinion words [14].

Table 2 The feature set used in our experiment

Feature name	Feature description
NumWord	Number of words
NumSent	Number of sentences
AvgSentWord	The average number of words of each sentence
POS_A	Ratio of non-predicate adjective
POS_ADV	Ratio of adverb
POS_N	Ratio of noun
POS_DET	Ratio of determiner
POS_M	Ratio of measure
POS_P	Ratio of preposition
POS_Vi	Ratio of intransitive verb
POS_Vt	Ratio of transitive verb
NumPos	Number of positive
NumNeg	Number of negative
NumStar	Number of star

In Li's paper [15] referred NTUSD as a dictionary that contains words and polar opinions, which contains 2812 positive terms and 8276 negative terms. Thus, our system uses the NTUSD opinion-word dictionary to screen the number of positive and negative words.

3.5 Evaluation Index

In this paper, we use four kinds of the evaluation index. The most basic indicator is obtained from the ratio of helpful voting. Amazon.cn review platform provides a mechanism for consumers to vote whether the review is helpful as shown in Fig. 1, where the number 35 is the amount of people who think the review is helpful, "think helpful," and number 36 is the number of how many people vote, "Total people," we can define confidence as follows:

$$\text{Confidence} = \frac{\text{think helpful}}{\text{Total people}} \tag{5}$$

However, Zeng [16] pointed out that the high confidence of reviews with less total number is not reliable. So Zeng proposed another evaluation index, log-support confidence (LSC), which is defined as follows:

$$\text{LSC} = \log_{10} * (\text{think helpful}) * \left(\frac{\text{Think helpful}}{\text{Total people}} \right) \tag{6}$$

For similar reason, Hsieh [14] took date into consideration to define the following two indexes: the date-related, log-date confidence (LDC) and date confidence (DC), which are defined as follows:

$$\text{LDC} = \log_{10} * \left(\frac{\text{think helpful}}{\text{Total people} * \text{MD}} \right) \tag{7}$$

$$\text{DC} = \frac{\text{think helpful}}{\text{Total people} * \text{MD}} \tag{8}$$

where month difference (MD) is how many months the review has been posted.

4 Experiments

Since Hsieh [14] suggests that DC is the most suitable index in most cases, we focus on the comparison between *confidence* and DC in our work.

Table 3 The number of
reviews in each category

	Number of reviews
Books	172
Digital cameras	664
Tablet PC	777
Backpacks	278
Movies	132
Men shoes	181
Toys	254
Cell phones	1272
Total	3730

4.1 Authors and Affiliations of Chinese Customer Review Corpus

Our corpus is collected from the Amazon.cn, an online e-commerce website. Customer reviews are collected from eight categories: books, digital cameras, tablet PC, backpacks, movies, men shoes, toys, and cell phones. In each category, we focus on the top 10 hot product items, and there are 3730 reviews in our collection. Table 3 shows the number in each category.

4.2 Experimental Tools

We conduct our experiment with the R language regression model toolkit. We use the same data set to build the regression model for confidence and DC. A snapshot of our example is shown in Figs. 3 and 4.

As we can see from the two figures above, the detail results-residual standard error, freedom (degrees of freedom), R-squared, adjusted R-squared coefficient, and other statistic numbers have been significantly improved: from the comparison between two models, the residuals in DC model are smaller, which means fitting error is less, while the *adjusted R^2* are bigger.

4.3 Experimental Results

We perform the training and test experiment in each category. In the experiment, the reviews of the first six products in each category are treated as the training set. The reviews of the last four products in each category are treated as the test set. The test data is unseen in the training set; therefore, this is an open test. The regression result of performance index of the test set is compared with the four different gold standards. We use the residual standard error (RSE) to evaluate the regression result.

```
Coefficients:
                Estimate Std. Error t value Pr(>|t|)
(Intercept)    9.770e-01  1.061e-01   9.208 2.26e-14
x1            -6.560e-03  1.654e-02  -0.397  0.69262
x2             7.221e-03  7.355e-03   0.982  0.32906
x3             6.013e-03  9.367e-03   0.642  0.52265
x4             5.898e-03  9.547e-03   0.618  0.53838
x5             3.362e-01  1.018e+00   0.330  0.74196
x6            -5.862e+00  8.126e+00  -0.721  0.47266
x7            -6.141e+00  1.486e+01  -0.413  0.68039
x8            -1.790e+00  2.317e+00  -0.773  0.44183
x9             5.915e+00  2.604e+00   2.272  0.02565
x10            2.543e+00  3.129e+00   0.813  0.41871
x11           -1.499e+01  6.474e+00  -2.316  0.02302
x12           -2.763e+01  1.027e+01  -2.692  0.00858
x13            4.349e-04  1.170e-02   0.037  0.97044
x14            1.662e-02  1.522e-02   1.091  0.27818
---
Signif. codes:  0 '***' 0.001 '**' 0.01 '*' 0.05 '

Residual standard error: 0.1459 on 84 degrees of f
Multiple R-squared:  0.235,     Adjusted R-squared
F-statistic: 1.843 on 14 and 84 DF,  p-value: 0.04
```

Fig. 3 A snapshot of our experiment conducted in *R* language, where we test the data in movie category to fit confidence

RSE is defined as follows:

$$RSE = \sqrt{\frac{SSE}{(n-2)}} = \sqrt{\sum (y_i - \widehat{y_i})^2 \Big/ (n-2)} \tag{9}$$

where y_i is the gold standard of one performance index out of the four performance indexes, and $\widehat{y_i}$ is the prediction result of linear regression model, and n is the number of test data. The training AIC of the two performance indexes is shown in Table 4 and V. The test RSE of the two performance indexes is shown in Table 5.

```
Coefficients:
              Estimate  Std. Error  t value  Pr(>|t|)
(Intercept)   4.749e-02  1.042e-02    4.558  1.74e-05
x1           -2.321e-03  1.624e-03   -1.429    0.1567
x2           -1.010e-03  7.223e-04   -1.398    0.1657
x3           -8.017e-04  9.199e-04   -0.872    0.3859
x4            4.173e-04  9.375e-04    0.445    0.6574
x5            2.208e-01  9.995e-02    2.209    0.0299
x6            3.042e-01  7.980e-01    0.381    0.7040
x7            1.748e+00  1.459e+00    1.198    0.2342
x8            1.908e-01  2.275e-01    0.839    0.4040
x9            6.632e-01  2.557e-01    2.594    0.0112
x10           3.026e-01  3.073e-01    0.985    0.3276
x11           8.916e-02  6.358e-01    0.140    0.8888
x12           1.220e+00  1.008e+00    1.210    0.2297
x13          -7.432e-04  1.149e-03   -0.647    0.5195
x14           2.435e-05  1.495e-03    0.016    0.9870
---
Signif. codes:  0 '***' 0.001 '**' 0.01 '*' 0.05 '.

Residual standard error: 0.01433 on 84 degrees of f
Multiple R-squared:  0.2406,     Adjusted R-squared:
F-statistic: 1.901 on 14 and 84 DF,  p-value: 0.037
```

Fig. 4 A snapshot of our experiment conducted in R language, where we test the data in movie category to fit DC

Table 4 The AIC result of the training set

AIC	Confidence	DC
Movies	−84.44796	**−543.95**
Men shoes	**83.112764**	114.568
Backpacks	−23.30453	**−566.21**
Tablet PC	398.32183	**−317.57**
Cell phones	**−6.520892**	317.348
Digital cameras	206.03682	**−930.23**
Books	126.23769	**71.1737**
Toys	224.32756	**−235.87**

Bold case means lower value

4.4 Discussion

According to Tables 4 and 5, we find that confidence and DC are good performance indexes. Both the traditional performance index confidence and our new performance index DC get stable result on training set and test set. This result suggests

Table 5 The RSE result of the test set

RSE	Confidence	DC
Movies	0.1458892	**0.01433**
Men shoes	**0.343772**	0.40497
Backpacks	0.218776	**0.05515**
Tablet PC	0.3306357	**0.18404**
Cell phones	**0.2386021**	0.28973
Digital cameras	0.2914104	**0.09545**
Books	0.3977811	**0.3104**
Toys	0.400788	**0.13116**

Bold case means lower value

Table 6 MSE of confidence and DC with SVR

MSE	Confidence	DC
Books	0.352642	**0.126242**
Digital cameras	0.094439	**0.026977**
Tablet PC	1.59539	**0.051485**
Backpacks	0.041984	**0.012494**
Movies	0.011548	**0.000271**
Men shoes	**0.024875**	0.873824
Toys	**0.018122**	0.097265
Cell phones	**0.089102**	2.16336

Bold case means lower value

that our assumption is partially correct, i.e., the old reviews will gather more vote. Therefore, the weight should be adjusted according to how old a review is. We further investigate the time difference of each review. To compare the regression result of linear regression and support vector regression (SVR) [14], we conduct another experiment as shown in Table 6. According to Table 6, we find that the traditional performance index confidence and our new performance index DC get better result in different product categories. This result also leads to the same conclusion as stated in Tables 4 and 5: the older the reviews are, the more votes they get. For this reason, the weight should be adjusted according to how old a review is.

5   Conclusion and Future Works

In this paper, we find that temporal issue should be considered when defining the performance index for online review regression. For some product categories in which new products come in very often, the old comments will not be that helpful. Therefore, the performance index DC will be a better one for a system that can predict the helpfulness of a review.

After finding suitable performance indexes, our research goal will go back to the features that can reveal the quality of reviews. Features used in automatic essay scoring system might be involved, which includes the grammar features, language model features, and syntactical features. In the future, we will use a non-linear regression method to compare the results [17, 18].

References

1. J. Mackiewicz, D. Yeats, Product review users' perceptions of review quality: the role of credibility, informativeness, and readability. IEEE Trans. Prof. Commun. **57**(4), 309–324 (2014)
2. J. Iio, Evaluating the usefulness of online reviews, in *15th International Conference on Network-Based Information Systems (NBiS)*, 26–28 September 2012
3. R. Zhang, X. He, A. Zhou, C. Sha, Online evaluation re-scoring based on review behavior analysis, in *IEEE/ACM International Conference on Advances in Social Networks Analysis and Mining (ASONAM)*, 17–20 August 2014
4. W. Hui-Po, The evolution analysis of the opinion network of Chinese farmers' adoption of mobile commerce, in *20th International Conference on Management Science and Engineering*, 17–19 July 2013
5. Y. Li, W. Mao, D. Zeng, L. Huangfu, C. Liu, Extracting opinion explanations from chinese online reviews, in *IEEE International Conference on Intelligence and Security Informatics (ISI)*, 11–14 June 2012
6. T.C. Peng, C.C. Shih, *Using Chinese Part-of-Speech Patterns for Sentiment Phrase Identification and Opinion Extraction in User Generated Reviews*. To appear in ICDIM, 2010
7. W. Wei, H. Liu, J. He, H. Yang, X. Du, Extracting feature and opinion words effectively from Chinese product reviews, in *Fifth International Conference on Fuzzy Systems and Knowledge Discovery FSKD'08*, 18–20 October 2008
8. Z. Zhang, J. Qi, G. Zhu, Mining customer requirement from helpful online reviews, in *Second International Conference on Enterprise Systems* (2014)
9. J.P. Lander, *R for Everyone: Advanced Analytics and Graphics*, 1st edn. (Addison-Wesley Professional, Boston, 2013)
10. GooSeeker, http://www.gooseeker.com/
11. CKIP, Chinese online parser service. http://parser.iis.sinica.edu.tw/
12. Y. Lu, P. Tsaparas, A. Ntoulas, L. Polanyi, Exploiting social context for review quality prediction, in *Proceedings of the 19th International Conference on World wide Web* (Raleigh, North Carolina, USA, 2010)
13. L.-W. Ku, T.-H. Huang, H.-H. Chen. Using morphological and syntactic structures for Chinese opinion analysis, in *Proceedings of the 2009 Conference on Empirical Methods in Natural Language Processing* (Singapore, 2009), vol. 3
14. H.-Y. Hsieh, V. Klyuev, Q. Zhao, S.-H. Wu, SVR-based outlier detection and its application to hotel ranking, in *IEEE 6th International Conference on Awareness Science and Technology (iCAST)* (2014)
15. C.-R. Li, Y. Chi-Hsin, H.-H. Chen, Predicting the semantic orientation of terms in E-HowNet. Comput. Linguistics Chinese Lang. Process. **17**(2), 21–36 (2012). (in Chinese)
16. Y.-C. Zeng, S.-H. Wu, Modeling the helpful opinion mining of online consumer reviews as a classification problem, in *IJCNLP Workshop on Natural Language Processing for Social Media (SocialNLP)* (2013), pp. 29–35
17. H.-X. Shi, X.-J. Li, A sentiment analysis model for hotel reviews based on supervised learning, in *Proceedings of the International Conference on Machine Learning and Cybernetics* (Guilin, 2011)
18. S. Tan, J. Zhang, An empirical study of sentiment analysis for Chinese documents. Expert Syst. Appl. **34**(4), 2622–2629 (2008)

Traits of Leaders in Movement Initiation: Classification and Identification

**Chainarong Amornbunchornvej, Margaret C. Crofoot,
and Tanya Y. Berger-Wolf**

1 Introduction

Leadership is one of the processes that both human and other social animal species use to solve complicated tasks to collectively achieve a goal [6, 8]. Understanding how leadership emerges and what behavioral mechanisms translate into leadership provides an insight into the complex organization of problem-solving and decision-making strategies in nature. In a movement context, leaders are individuals who successfully initiate movement, which the group then follows [6, 18]. In the leadership inference literature, there are many approaches for inferring leadership based on social network action-log data [9, 10], position-tracking information [2, 3, 13, 16], and others. There are also many approaches that define the traits of a "leader" a priori and extract data from individuals that fit the model's definition, such as influence maximization model [10, 11], implicit leadership model [6, 19], and flock model [3]. However, are these traits evident in real instances of leadership? Conversely, are the individuals defined by these traits indeed leaders? In this work, we propose an explicit framework for testing hypotheses about the behavioral traits of leaders by combining leader identification approaches with leadership characterization. We first identify leaders and then evaluate behavioral traits that purportedly characterize a leader. In the context of movement initiation, we focus on three behavioral traits commonly assumed to be associated with leadership of group movements: (1) being at the front of the group [3], (2) being the first to start

C. Amornbunchornvej (✉) · T. Y. Berger-Wolf
Department of Computer Science, University of Illinois at Chicago, Chicago, IL, USA
e-mail: camorn2@uic.edu; tanyabw@uic.edu

M. C. Crofoot
Department of Anthropology, University of California, Davis, Davis, CA, USA
e-mail: mccrofoot@ucdavis.edu

© Springer Nature Switzerland AG 2019
M. Kaya, R. Alhajj (eds.), *Influence and Behavior Analysis in Social Networks
and Social Media*, Lecture Notes in Social Networks,
https://doi.org/10.1007/978-3-030-02592-2_3

moving [6], and (3) being the first to move in the new direction [4]. The framework is general enough to incorporate any set of traits as the set of hypotheses of leader characterization.

LEADER TRAIT CHARACTERIZATION PROBLEM: **Given a time series of individual activities and target traits, the goal is to find a set of leaders during decision-making periods and a set of traits that best characterize these leaders.**

We propose a two-step approach for the LEADER TRAIT CHARACTERIZATION PROBLEM:

1. We find instances of leadership and identify leaders, using an agnostic and assumption-free leadership inference framework FLICA [1, 2];
2. We evaluate traits of interest for all identified leaders and perform hypothesis testing to infer which traits are significant.

In the following section, we describe the FLICA approach for leadership inference as well as the justification and the approach for testing particular behavioral traits—position, velocity, and directionality—to characterize leaders.

We demonstrate our approach using simulation datasets for sensitivity analysis and a publicly available position tracking dataset from a troop of wild olive baboons (*Papio anubis*) from Mpala Research Centre, Kenya [7, 17], as well as a fish school of golden shiners (*Notemigonus crysoleucas*), which is another publically available dataset [16]. Our results show that the framework is robust to noise in the classification task of trait models. In baboons, movement initiators are not the first to move but, instead, are the first to explore new areas and that the group quickly aligns itself with the direction of the leader's movement. On the contrary, in a school of fish, movement initiators are the first to move and the first to explore new areas before others, and the group then too aligns its direction with initiators quickly.

2 The Proposed Approach

As stated earlier, there are many aspects of leader identity that may be used as the defining traits of the leader: the individual may be the oldest, biggest, wisest, or loudest. However, here we focus on the *behavioral* aspects of successful leadership, particularly in movement initiation. Are the leaders the ones who move first, move in the new direction, stay at the front, etc.? These are aspects of leadership behavior that also are inferable from the spatiotemporal time series data directly. We use the notion of a convex hull of the variable of interest for the group versus an individual, particularly the leader individual.

2.1 Bidirectional Agreement in Multi-Agent Systems

The use of convex hull to analyze traits of a leader in this paper is motivated by the work on bidirectional agreement dynamics in multi-agent systems by Chazelle [5]. Chazelle showed that in a multi-agent system, the states of all individuals converge to a group consensus if each individual changes its state for each time step under what he calls the "bidirectional agreement condition." The bidirectional agreement condition constrains an individual's choice of the state at each time step within the convex hull of the states of its neighbors (in the arbitrary agent network) in the previous time step. Thus, to break the group consensus state, some individual must break the convex hull condition at some time point. In the collective movement context, a state of an individual at time t can be the individual's position, direction of movement, velocity, or acceleration.

Initially, all individuals' state is within the convex hull of the group's state. However, when the group initiates movement, the group changes its state from the initial state to unstable state. Leaders who initiate movement must break the convex hull of the group state to change the state of the group from one state to another state. After movement initiation, under "bidirectional agreement condition," the group converges to a stable state, and everyone stays within the convex hull of the group's state again unless the convex hull is breached. In other words, we hypothesize that leaders are the state changers who start breaking the convex hull before others, and we test that hypothesis. For example, suppose we define a state as a position of each individual. Initially, by definition, all individuals are within the convex hull of an individual's positions. When leaders initiate movement by leading at the front, they must step outside the convex hull of group's positions.

We can define individual states to be any variable directly derivable from the time series data, including individual positions, velocities, or directions. However, the question is which of these variables' convex hull of the group states that leaders actually break when they initiate movement that everyone follows. In this paper, we consider the type(s) of convex hull that leaders break as behavior traits, and we aim to infer these traits from time series data of group movement.

2.2 Bidirectional Agreement Condition

First, we start with the one-dimensional states of bidirectional agreement condition. At any time t, suppose $S_t = \{s_{1,t}, \ldots, s_{n,t}\}$ is a set of individual states at current time where $s_{i,t} \in \mathbb{R}$ is a one-dimensional state of individual i at time t, $m_{i,t}$ is a point in S_t that is closest to $s_{i,t}$ but has a value at most $s_{i,t}$, and $M_{i,t}$ is a point in S_t that is closest to $s_{i,t}$ but has a value at least $s_{i,t}$ and a constant $\rho \in (0, 1/2]$. The work by Chazelle [5] defines a bidirectional agreement condition as follows:

$$(1 - \rho)m_{i,t} + \rho M_{i,t} \leq s_{i,t+1} \leq \rho m_{i,t} + (1 - \rho)M_{i_t}. \tag{1}$$

The interpretation is that if all individuals change their state within the bound of their neighbor's states, the group will converge to a collective state, which is a stable state. In high-dimensional states, the bidirectional agreement condition still requires individuals to change their state from time to time within the bound of their neighbor's states, which is a convex hull of neighbor's states to make the group converge to a stable state. In other words, if all individual states always stay within their neighbor-state convex hull, then the group converges to a single point of collective state and stays there forever.

2.3   *Leaders as State Changers*

When leaders initiate a group movement, if leaders are state changers, then leaders are necessary to be the first who break the bidirectional agreement condition or step outside group's state convex hull. Figure 1 shows an example of state-changing situation in two-dimensional state. Suppose U is a state changer and a leader, while U initiates movement, U steps outside the group's state convex hull, which means U breaks the bidirectional agreement condition. In this paper, we infer whether leaders who initiate movement are state changers by observing the association between

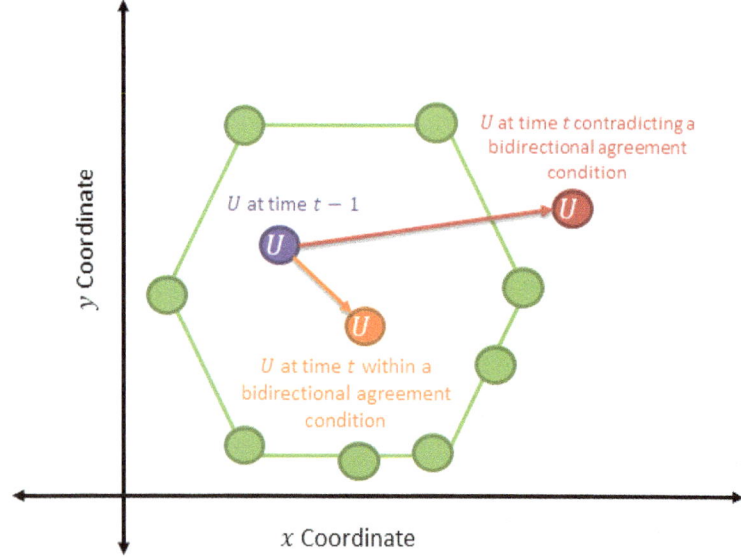

Fig. 1 An example of state-changing situation in the two-dimensional space. The green nodes are states of individuals at time $t - 1$, and the green polygon is a neighbor-state convex hull of individual U. If U changes its state under the bidirectional agreement condition, then the next state of U is always in the convex hull (orange). On the contrary, if U steps outside the convex hull (red) to make a group changes its state, then it breaks the bidirectional agreement condition

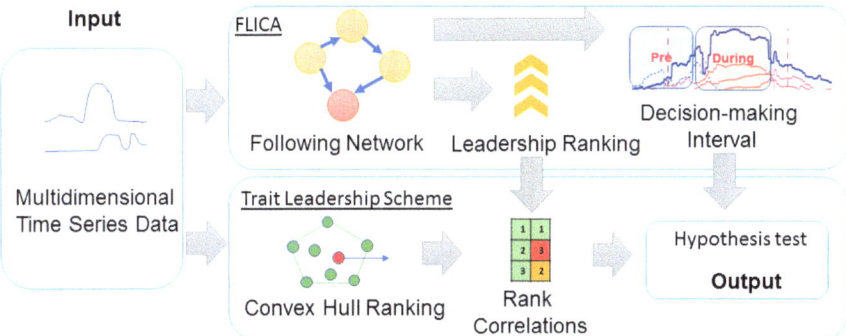

Fig. 2 High-level overview of trait leadership scheme using FLICA ([1, Figure 1] used and modified with permission). An arrow between elements represents a relationship that an element at the rear of the arrow is the input of an element at the head of the arrow. For example, rank correlations are calculated by taking leadership ranking and convex hull ranking as inputs

the time that individuals break the convex hull of states (velocity, position, and direction) compared to individual leadership ranking.

2.4 Approach Overview

The high-level overview of the proposed leadership trait characterization scheme using FLICA [1, 2] is shown in Fig. 2. Given a time series of GPS positions of baboons, we use FLICA to report a dynamic following network, leadership ranking, and decision-making intervals. Then, in this work, we propose measures of velocity, position, and direction convex hull containment as traits of leadership and conduct the experiments to find any significant positive/negative correlations between leadership ranking and those measures.

Let $D = \{Q_1, \ldots, Q_n\}$ be a set of time series of positions where D consists of n time series where each $Q_i \in D$ has length T (the number of time steps) and each Q_{it} is a position coordinate of the individual i at time t.

2.5 FLICA

Construction of the Network of Following Relations To infer the following relations between time series, dynamic time warping (DTW) [15] was deployed to measure the similarity between the shape (not the exact position) and the shift in the trajectories. Figure 3 demonstrates an example of following relation inference between time series Q and U. In this figure, U follows Q which has time delay Δt. By considering an optimal warping path within DTW, we can infer a following

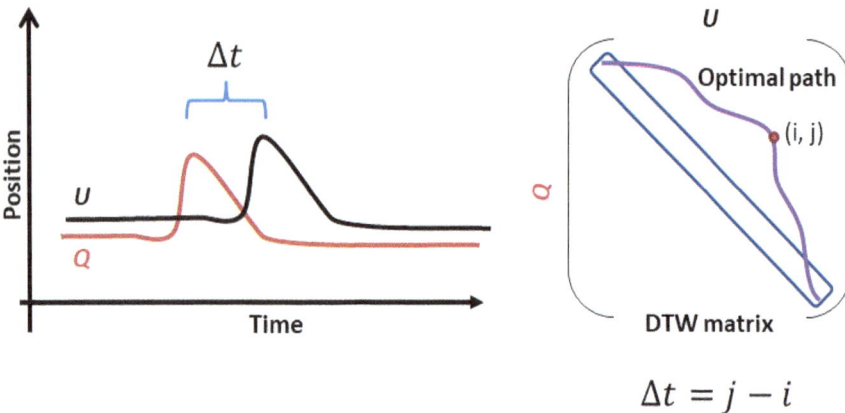

$$\Delta t = j - i$$

Fig. 3 An example of a following relation between time series U and Q. (Left) Time series U follows Q. (Right) The optimal warping path on the DTW dynamic programming matrix, shifting U backward in time onto Q

relation between time series. For each pair of time series, we calculate an average of differences between indices within an optimal warping path of DTW to extract the average time delay between time series. If a time delay is positive, then U follows Q, negative if Q follows U, and zero if neither U nor Q follows each other.

To construct a dynamic following network, we split time series into subintervals to infer following networks, and then we combine following networks from these subintervals to be a single dynamic following network. Let ω be a time window that defines a subinterval and $\delta = 0.1\omega$ be a sliding window parameter. Let a kth window be an interval given by $w(k) = [k \times \delta, k \times \delta + \omega]$. A following network $G_k = (V, E_k)$ at time interval $w(k)$ is a directed graph where V is a set of time series nodes (that do not change), which has one-to-one mapping to each individual time series, and E_k is a set of following edges. If $e(U, Q) \in E_k$, then a time series U follows Q at time interval $w(k)$. FLICA computes the networks of following relations from $w(0)$ to $w(m)$ to cover the entire time series intervals T, and then it reports the entire dynamic following network.

Leadership Ranking To rank a degree of leadership, given a following network, FLICA uses PageRank [14]. An individual with a high PageRank score has many followers and is followed by individuals who themselves have many followers, which matches the intuitive notion of leadership. We prefer PageRank rather than any other centrality measure, such as degree or betweenness, because PageRank captures the transitive nature of following relations and the end-to-end aspect of the individual to leader path. Leaders are nodes that have a high number of reachable paths to them in a following network. Ultimately, leaders are the nodes to whom *everyone* has a reachable path. Hence PageRank is the most appropriate measure in our leadership setting.

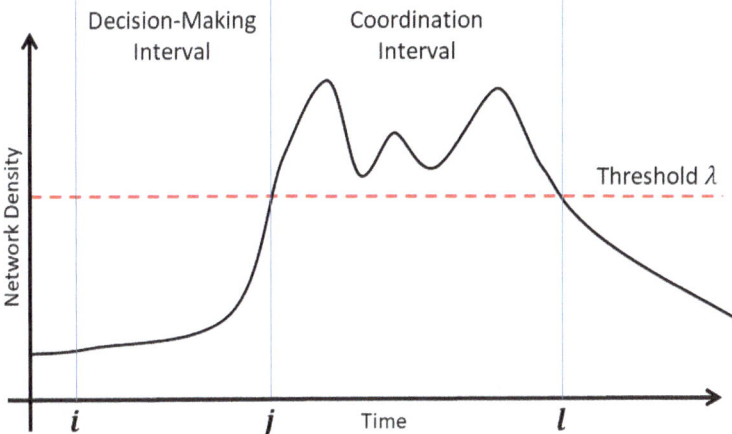

Fig. 4 An example of a coordination event identified based on a network density time series ([1, Figure 4] used and modified with permission). Based on a threshold λ, we identify a decision-making interval, followed by a coordination interval

Decision-Making Interval Detection After constructing a dynamic following network, FLICA uses network density as the measure of the level of coordination within the group to extract intervals of coordinated activity and the decision-making period that preceded it. Let λ be a decision-making threshold parameter. We set a threshold of network density at a percentile λth for the values of dynamic following network densities to separate between two types of intervals: coordination events and non-coordination interval. Figure 4 shows the example of coordination event that has its peak greater than λ. In other words, a coordination event represents an interval which has a high number of following edges. The intervals outside coordination events are non-coordination intervals. The interval directly preceding the coordination event is referred to as a decision-making interval; FLICA reports the initiator of each of these coordinated events. Now, for each instance of coordination and the resulting of significantly following in the group, FLICA reports the ranks of all the individuals during the initiation of that event. We use that ranking to evaluate the corresponding ranking by the proposed leadership traits.

2.6 Leadership Trait Characterization Scheme

The Quantification of the Traits of Interests We focus on three common characterizations of a leader: being the first to move, being at the front of a group, and being the first to move in the new direction. We use the notion of the convex hull to measure the similarity of the trait value for an individual versus the group as a whole.

First, to measure the notion of being the *first to move*, we need to consider the velocity of all individuals at the previous time step. If any individual moves before others, its velocity is higher than others' velocity at the previous time step. That is, it is higher than the maximum previous velocity of any individual, or, to put it in other words, it is outside of the convex hull of the velocities in the previous time step in the positive direction (since velocity is a one-dimensional measure).

Second, to measure the notion of being at the *front of the group*, we need to consider both direction of individuals and their positions. If any individual moves toward the front of the group, then its direction of movement is the same as the group's direction, but its position is outside the group's area of the previous time step. That is, the coordinates of the individual at the front of the group are outside of the convex hull of the coordinates of the individuals in the previous time step but aligned with the direction vector of the group.

Third, to measure the notion of being the *first to move in the new direction*, we need to consider direction vectors of all the individuals. If any individual moves in the new direction, which is not the same as the group's direction, then the angle between its current direction vector and the group's direction vector at the previous time step must be high. That is, the current (angle of the) direction vector of the individual is outside the convex hull of the direction vectors of the individuals in the previous time step.

Convex Hull Ranking Measures   For each of the three measures, we construct the convex hull in each time step and rank the individuals by the frequency with which their value in the current step is outside the convex hull of the values of all the individuals in the previous step for the same measure.

The velocity convex hull (VCH) ranking score measures the frequency with which the discrete time series derivative (dQ_i/dt) associated with an individual i is outside the bounds of the population's (including i) discrete derivative interval in the previous time step. The highest rank of this measure indicates an individual who is the first to move in the group. Let $n \times T$ matrix VCH be a velocity convex hull score matrix where $\text{VCH}(Q_i, t) = 1$ if a time series Q_i at time t has its velocity greater than a maximum velocity of the entire group at time $t - 1$ and $\text{VCH}(Q_i, t) = -1$ if Q_i has its velocity less than a minimum velocity of the entire group at time $t - 1$, and otherwise $\text{VCH}(Q_i, t) = 0$.

The position convex hull (PCH) ranking score measures the frequency with which a position and direction associated with an individual i are outside the bounds of the population's position convex hull in the previous time step. A high rank of this measure indicates which individual first explores a new area before others. Let $n \times T$ matrix PCH be a position convex hull score matrix where $\text{PCH}(Q_i, t) = 1$ if a time series Q_i at time t has its direction toward the group's direction and i's position at time t is outside the group's position convex hull at time $t - 1$ (see Fig. 5). In contrast, if Q_i is outside the convex hull but moving in the opposite way of group direction, then $\text{PCH}(Q_i, t) = -1$ (see Fig. 5); otherwise $\text{PCH}(Q_i, t) = 0$. We consider that i is moving toward the group direction if the angle between i's

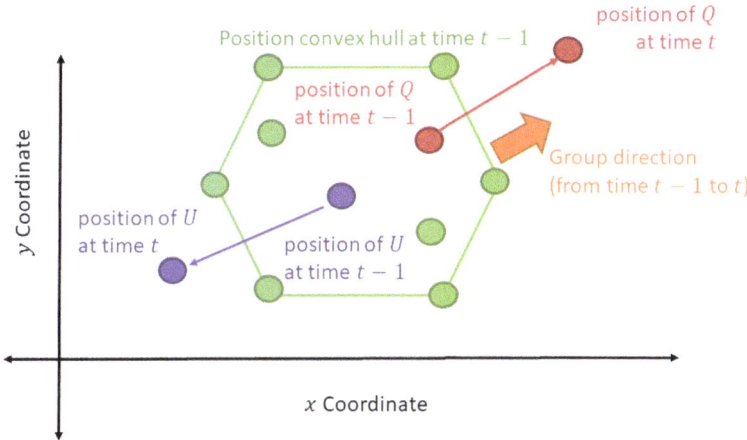

Fig. 5 An example of position convex hull. Each point represents an individual, and the polygon represents a convex hull boundary at time $t - 1$. In this example, Q steps outside the convex hull at time t toward the group direction, while U steps outside the convex hull in the opposite direction. In this case, Q gets a score +1, and U gets a score -1 for time step t. If an individual is still in the convex hull, it gets zero score

direction vector and group's direction vector is between $-90°$ and $90°$. Otherwise, we consider that i is moving in the opposite direction from its group movement.

The direction convex hull (DCH) ranking score measures the frequency with which the angle between individual's direction vector and group's direction vector is outside the bound of the set of angles between each individual and the group's direction vector in the previous time step. A high rank of this measure indicates an individual that frequently deviates from the group's direction of travel. Let $n \times T$ matrix DCH be a direction convex hull score matrix where $\mathrm{DCH}(Q_i, t) = 1$ if a time series Q_i at time t has its individual-group direction angle greater than a maximum individual-group direction angle of the entire group at time $t - 1$ and $\mathrm{DCH}(Q_i, t) = -1$ if i has its individual-group direction angle lower than a minimum individual-group direction angle of the entire group at time $t - 1$, and otherwise $\mathrm{DCH}(Q_i, t) = 0$.

Rank Correlation We deploy the Kendall rank correlation coefficient $\tau(x, y)$ [12] to infer correlation between PageRank leadership ranking (see paragraph "Leadership Ranking") and the convex hull ranking.

Further, for any given threshold λ used to determine coordination events, we focus on only decision-making intervals to measure the rank correlations. We define two levels of analysis: **time-point level** and **interval level**. First, for a **time-point-level** correlation, we compute a rank correlation for each time t within any decision-making interval as follows.

Let $R_{\mathrm{PR},t} = \mathrm{argsort}(\mathrm{PR}(:, t))$ be a PageRank rank ordered list at time t such that $R(Q_i)_{\mathrm{PR},t} = q$ if an individual i is at qth rank at time t and $R(Q_i)_{\mathrm{PR},t} = 1$ if i is a leader at time t. Note that we always use argsort to represent the descending sort order for the entire paper since the higher score implies the better rank.

$R_{\text{VCH},t} = \text{argsort}(\text{VCH}(:,t))$, $R_{\text{PCH},t} = \text{argsort}(\text{PCH}(:,t))$, and $R_{\text{DCH},t} = \text{argsort}(\text{DCH}(:,t))$ are velocity, position, and direction convex hull rank order lists, respectively. A rank correlation between PageRank and VCH is $\tau(R_{\text{PR},t}, R_{\text{VCH},t})$. A rank correlation between PageRank and PCH is $\tau(R_{\text{PR},t}, R_{\text{PCH},t})$. And a rank correlation between PageRank and DCH is $\tau(R_{\text{PR},t}, R_{\text{DCH},t})$. We define a set of time-point PageRank-VCH correlations as follows:

$$\Phi_{\text{PR,VCH}} = \{\tau(R_{\text{PR},t_1}, R_{\text{VCH},t_1}), \tau(R_{\text{PR},t_2}, R_{\text{VCH},t_2}), \ldots\} \tag{2}$$

where t_i is a time point within any decision-making interval. Similarly, we can also define a set of time-point PageRank-PCH correlations and PageRank-DCH correlations in the similar way.

$$\Phi_{\text{PR,PCH}} = \{\tau(R_{\text{PR},t_1}, R_{\text{PCH},t_1}), \tau(R_{\text{PR},t_2}, R_{\text{PCH},t_2}), \ldots\} \tag{3}$$

$$\Phi_{\text{PR,DCH}} = \{\tau(R_{\text{PR},t_1}, R_{\text{DCH},t_1}), \tau(R_{\text{PR},t_2}, R_{\text{DCH},t_2}), \ldots\} \tag{4}$$

Second, for an **interval-level** rank correlation, we compute the representative correlation of the entire decision-making interval for each coordination event. Let $I = (i, j, l)$ be any coordination event, and we define $\tilde{R}_{\text{PR},I} = \text{argsort}(\sum_{t \in [i,j]} R_{\text{PR},t})$ as a PageRank rank ordered list during decision-making interval of coordination event I. $\tilde{R}_{\text{VCH},I} = \text{argsort}(\sum_{t \in [i,j]} R_{\text{VCH},t})$, $\tilde{R}_{\text{PCH},I} = \text{argsort}(\sum_{t \in [i,j]} R_{\text{PCH},t})$, and $\tilde{R}_{\text{DCH},I} = \text{argsort}(\sum_{t \in [i,j]} R_{\text{DCH},t})$ are defined to be VCH, PCH, and DCH rank ordered lists of I, respectively. The PageRank-VCH rank correlation at decision-making interval of I is $\tau(\tilde{R}_{\text{PR},I}, \tilde{R}_{\text{VCH},I})$, the PageRank-PCH rank correlation is $\tau(\tilde{R}_{\text{PR},I}, \tilde{R}_{\text{PCH},I})$, and the PageRank-DCH rank correlation is $\tau(\tilde{R}_{\text{PR},I}, \tilde{R}_{\text{DCH},I})$. We define a set of interval PageRank-VCH correlations as follows:

$$\tilde{\Phi}_{\text{PR,VCH}} = \{\tau(\tilde{R}_{\text{PR},I_1}, \tilde{R}_{\text{VCH},I_1}), \tau(\tilde{R}_{\text{PR},I_2}, \tilde{R}_{\text{VCH},I_2}), \ldots\} \tag{5}$$

where I_i is an ith coordination event. We can also define PageRank-PCH correlations and PageRank-DCH correlations in the similar way.

$$\tilde{\Phi}_{\text{PR,PCH}} = \{\tau(\tilde{R}_{\text{PR},I_1}, \tilde{R}_{\text{PCH},I_1}), \tau(\tilde{R}_{\text{PR},I_2}, \tilde{R}_{\text{PCH},I_2}), \ldots\} \tag{6}$$

$$\tilde{\Phi}_{\text{PR,DCH}} = \{\tau(\tilde{R}_{\text{PR},I_1}, \tilde{R}_{\text{DCH},I_1}), \tau(\tilde{R}_{\text{PR},I_2}, \tilde{R}_{\text{DCH},I_2}), \ldots\} \tag{7}$$

Leadership Model Classification Using Trait-Rank Correlation For model classification, we use three interval-level rank correlations from paragraph "Rank

Correlation" as features to train a classifier. For each dataset, our framework provides a vector of features $v = (\tau(\tilde{R}_{PR}, \tilde{R}_{VCH}), \tau(\tilde{R}_{PR}, \tilde{R}_{PCH}), \tau(\tilde{R}_{PR}, \tilde{R}_{DCH}))$, which represents trait characteristic of leadership model. We use multiclass support vector machine (SVM) as our main classifier.

3 Experimental Setup

3.1 Trait of Leadership Model

In this section, we provide three different models of trait leadership. We use these models to demonstrate that our rank correlations in paragraph "Rank Correlation" can be used as features to classify these models, which have different traits of leadership. All these models are in two-dimensional space. Initially, there are 20 individuals within a unit cycle. Positions of individuals are uniformly distributed within this unit cycle. Then the group moves toward a collective target.

Moving First Model In this model, high-rank individuals move earlier than low-rank individuals. A leader moves toward target trajectory, and everyone follows its hierarchy. We have ID(1) as a leader. ID(k) moves first; then it is followed by ID($k + 1$) with a constant time delay. The acceleration of movement for all individuals is constant. We aim to use this model as a representative model that high-rank individuals always move earlier than low-rank individuals. For this model, we set the initial velocity at 1 unit/time step and acceleration at 0.001 unit/time step^2.

Moving Front Model This model also has an ordered hierarchy of following the same as the previous model. Nevertheless, there is no order of movement initiation. In other words, all individuals have uniformly time delay before they start moving. The group moves along a target trajectory with a constant velocity, and a leader is always in the front of the group followed by high-rank individuals. Lower-rank individuals follow higher-rank individuals. We aim to use this model as a representative model that high-rank individuals always explore new areas before low-rank individuals. For this model, we set the initial velocity at 1 unit/time step and acceleration at 0 unit/time step^2.

Reversible Agreement Model Compared to previous models, this model has no leader and any following hierarchy. All individuals move toward the average of group's direction with a constant velocity. This model is one of the bidirectional agreement systems that have convergence property [5]. In our case, all individual's directions converge to an average group direction, which implies the existence of coordinated movement of the group. We aim to use this model as a representative model that the group has coordinated movement without leadership hierarchy. We expect that any leadership model classification should be able to at least distinguish between leadership models and this non-leadership model. For this model, we set the initial velocity at 1 unit/time step and acceleration at 0 unit/time step^2.

3.2 Datasets

Simulation Datasets for Sensitivity Analysis We create simulation datasets with the difference level of noises. We have two types of noise here: direction noise and position noise. For direction noise, instead of moving to a target direction at degree D, an individual moves toward direction $D + a$. The direction noise a is drawn randomly from normal distribution with zero mean and γ standard deviation where $\gamma \in \{0, 1, 10, 30, 60\}$. For position noise, suppose (x, y) is the next position that an individual should move to, with position noises, the actual position that the individual moves is $(x + b_1, y + b_2)$. The position noises b_1, b_2 are drawn randomly from a normal distribution with zero mean and β standard deviation where $\beta \in \{0.0001, 0.001, 0.01, 0.1, 1\}$.

For each noise setting (γ, β), we create 100 for each trait of leadership model. Each dataset contains 20 time series of individuals, which have the length as 300 time steps. In total, since we have three leadership models and 25 possible different (γ, β), we have 7500 datasets.

Simulation Datasets for Degree of Hierarchy Structure Analysis We use simulated datasets that can be found in [2]. There are three leadership models we use in this paper: dictatorship, hierarchical model, and random model. Each model consists of 100 datasets. Each dataset has two-dimensional time series of 20 individuals. Each time series has its length at 12,000 time steps. There are 20 coordination events within each dataset.

Initially, all individuals are at their starting point. In dictatorship model (DM), a leader moves first, and then everyone else follows its leader with some time delay. In hierarchical model (HM), there are four high-rank individuals, ID1, ID2, ID3, and ID4. Other non-high-rank individuals get assigned by their leaders to be one of the high-rank individuals. ID1 is a global leader of all high-rank individuals that always moves first. ID2 and ID3 follow ID1 with some time delay. Then ID4 follows ID1. Lastly, the followers of ID1, ID2, ID3, and ID4 follow their leaders.

For the random model, all individuals move together toward a target direction. However, these individuals never follow any specific individuals. Hence, there are coordination events in this model, but there are no leaders.

Baboon Dataset The baboon dataset is a publically available dataset that contains GPS tracking information from 26 members of an olive baboon (*Papio anubis*) troop recorded from 6 a.m. to 6 p.m. between August 01, 2012 and August 10, 2012. These baboons live in the wild at the Mpala Research Centre, Kenya [7, 17]. For each individual, the GPS collar recorded its latitude and longitude position for every second. Then these latitude and longitude time series were converted to be the $X - Y$ coordinate trajectories.

We preprocessed the GPS data, removing some individuals whose GPS collars were active only in a short period of time. The final dataset consists of 16 individuals, each of whose trajectory has a length of 419,095 time steps. The composition of the baboon group includes individuals who vary in sex (male and female) and age (juvenile, subadult, and adult). This dataset includes a variety of baboon activities, including sleeping, foraging, traveling, and resting.

Fish Dataset The fish school dataset of golden shiners (*Notemigonus crysoleucas*) is another publically available dataset. The two-dimensional fish movement trajectories are recorded by video in order to study information propagation over the visual fields of fish [16]. The number of individuals within each population is 70 individuals, but only 10 individuals are labeled with a trained class. A trained fish is able to lead the school to feeding sites. The dataset contains 24 coordination events. The fish trajectories have their length between 550 and 600 time steps. Our task is to identify the traits of trained fish.

3.3   Sensitivity Analysis in Model Classification

We separate simulation dataset into the groups based on the value of noise setting (γ, β). For each group, it consists of 100 datasets of moving first model, 100 datasets of moving front model, and 100 datasets of reversible agreement model. We report tenfold cross-validation of model classification for each group of datasets having the same noise level (γ, β). We also report the rank correlation between the ground-truth leadership rank and inferred leadership rank from our framework to measure the ability of leadership inference within difference level of noises.

3.4   Hypotheses Tests

In this section, we aim to design a hypothesis testing scheme to address three hypotheses: (1) individuals who act as leaders (identified by FLICA) are individuals who move first, initiating their movements before others in their group in the decision-making period prior to coordinated movement, (2) individuals who act as leaders are individuals who always explore a new area before others prior to a coordinated movement, and (3) individuals who act as leaders are individuals who always align with the group direction. We define leaders as individuals who possess a highly ranked position in a PageRank rank ordered list. The hypothesis testing methods we used can be categorized into two categories: zero mean/median test and normality test. For the zero mean/median hypothesis test, we aim to test whether a positive/negative correlation exists between PageRank and convex hull ranking in both time-point and interval levels. For normality tests, we aimed to determine whether correlation samples come from a normal distribution. If not, the interpretation of tests which assume normally distributed data, e.g., t-test, should be considered carefully. The full list of hypothesis testing methods we used is in Table 1. We set significance level at $\alpha = 0.001$ for all tests.

Table 1 Description of hypothesis tests used in this paper

	Method	Null hypothesis H_0
zero mean/median hypothesis test	t-Test	A sample has a normal distribution with zero mean and unknown variance
	Sign test	A sample has a distribution with zero median
	Wilcoxon signed-rank test	A sample has a symmetric distribution around zero median
Normality test	Kolmogorov-Smirnov test	A sample comes from a normal distribution
	Chi-square goodness-of-fit test	A sample comes from a normal distribution with a mean and variance estimated from a sample itself
	Jarque-Bera test	A sample comes from a normal distribution with an unknown mean and variance
	Anderson-Darling test	A sample comes from a normal distribution

A significance level has been set at $\alpha = 0.001$ for all experiments

3.5 Parameter Setting

For simulation datasets, we set the time window $\omega = 60$ and $\delta = 6$, which is the optimal setting since the simulation dataset has time delay less than 5 time steps by design. For the analysis in baboon dataset, we set the time window $\omega = 240$ and $\delta = 24$. For the fish datasets, we set the time window $\omega = 285$ and $\delta = 28$. Both parameter settings of baboon and fish datasets are set based on the fact that these settings can infer the highest number of following relations per following group on average. The time sliding window parameter δ serves to trade off computation versus the sampling rate of the time series process. The FLICA has time complexity $\mathcal{O}(n^2 \times t \times \omega)$. The network density decision-making threshold λ was set at 25th, 50th, 75th, and 99th percentile of network density values for the baboon dataset to detect decision-making intervals. For the simulation and fish datasets, we already have the decision-making intervals, so we do not need to set λ.

4 Results

4.1 Traits of Leader Classification: Sensitivity Analysis

Figure 6 shows the result of sensitivity analysis in the model classification. Loss values of tenfold cross-validation are shown in the figure at the top. A loss value is a percentage of datasets that the classifier predicted them into wrong classes. Figure 6 (top) shows that when the level of noises increases, classifier produces more errors. According to the cross-validation result, our framework can distinguish between

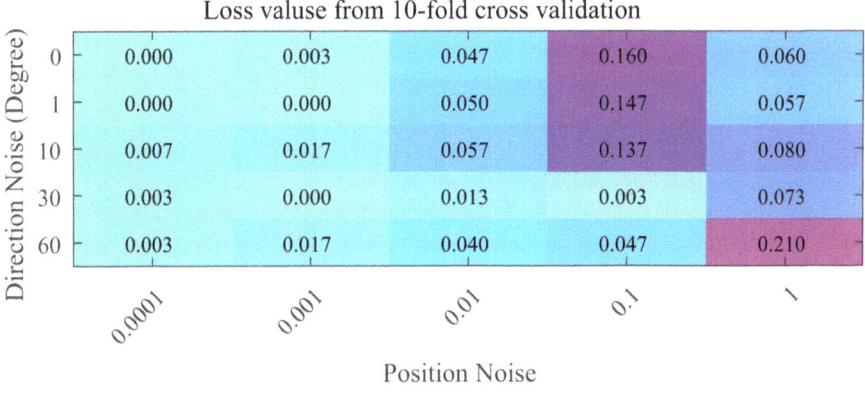

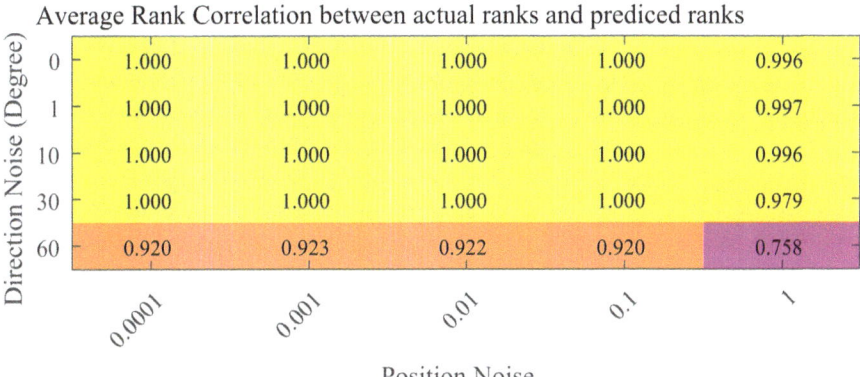

Fig. 6 Sensitivity analysis in model classification task from simulation datasets with different noise levels. (Top) Tenfold cross-validation loss values. Each element in the table represents the loss value of each noise setting (γ, β). (Bottom) Rank correlation between actual leadership ranking and predicted ranking from moving first and moving front models

leadership models (moving first and moving front models) and non-leadership model (reversible agreement model). Additionally, the result suggests that position noise affected the classification result than direction noise. When the position noise level reach at 1, which is the diameter of group movement, the leadership rank is less consistent with the ground-truth rank (Fig. 6 bottom). This indicates that both leadership ranking and traits of leadership inference are hard to perform under high-level of position noise. In general, this result shows that our framework performs accurately even if an input data is noisy until a certain degree of noises.

4.2 Trait Identification of Baboon Movement

The distributions of rank correlations inferred from the baboon dataset are in Fig. 7. At the time-point level, the distribution of PageRank and velocity convex hull (PR-VCH) correlation $\Phi_{PR,VCH}$ is at the top left of the figure, the distribution of PageRank and position convex hull (PR-PCH) correlation $\Phi_{PR,PCH}$ is at the top middle, and the distribution of PageRank and direction convex hull (PR-DCH) $\Phi_{PR,DCH}$ is at the top right of the figure. For the interval-level correlations, the distribution $\tilde{\Phi}_{PR,VCH}$ is at the bottom left, the distribution $\tilde{\Phi}_{PR,PCH}$ is at the bottom middle, and the distribution $\tilde{\Phi}_{PR,DCH}$ is at the bottom right. Table 2 illustrates the means and standard deviations of these correlation distributions.

Figure 7 and Table 2 suggest that there is no correlation between PageRank and velocity convex hull ranking at both the time-point level (Fig. 7's top left) and the interval level (Fig. 7's bottom left). In contrast, positive correlations exist between PageRank and position convex hull in both levels (Fig. 7, top and bottom middle). Moreover, negative correlations exist between PageRank and direction convex hull in interval level (Fig. 7, bottom right). When we set a higher percentile threshold, we get stronger coordination events; a stronger coordination event has a higher number of following relations. Both Fig. 7 and Table 2 illustrate that the rank correlations between PageRank and position convex hull ranking are higher, while the rank correlations between PageRank and direction convex hull ranking are lower

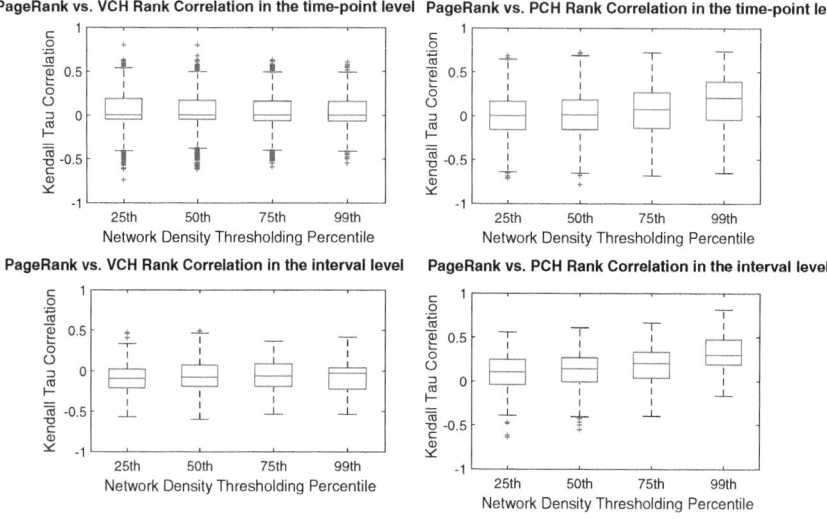

Fig. 7 Comparison of PR-VCH, PR-PCH, and PR-DCH rank correlations under different thresholds. For PR-VCH correlation, the results in both time-point level (top left) and interval level (bottom left) show that there are no strong correlations between leadership and VCH ranking. In contrast, leadership and PCH rankings have positive correlations in both time-point level (top middle) and interval level (bottom middle), as well as PR-DCH correlation which has a negative correlation at the interval level (bottom right)

Table 2 PR-VCH, PR-PCH, and PR-DCH rank correlations from the baboon dataset under different thresholds

		Time-point level		Interval level	
	Percentile	Mean	STD	Mean	STD
PR-VCH corr.	25th	0.03	0.20	−0.09	0.18
	50th	0.03	0.19	−0.07	0.18
	75th	0.03	0.19	−0.06	0.19
	99th	0.03	0.19	−0.07	0.21
PR-PCH corr.	25th	0.00	0.23	0.09	0.20
	50th	0.01	0.25	**0.12**	0.21
	75th	0.06	0.27	**0.18**	0.22
	99th	**0.15**	0.30	**0.32**	0.22
PR-DCH corr.	25th	−0.0082	0.1739	0.03	0.22
	50th	−0.0098	0.1745	−0.01	0.23
	75th	−0.0251	0.1818	−0.09	0.25
	99th	−0.0552	0.1827	**−0.24**	0.24

when we set a stronger threshold. However, there is not a large difference in the correlations of PageRank and velocity convex hull when we varied the threshold value.

Based on this result, due to weak correlations of PR-VCH in both time-point and interval levels and PR-DCH in the time-point level, we decided to conduct the hypothesis tests only in the PR-PCH rank correlation samples in both levels while conducting the hypothesis tests for PR-DCH in the interval level.

The result of these hypotheses tests are shown at Table 3. In the aspect of normality test results, correlations at time-point level of PCH are less normal compared to the PCH's and DCH's correlations at the interval level. This implies that the result of t-test at the PCH's time-point level should be interpreted carefully.

In the aspect of zero mean/median hypothesis test, with the significance level at $\alpha = 0.001$, PageRank and position convex hull ranking have positive correlations far from 0. This implies that individuals who act as leaders tend to explore new areas before other individuals during decision-making intervals.

In contrast, PageRank and direction convex hull ranking have negative correlations far from 0 at the 75th and 99th percentile thresholds. This implies that individuals who act as leaders tend to align with the group's direction (or, more intuitively, the group is aligned with the leader's direction), while non-leaders frequently attempt to change the direction, but nobody follows. In other words, high-rank individuals control the group direction, and this is why they are almost always inside the direction convex hull. When high-rank individuals move in any given direction, the group follows almost immediately, and this makes the group's direction the same as the leading individuals' direction.

Finally, for interval-level correlations of PR-PCH and PR-DCH ranking, we reported the normal confidence intervals at Table 4. We only reported the confidence intervals of interval-level correlations because of the normality test results; time-

Table 3 Hypothesis test results of PR-PCH and PR-DCH correlation

	Tests/percentile THS	PR-PCH corr. at a time-point level				PR-PCH corr. at an interval level				PR-DCH corr. at an interval level			
		25th	50th	75th	99th	25th	50th	75th	99th	25th	50th	75th	99th
Zero mean/ median test	t-Test	0	1	1	1	1	1	1	1	0	0	1	1
	Sign test	0	1	1	1	1	1	1	1	0	0	1	1
	Wilcoxon signed-rank test	0	1	1	1	1	1	1	1	0	0	1	1
Normality test	Kolmogorov-Smirnov test	1	1	1	1	1	1	1	1	1	1	1	1
	Chi-square test	1	1	1	1	0	0	0	0	0	0	0	0
	Jarque-Bera test	1	1	1	1	0	0	0	0	0	0	0	0
	Anderson-Darling test	1	1	1	1	0	0	0	0	0	0	0	0

The zero value implies that a test fails to reject H_0, while one implies a test successfully rejects H_0 with $\alpha = 0.001$

Table 4 Normal confidence intervals of PR-PCH and PR-DCH correlations from the baboon dataset at the interval level with $\alpha = 0.001$

	Percentile threshold	Normal confidence interval			
		Mean μ		STD	
		Lower bound	Upper bound	Lower bound	Upper bound
PR-PCH	25th	0.06	0.13	0.18	0.23
	50th	0.08	0.16	0.18	0.23
	75th	0.13	0.23	0.19	0.25
	99th	0.19	0.44	0.16	0.35
PR-DCH	25th	−0.01	0.07	0.20	0.25
	50th	−0.05	0.03	0.21	0.27
	75th	−0.14	−0.04	0.21	0.29
	99th	−0.38	−0.11	0.17	0.37

point level of PR-PCH correlation distributions seems not to be normal (see Table 3), while the rest of the cases are normal. All normal confidence intervals of PR-PCH correlation distributions have their lower bound greater than 0, while the upper bounds of PR-DCH correlation at the 75th and 99th percentile thresholds are below 0. This supports the hypotheses that there exist a positive correlation between PageRank and PCH ranking and a negative correlation between PageRank and DCH at the interval level.

4.3 Trait Identification of Fish Movement

The distributions of rank correlations inferred from the fish dataset are in Fig. 8. At the time-point level, the distributions of $\Phi_{PR,VCH}$, $\Phi_{PR,PCH}$, and $\Phi_{PR,DCH}$ are at the left of the figure, while the right of the figure contains rank correlations at the interval level. Table 5 illustrates the means and standard deviations of these correlation distributions.

At the time-point level, Fig. 8 and Table 5 suggest that there is no correlation between PageRank vs. VCH ranking and PageRank vs. DCH ranking, while we have positive rank correlations of PageRank vs. PCH on average. At the interval level, $\tilde{\Phi}_{PR,VCH}$ and $\tilde{\Phi}_{PR,PCH}$ have positive values on average, while $\tilde{\Phi}_{PR,DCH}$ has negative values on average.

Based on this result, due to the weak correlations of PR-VCH and PR-DCH in a time-point level, we decided to conduct the hypothesis tests only in the PR-PCH rank correlation samples in both levels while conducting the hypothesis tests for PR-VCH and PR-DCH in the interval level.

The result of hypotheses tests from the fish dataset is shown in Table 6. In the aspect of normality test results, correlations at time-point level of PCH are less

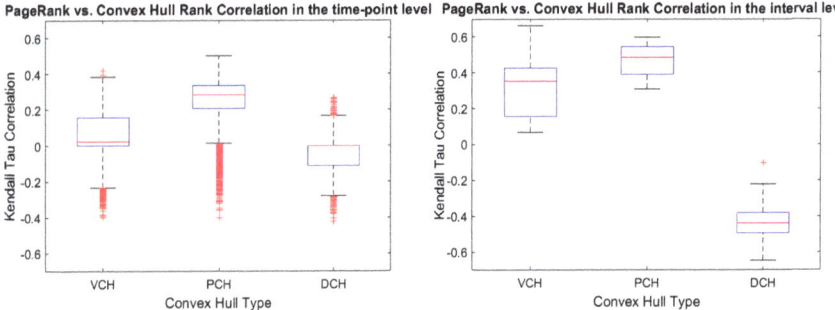

Fig. 8 Comparison of PR-VCH, PR-PCH, and PR-DCH rank correlations in both time-point and interval levels from the fish movement dataset. In the time-point level (left), the result shows that leadership vs. VCH and leadership vs. PCH rankings have positive correlations, while leadership and DCH has negative correlation. In the interval level (right), leadership vs. VCH and leadership vs. PCH rankings have stronger positive correlations than time-point level, while leadership and DCH also have stronger negative correlation

Table 5 PR-VCH, PR-PCH, and PR-DCH rank correlations from the fish dataset		Time-point level		Interval level	
		Mean	STD	Mean	STD
	PR-VCH corr.	0.05	0.12	0.32	0.16
	PR-PCH corr.	0.26	0.12	0.47	0.09
	PR-DCH corr.	−0.05	0.08	−0.43	0.12

Table 6 Hypothesis test results of PR-VCH, PR-PCH, and PR-DCH correlations in time-point level and interval level from the fish movement dataset

		Time-point level	Interval level		
		PR-PCH corr.	PR-VCH corr.	PR-PCH corr.	PR-DCH corr.
Zero mean/ median test	t-Test	1	1	1	1
	Sign test	1	1	1	1
	Wilcoxon signed-rank test	1	1	1	1
Normality test	Kolmogorov-Smirnov test	1	1	1	1
	Chi-square goodness-of-fit test	1	0	0	0
	Jarque-Bera test	1	0	0	0
	Anderson-Darling test	1	0	0	0

The zero value implies that a test fails to reject H_0, while one implies a test successfully rejects H_0 with $\alpha = 0.001$

Table 7 Normal confidence intervals of PR-VCH, PR-PCH, and PR-DCH correlations from the fish dataset at the interval level with $\alpha = 0.001$

	Normal confidence interval			
	Mean μ		STD	
	Lower bound	Upper bound	Lower bound	Upper bound
PR-VCH	0.20	0.45	0.11	0.30
PR-PCH	0.41	0.54	0.06	0.16
PR-DCH	−0.52	−0.34	0.08	0.21

normal compared to the VCH's, PCH's, and DCH's correlations at the interval level. This implies that the result of t-test at the PCH's time-point level should be interpreted carefully.

In the aspect of zero mean/median hypothesis test, with the significance level at $\alpha = 0.001$, both PageRank vs. velocity convex hull ranking and PageRank vs. position convex hull ranking have positive correlations far from zero on average. The result demonstrates that individuals who act as trained fish tend to move earlier and explore new areas before other individuals during coordination events. On the contrary, PageRank vs. Direction convex hull ranking has negative correlations far from zero on average. The result implies that when trained fish moves in any given direction, the group follows almost immediately, and this makes the group's direction the same as a trained fish's direction.

We also reported the normal confidence intervals at Table 7. We only reported the confidence intervals of interval-level correlations because of the normality test results; time-point level of PR-PCH correlation distributions seems not to be normal (see Table 6), while the rest of the cases are normal.

According to Table 7, the normal confidence intervals of PR-VCH and PR-PCH correlation distributions have their lower bound greater than zero, while the upper bound of PR-DCH correlation is below zero. This supports the hypotheses that there exist a positive correlation between PageRank and VCH ranking as well as PageRank and PCH ranking, while there is a negative correlation between PageRank and DCH at the interval level.

4.4 Traits of Leaders as Measure of Degree of Hierarchy Structure

Another application of trait-rank correlations we proposed here is to use these correlations to measure the degree of hierarchy structure in the datasets. The hierarchy structure here is the order of early movement. If the datasets contain a high degree of order of movement, then some specific individuals (e.g., high-rank individuals) always move before other individuals. In contrast, if datasets contain no order of movement, then there is no specific order of individuals who move before others. Figure 9 illustrates the distributions of PR-VCH rank correlations of datasets (paragraph "Simulation Datasets for Degree of Hierarchy Structure Analysis") from three leadership models. As we expected, since hierarchical model has a higher degree of structure than the dictatorship model, hence, it has the highest value of PR-VCH rank correlations. The dictatorship model has the second highest value of PR-VCH rank correlations since there is a weak order of early movement; a leader

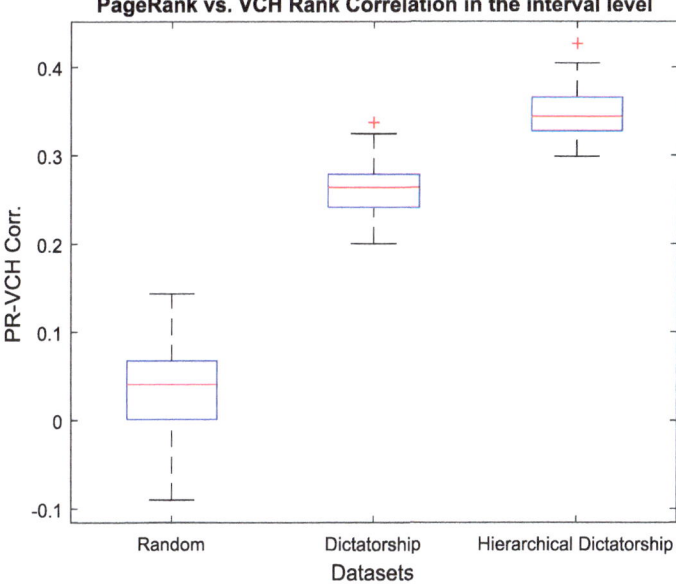

Fig. 9 The distributions of PR-VCH rank correlations of datasets from three leadership models. The higher-rank correlation implies the higher degree of hierarchy structure of early movement order in the model

Table 8 The means and
standard deviations of
PR-VCH rank correlations
from both simulated and
biological datasets

Datasets	Mean	STD
Hierarchical model	0.35	0.03
Dictatorship model	0.26	0.03
Random	0.04	0.05
Baboon (25th THS)	−0.09	0.18
Baboon (50th THS)	−0.07	0.18
Baboon (75th THS)	−0.06	0.19
Baboon (99th THS)	−0.07	0.21
Fish	0.32	0.16

always moves first. Lastly, the random model has the PR-VCH rank correlations around zero since it has no order of early movement.

In conclusion, the result implies that the higher-rank correlation implies the higher degree of hierarchy structure of early movement order in the model.

Table 8 shows the mean and standard deviation of PR-VCH rank correlations from both simulated and biological datasets. The result shows that baboon datasets have PR-VCH rank correlations nearly zero in all threshold of coordination events, while fish datasets have PR-VCH rank correlations nearly the Hierarchical model's correlations. This implies that baboons have no hierarchy of early movement, while schools of fish have pretty high degree of movement order.

5 Conclusions

In this paper, we proposed a framework for testing the correspondence between behavioral traits and leader individuals in the context of movement initiation. We focused on three hypotheses. First, individuals who act as leaders tend to move before others in their group in the period preceding coordinated movement. Second, individuals who act as leaders tend to move into new areas before others prior to a coordinated movement. Third, individuals who act as leaders tend to set the group's direction of travel. We constructed a dynamic following network and used the simple notion of convex hull as the measure of degree of difference of the velocity, position, and direction of an individual from its group. We use proposed traits of leaders for model classification. We evaluated the classification task on simulated movement data. We tested our proposed approach in baboon movement and fish movement datasets using the time series leadership inference framework, FLICA.

We found that during baboon decision-making intervals before a period of coordinated troop movement, there was a positive correlation between an individual's leadership ranking and the frequency with which an individual decided to step outside the group to explore a new area. Moreover, there was a negative correlation between leadership ranking and the frequency which individuals misaligned with the group's direction. We drew this conclusion from the hypothesis testing of the distribution of correlations between leadership ranking and convex hull measures, constructed by the proposed framework. However, there was no strong correlation between the frequency of early movement and leadership ranking.

In the fish dataset, we found that there were a positive correlation between the leadership ranking and the order of movement ranking, as well as leadership vs. order of exploring new areas ranking. On the contrary, on average, there was a negative correlation between the leadership ranking and the frequency which individuals misaligned with the group's direction. These results suggest that trained fish seems to move earlier than other fish to the new area and the untrained fish aligns with trained fish quickly.

Our work establishes a general framework to draw conclusions about leadership characteristics of individuals initiating movement and to test long-standing common assumptions about the behavioral traits the leaders possess. Our framework is sufficiently general to be applied to any movement dataset and any set of traits directly computable from the data.

Acknowledgements This work was supported in part by the NSF grants III-1514126 (Berger-Wolf, Crofoot), III-1514174 (Crofoot), IOS-1250895 (Crofoot), SMA-1620391 (Crofoot), and CNS-1248080 (Berger-Wolf) and the David and Lucile Packard Foundation 2016-65130 (Crofoot).

References

1. C. Amornbunchornvej, I. Brugere, A. Strandburg-Peshkin, D. Farine, M.C. Crofoot, T.Y. Berger-Wolf, Flica: a framework for leader identification in coordinated activity (2016). Preprint. arXiv:1603.01570
2. C. Amornbunchornvej, I. Brugere, A. Strandburg-Peshkin, D. Farine, M.C. Crofoot, T.Y. Berger-Wolf, Coordination event detection and initiator identification in time series data. ACM Trans. Knowl. Discov. Data **12**(5), 1–33 (2018). http://doi.acm.org/10.1145/3201406
3. M. Andersson, J. Gudmundsson, P. Laube, T. Wolle, Reporting leaders and followers among trajectories of moving point objects. GeoInformatica **12**(4), 497–528 (2008)
4. C. Brown, E. Irving, Individual personality traits influence group exploration in a feral guppy population. Behav. Ecol. **25**(1), 95 (2014). http://dx.doi.org/10.1093/beheco/art090
5. B. Chazelle, The total s-energy of a multiagent system. SIAM J. Control. Optim. **49**(4), 1680–1706 (2011). https://doi.org/10.1137/100791671
6. I.D. Couzin, J. Krause, N.R. Franks, S.A. Levin, Effective leadership and decision-making in animal groups on the move. Nature **433**(7025), 513–516 (2005)
7. M.C. Crofoot, R.W. Kays, M. Wikelski, Data from: shared decision-making drives collective movement in wild baboons. Movebank Data Repository (2015). https://doi.org/10.5441/001/1.kn0816jn
8. J.R. Dyer, A. Johansson, D. Helbing, I.D. Couzin, J. Krause, Leadership, consensus decision making and collective behaviour in humans. Philos. Trans. R. Soc. Lond. B: Biol. Sci. **364**(1518), 781–789 (2009)
9. A. Goyal, F. Bonchi, L.V. Lakshmanan, Discovering leaders from community actions, in *Proceedings of the 17th ACM Conference on Information and Knowledge Management* (ACM, New York, 2008), pp. 499–508

10. A. Goyal, F. Bonchi, L.V. Lakshmanan, Learning influence probabilities in social networks, in *Proceedings of the Third ACM International Conference on Web Search and Data Mining* (ACM, New York, 2010), pp. 241–250
11. D. Kempe, J.M. Kleinberg, É. Tardos, Maximizing the spread of influence through a social network. Theory Comput. **11**(4), 105–147 (2015)
12. M.G. Kendall, A new measure of rank correlation. Biometrika **30**(1/2), 81–93 (1938). http://www.jstor.org/stable/2332226
13. M.B. Kjargaard, H. Blunck, M. Wustenberg, K. Gronbask, M. Wirz, D. Roggen, G. Troster, Time-lag method for detecting following and leadership behavior of pedestrians from mobile sensing data, in *Proceedings of the IEEE PerCom* (IEEE, Piscataway, 2013), pp. 56–64
14. L. Page, S. Brin, R. Motwani, T. Winograd, The pagerank citation ranking: bringing order to the web. Technical Report 1999-66, Stanford InfoLab (November 1999). http://ilpubs.stanford.edu:8090/422/
15. H. Sakoe, S. Chiba, Dynamic programming algorithm optimization for spoken word recognition. IEEE Trans. Acoust. Speech Signal Process. **26**(1), 43–49 (1978)
16. A. Strandburg-Peshkin et al., Visual sensory networks and effective information transfer in animal groups. Curr. Biol. **23**(17), R709–R711 (2013)
17. A. Strandburg-Peshkin, D.R. Farine, I.D. Couzin, M.C. Crofoot, Shared decision-making drives collective movement in wild baboons. Science **348**(6241), 1358–1361 (2015)
18. S. Stueckle, D. Zinner, To follow or not to follow: decision making and leadership during the morning departure in Chacma baboons. Anim. Behav. **75**(6), 1995–2004 (2008)
19. S. Wu, Q. Sun, Computer simulation of leadership, consensus decision making and collective behaviour in humans. PLoS One **9**(1), e80680 (2014)

Emotional Valence Shifts and User Behavior on Twitter, Facebook, and YouTube

Ema Kušen, Mark Strembeck, and Mauro Conti

1 Introduction

In online social networks (OSNs), news travel fast and reach a large number of users within a short period of time [24, 33]. Such a rapid information diffusion comes with valuable social benefits such as using OSNs to help save lives during the 2011 tsunami disaster in Japan [35] as well as the Red River flood and Oklahoma fires in 2009 [43]. However, although having a great potential to do good for the society, OSNs have also been recognized as a convenient tool to (positively or negatively) influence people. For example, a number of recent studies indicated that Twitter, Facebook, and YouTube have been used to spread terrorist propaganda [44] and negatively influence users (online radicalization) [2, 7, 26, 36].

In this context, emotions have generally been recognized as an important factor in influencing or manipulating people's opinions and beliefs [29]. In particular, recent studies indicated that emotions can be passed through online interactions from one user to another [11, 21], resulting in the so-called emotional contagion. In addition, numerous studies reported on user reactions to emotionally charged

E. Kušen
Vienna University of Economics and Business, Wien, Austria

M. Strembeck (✉)
Vienna University of Economics and Business, Wien, Austria

Secure Business Austria Research Center (SBA), Wien, Austria

Complexity Science Hub Vienna (CSH), Wien, Austria
e-mail: mark.strembeck@wu.ac.at

M. Conti
Università di Padova, Padua, Italy

© Springer Nature Switzerland AG 2019
M. Kaya, R. Alhajj (eds.), *Influence and Behavior Analysis in Social Networks and Social Media*, Lecture Notes in Social Networks,
https://doi.org/10.1007/978-3-030-02592-2_4

messages. For example, Faraon et al. [10] and Stuart [38] found that users tend to pay more attention to the negative messages, while Bayer et al. [4] and Stieglitz and Linh [37] presented a contradictory finding (i.e., positive messages receive more attention). The common denominator in either case is that emotions conveyed in OSN messages have the potential to trigger a strong emotional reaction in people [5, 9, 25, 28].

This paper extends our prior analysis presented in [23]. In particular, we study the impact of emotions on the messaging behavior of OSN users on Twitter, Facebook, and YouTube. To this end, we performed an emotion analysis over 5.6 million social media messages that occurred in 24 systematically chosen real-world events. For each of these messages, we derived emotion scores concerning the eight basic emotions according to Plutchik's wheel of emotions [32]. In general, we found that people tend to conform to the base emotion of a particular event. However, we also found empirical evidence that in all three OSNs prospectively, negative real-world events are accompanied by a substantial amount of shifted (i.e., positive) emotions in the corresponding messages. In order to explain this finding, we use the theory of *social connection* and *emotional contagion*. To the best of our knowledge, this is the first study that provides empirical evidence for the *undoing hypothesis* in online social networks (OSNs).

The remainder of this paper is organized as follows. In Sect. 2, we discuss related work. Next, Sect. 3 describes our data analysis procedure followed by a detailed report on our results in Sect. 4. Subsequently, Sect. 5 discusses our findings, and Sect. 6 concludes the paper.

2   Related Work

Prior studies predominantly examined the impact of sentiment polarities and emotions on information diffusion over OSNs. For example, Zhang and Zhang [46] examine the impact of *emojis* on message diffusion patterns over a data set containing about 12 million Weibo messages. In particular, they found that positive and negative emojis result in the same effects with respect to retweets and replies. In fact, both groups of emojis have a positive effect on the number of replies a message receives and a negative effect on the retweet count. Other studies examined textual cues to identify a set of emotions or sentiment polarities. For example, Kim et al. [20] conducted a questionnaire-based study to examine the role of emotional valence on the diffusion of anti-tobacco messages. They found that positive emotions boost the transmission of messages, while negative ones had the opposite effect.

In [12], Ferrara and Yang extracted emotion polarities for about 19 million tweets by applying the SentiStrength algorithm [40]. In particular, they studied four aspects of information diffusion over Twitter: retweet count, like count, the speed of diffusion, and the scope of the diffusion. The results of the study show a clear evidence of the *Pollyanna hypothesis* [8], which refers to the human preference to like positive messages more than negative and neutral ones. Moreover, in terms of the scope of the diffusion, the study showed that positive messages spread wider than negative and neutral ones. However, it also indicates that messages carrying negative and neutral sentiments spread faster than positive ones.

Another study that utilized SentiStrength to obtain emotion polarities [37] studied the effects of polarities on the retweet count and the speed of retweeting during the 2011 German state parliament elections. The findings suggest that emotionally charged tweets tend to be retweeted more often than the neutral ones, which is in line with the findings presented in [30, 41, 42]. In particular, tweets carrying a negative sentiment are strongly associated with an increase in the retweet rate.

In [16], Gruzd et al. analyzed sentiment polarities from tweets related to the 2010 Winter Olympics. They found that a user's position in the social network can be regarded as an indicator of the user's tendency to post positive or negative messages. Specifically, Gruzd et al. showed that users who tweeted predominantly positive messages generally have more followers on Twitter, while users who tweeted more negative messages exhibited a higher tweet-per-user rate.

In [41], Trung et al. assigned sentiment polarities to a data set of about 11,000 tweets by using a Bayesian classifier trained on the annotated tweets from three domains: news, industry, and entertainment. In particular, they studied three aspects of information diffusion: the number of retweets, speed of diffusion, and the scope of diffusion. In contrast to the findings from [12], Trung et al. found that all emotionally charged messages (i.e., positive as well as negative ones) spread wider (i.e., to more users) than the neutral ones. However, in terms of the speed of diffusion, they found no significant difference among the neutral, positive, and negative messages.

Such a dissonance in the findings might result from the fact that existing papers predominantly study the diffusion patterns only with respect to one particular domain of interest (such as health care, politics, popular culture, or sports; see, e.g., [20, 37]) which makes it difficult to generalize the respective findings across domain borders. While some papers report on diffusion patterns of messages belonging to different domains, the corresponding papers do not follow a systematic approach for studying the differences between domains with respect to information diffusion patterns (see, e.g., [12, 41]).

Even though a number of effects relating to sentiment polarities have been studied in the related work, aspects beyond the effects of sentiment polarities on the information diffusion in OSNs have rarely been investigated. For example, Berger [6] discusses the effects of emotional arousal on information sharing. In particular, the study distinguishes between dimensions of emotions other than emotion polarities only. Berger found that arousal increases the likelihood for sharing an information, regardless of whether the respective information conveys a positive or a negative sentiment. Two other studies [18, 39] consider anger, anxiety, awe, and sadness, as annotated by human encoders. The results of both studies indicate that anger and awe increase the content sharing behavior, while sadness and anxiety were negatively associated with content diffusion.

3 Data Analysis Procedure

In this section, we outline the four main phases of our study (see Fig. 1). In Sect. 3.1 we describe our data extraction procedure. Section 3.2 provides more details on cleaning the raw data set followed by Sect. 3.3 in which we outline the heuristics used to identify emotions and their corresponding emotion scores. Finally, Sect. 3.4 provides details on our data analysis procedure and the scope of this paper.

3.1 Data Extraction

In order to study the impact of emotional valence shifts on information diffusion, we systematically identified 24 real-world events that belong to five different domains (sports, politics, popular culture, war and terrorism, and others) and collected more than 5.6 million corresponding messages published on Twitter, Facebook, and YouTube. The 24 events have been selected such that they fall in one of the following categories:

1. events that potentially trigger positive emotions (e.g., birthday celebrations, festivities)
2. events that potentially trigger negative emotions (e.g., war, terror, death)
3. emotionally polarizing events (e.g., presidential elections, controversial topics)

We summarize the events extracted for each category in Table 1, where N refers to the number of messages in each category, followed by the relative size of each category in our data set (in percent).

To extract the public messages, we used the corresponding APIs offered by Twitter, Facebook, and YouTube. In particular, we used Twitter's Search API[1] to

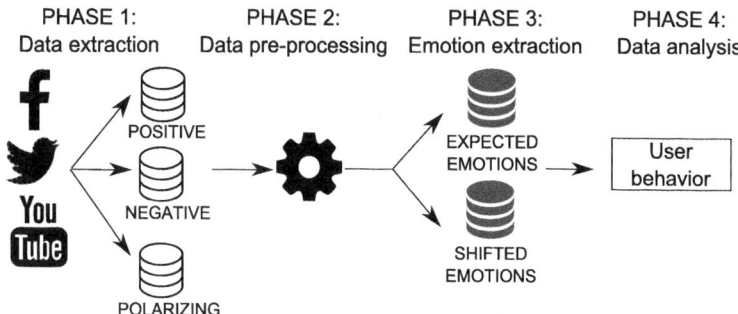

Fig. 1 Research phases

---

[1]https://dev.twitter.com/overview/api.

Table 1 List of events extracted from Twitter (T), Facebook (F), and YouTube (Y)

Event	T messages	F messages	Y messages
Negative	($N = 1,490,495$; 34%)	($N = 161,898$; 14%)	($N = 33,563$; 22%)
(1) Erdogan's threats to EU	804	36	1160
(2) Anti-Trump protests	381,982	218	5270
(3) Death of Leonard Cohen	89,619	43,808	11,820
(4) Death of Colonel Abrams	1253	6	18
(5) Aleppo bombings	995,561	94,116	8129
(6) Seattle shooting	73	2085	660
(7) Lufthansa strikes	3387	156	26
(8) Ransomware incidents	2564	1012	3724
(9) Yellowstone hotpot	15	9980	2156
(10) Earthquake central Italy	15,237	10,481	600
Positive	($N = 1,115,587$; 25%)	($N = 328,792$; 29%)	($N = 83,394$; 55%)
(11) Rosberg wins F1	215,703	586	804
(12) Murray wins ATP	62,184	169	495
(13) Rosberg retires	34,201	10,817	353
(14) "Beauty and the Beast" trailer	138,979	73,399	42,180
(15) Fantastic beasts trailer	64,264	51,468	17,829
(16) Vienna ComiCon	704	4693	57
(17) Miley Cyrus birthday	76,270	3014	197
(18) Pentatonix album release	9341	70	15,159
(19) Ellen Degeneres medal of freedom	73,854	184,519	4450
(20) Thanksgiving	440,087	57	1870
Polarizing	($N = 1,812,573$; 41%)	($N = 637,945$; 57%)	($N = 35,657$; 23%)
(21) Death of Fidel Castro	720,548	21,938	2068
(22) Austrian elections 2016	2558	3351	1096
(23) The Walking Dead S07 premiere	198,042	34,486	5136
(24) US elections 2016	891,425	578,170	27,357

extract publicly available tweets. For this extraction, we used a pre-defined list of hashtags and restricted the search to English-language tweets only. Moreover, we collected the tweets related to the 24 events by starting with the date of an event announcement and stopped 7 days after. In total, the extraction resulted in 4,418,655 tweets. Furthermore, we used YouTube Comment API[2] to extract 152,614 publicly available YouTube comments on a set of 98 manually selected YouTube videos

---

[2]https://github.com/philbot9/youtube-comment-api.

related to the 24 events in our study. In addition, we used Facebook's Graph API[3] to extract 1,128,635 publicly available Facebook comments on 69 manually selected Facebook posts related to the 24 events.

3.2 Data Preprocessing

After the data extraction, we cleaned the raw data set by removing entries that contained uninformative content with respect to emotion extraction (e.g., entries that consisted of URLs only). Thus, after preprocessing our data set included messages that contained either text, emoticons, or a combination of both. Moreover, since our Facebook and YouTube data sets included messages that were written in languages other than English, we used Python's *langdetect*[4] language detection library to identify the language of a particular message and removed messages that were not written in English.

The final number of messages for each OSN after preprocessing is shown in Table 1.

3.3 Emotion Extraction

After preprocessing the overall data sets, we further processed each message by lemmatizing it and tagging words to their corresponding part-of-speech category. We then identified the presence of specific emotions conveyed in the messages and computed an emotion intensity score for each message by applying a customized emotion extraction script (see [22] for further details on the heuristics used and an evaluation). In general, the procedure is encoded in the script:

1. identifies the presence of Plutchik's eight basic emotions (anger, fear, disgust, sadness, joy, trust, anticipation, surprise) [32] by relying on the NRC word-emotion lexicon [27],
2. assigns an intensity score for each emotion in every tweet by counting the number of words in the NRC lexicon that are associated with an emotion and multiplies them with a score provided in the AFINN lexicon[5] [31],
3. deals with negation (e.g., "I am *not* happy.") by shifting the valence of a word (e.g., the term *not happy* results in a negative emotion score for joy: $joy = -1$),

---

[3]https://developers.facebook.com/docs/graph-api.

[4]https://pypi.python.org/pypi/langdetect.

[5]The AFINN lexicon [31] contains scores corresponding to the emotional valence intensity of a given word. For example, words such as *sad* and *depressed* are classified as negative words, but the latter has a weaker intensity compared to the former word.

4. deals with intensifiers (e.g., *very* happy), downtoners (e.g., *hardly* happy), and maximizers (e.g., *absolutely* happy),
5. identifies misspellings and repeated letters to find "hidden" boosters (e.g., "I am *sooooo* happy" is regarded as "I am *so* happy."),
6. as noted in [19], emoticons are often used instead of words to express emotions. Thus, our script also identifies emoticons and categorizes them as positive (e.g., happy face :) and laughing face :D), negative (e.g., sad face :(and crying face :'(or broken heart </3), or conditional (heart <3) (see also [1]). Note that we regard a heart (<3) either as a positive or a negative emotion carrier because its meaning depends on the context of its use. For example, in a sentence "You will be missed <3," it is used in a negative context (sadness), while in the sentence "I love him so much <3," the emoticon is used in a positive context (joy). Thus, to correctly interpret the emoticon <3, we first identify the dominant emotion in the tweet and then assign the corresponding emotion score.

Moreover, for our analysis we also extended the NRC dictionary with a list of common acronyms used in social media (such as LOL, WTF, and YOLO).

3.4 Data Analysis and Research Questions

First, we analyzed how social network users express specific emotions during positive, negative, and polarizing events. Next, we separated each data set into a subset that conveys *expected emotions* and a subset that conveys *shifted emotions* in terms of their valence. In particular, we treat emotions of a shifted valence as *unexpected* emotions (e.g., a positive event receives messages that predominantly convey negative emotions). We then analyzed how the user behavior in each subset is influenced by expected and shifted emotions.

Our analysis was guided by the following research questions.

RQ1: Which emotions are expressed during positive, negative, and polarizing events?

For RQ1, we searched for emotions communicated during positive, negative, and polarizing events. For this research question, it was of particular interest whether emotions belonging to a specific emotional valence (i.e., positive or negative) dominate in an event category.

To answer the first research question, we obtained the average intensity of each of the eight basic emotions for each event (see Table 1). Moreover, we computed the bivariate correlation between each pair of emotions.

RQ2: Which messaging behavior do users exhibit during positive, negative, and polarizing events?

For RQ2, we studied how users react to the three types of events (positive, negative, polarizing) in terms of platform-specific user actions. Thus, for Twitter we consider the number of retweets, number of likes, tweeting rate, tweeting count per user, and one-to-one communication. For Facebook, we study the number of replies to a comment, like count, daily time rate, and number of comments per user. And for YouTube, we examine the number of replies and likes to a comment, as well as a daily time rate, and the number of comments per user.

RQ3: Are there differences in the messaging behavior when users are faced with messages that convey expected emotions and those with a shifted emotional valence?

For RQ3, we study how users respond to the emotions conveyed in messages. In particular, we contrast the behavior toward the expected emotions and the shifted emotions and provide a time series analysis of each.

4 Results

In this section, we first show the intensities of emotions expressed in each OSN during positive, negative, and polarizing events (Sect. 4.1). We then examine the user behavior as a reaction to emotionally charged messages and show a time series analysis of the shifted emotions with respect to the expected emotions (Sect. 4.2).

4.1 Emotion Intensity During Positive, Negative, and Polarizing Events

Our analysis shows that OSN users express emotions with a similar intensity over Twitter, Facebook, and YouTube upon encountering polarizing, positive, and negative events (see Figs. 2, 3, and 4 where negative emotions are colored red (anger,

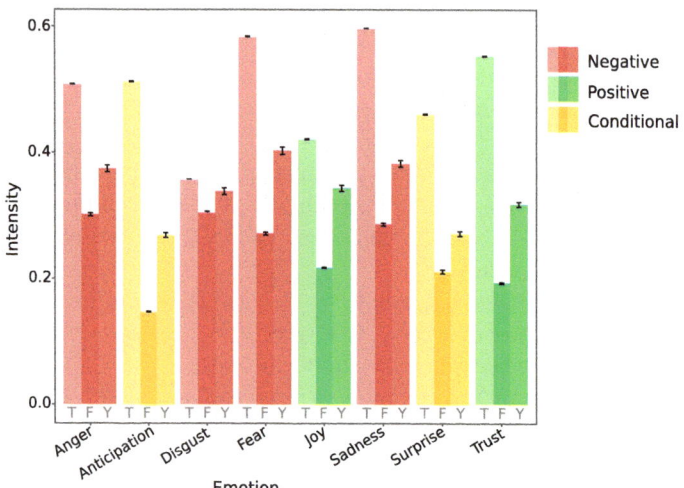

Fig. 2 Emotions expressed during polarizing events on Twitter (T), Facebook (F), and YouTube (Y)

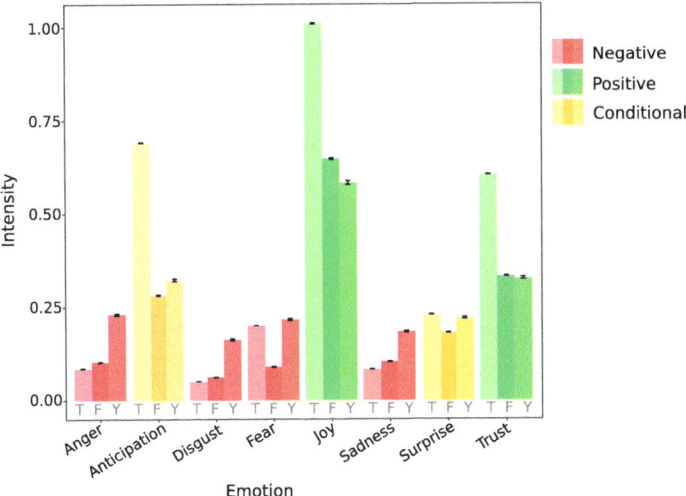

Fig. 3 Emotions expressed during positive events on Twitter (T), Facebook (F), and YouTube (Y)

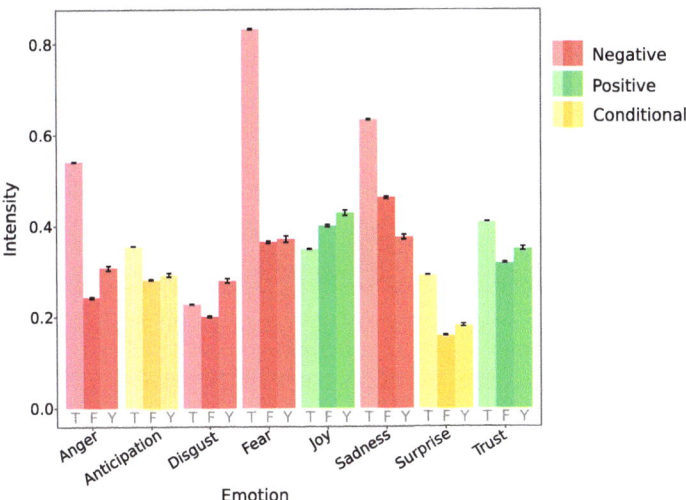

Fig. 4 Emotions expressed during negative events on Twitter (T), Facebook (F), and YouTube (Y)

sadness, disgust, fear), positive are green (joy, trust), and conditional (i.e., context-dependent) are yellow (surprise, anticipation)).

Furthermore, for each category (positive, negative, polarizing), Fig. 5 shows the respective difference between the *expected* and the *shifted* emotions. Thus, in positive events, the negative emotion score (shifted) is subtracted from the positive emotion score (expected). In negative events, the positive emotion score (shifted) is subtracted from the negative emotion score (expected). Moreover, since there is no expected emotion for polarizing events, we chose to subtract the positive emotion score from the negative emotion score.

To mitigate bias in the results which may emerge due to the length of a message (i.e., tweets are restricted to 140 characters,[6] while Facebook and YouTube posts can be considerably longer), we present the scores of each emotion averaged over the sentence count. Finally, to show the relative presence of each emotion in the data set, we divide the averaged emotion scores e (based on the sentence count S) with the message count in the data set (N):

$$\frac{\sum_{i=1}^{n} \frac{e_i}{S_i}}{N}.$$

We found that messages sent during polarizing events exhibited no tendency of a particular group of emotions to greatly dominate over the other, as compared to the positive and negative events. As shown in Fig. 2, OSN users expressed positive and negative emotions with a similar intensity. For polarizing events, Fig. 5 further shows that the relative difference between the scores assigned to negative and positive emotions only exhibits a low difference (0.02 for Twitter, 0.08 for Facebook, and 0.04 and YouTube). These results were expected to a certain degree, as users tend to either approve/support or disapprove/oppose a topic of interest during polarizing events (e.g., political campaigning).

With respect to OSN-related differences in emotional intensities during polarizing events, we found that our Facebook data set contained 39% emotionally neutral messages, while YouTube and Twitter messages were more emotionally charged (24% and 21% emotionally neutral messages, respectively). These platform-related differences are depicted in Fig. 2.

In contrast, and as shown in Fig. 3, positive events exhibited a higher intensity of positive emotions (joy, trust) as compared to negative emotions (anger, fear, disgust, sadness). In fact, in positive events the differences between the intensities of positive and negative emotions are considerably higher (0.70 for Twitter, 0.40 for Facebook, and 0.26 for YouTube) as compared to the data sets for polarizing and negative events.

Interestingly, when comparing the intensities of specific emotions communicated over the three OSN platforms, we found that a single tweet carries on average a more intense positive emotion, when compared to messages sent via the other two platforms. However, when observing the shifted emotions in positive events (i.e., negative emotions related to positive events), our results reveal that YouTube users tend to express (on average) more intense negative emotions as compared to Facebook and Twitter users. This difference is particularly evident in Fig. 5, where

---

[6]Note that the increased limit of 280 characters that has been introduced by Twitter in November 2017 was not in effect during our data extraction period.

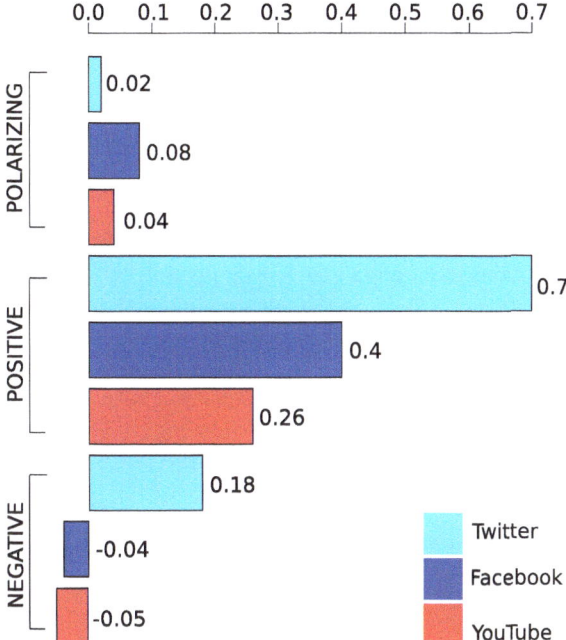

Fig. 5 Difference between the emotional intensity of expected and shifted emotions

the difference between positive and negative emotional intensities on YouTube is only 0.26, compared to 0.70 on Twitter and 0.40 on Facebook.

Figure 4 shows emotional intensities communicated during negative events. As expected, negative events showed a comparatively higher intensity of negative (expected) emotions on Twitter. However,we also found a considerable presence of positive emotions (see Fig. 4) and only a low difference between the intensities of negative and positive emotions (see Fig. 5). In contrast to Twitter, emotions in messages related to negative events communicated on YouTube and Facebook are even predominantly positive on average (see Fig. 5, the difference between negative and positive emotions is −0.05 on YouTube and −0.04 on Facebook, i.e., the shifted emotion is slightly dominant over the expected emotion).

Next, we examine whether different emotions belonging to the same emotional valence are communicated jointly in a single message. To this end we performed a bivariate correlation analysis for each pair of emotions (e.g., anger with disgust, anger with joy). Our results show a high Spearman's ρ coefficient between *disgust* and *anger* ($\rho = 0.81$) as well as *sadness* and *fear* ($\rho = 0.87$) on YouTube, between *sadness* and *anger* ($\rho = 0.92$) as well as *joy* and *trust* ($\rho = 0.86$) on Facebook, and between *sadness* and *anger* ($\rho = 0.70$) on Twitter.

During positive events, *anger* and *disgust* were highly correlated ($\rho = 0.83$) on YouTube, while the same holds for *sadness* and *fear* ($\rho = 0.89$) on Facebook. Negative events exhibited a high correlation between *disgust* and *anger* ($\rho = 0.83$), as well as *fear* and *sadness* ($\rho = 0.82$) on YouTube, a high correlation between *fear* and *anger* ($\rho = 0.83$) as well as *fear* and *sadness* ($\rho = 0.81$) on Facebook, and a high correlation between *sadness* and *fear* ($\rho = 0.71$) on Twitter.

Based on the aforementioned results, we conclude that emotions belonging to the same emotional valence tend to be communicated together in a single OSN message. This observation is particularly evident in our Twitter data set (see Fig. 6a), where users are limited to 140 characters only, i.e., Twitter users only have limited space to express their emotions and opinions. We also observed that when users are allowed to post longer messages, there is a higher correlation between positive and negative emotions (e.g., posts that convey joy also convey anger) (see Fig. 6b, c).

However, it is worth mentioning that emotions belonging to two different categories in terms of emotional valence (positive vs. negative) are weakly or at most moderately correlated as compared to emotions belonging to the same emotional valence (e.g., joy and trust; anger and disgust). In a similar way, we found that different negative emotions are only weakly or moderately correlated during positive and polarizing events.

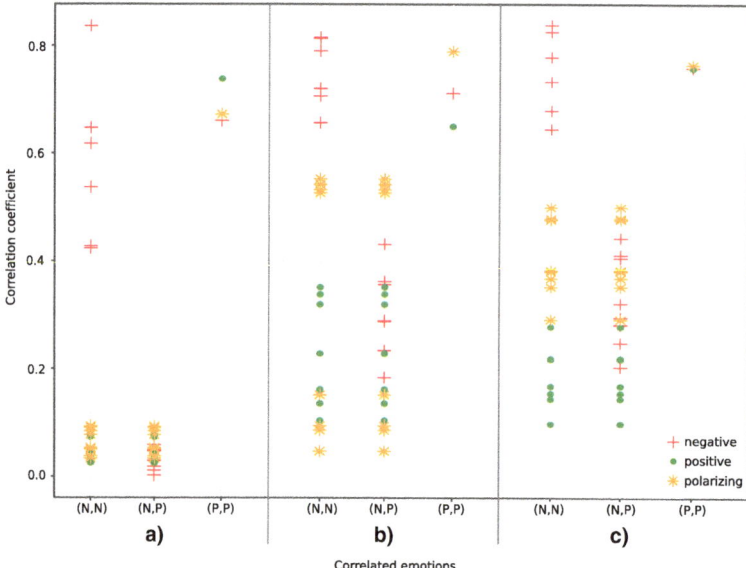

Fig. 6 Correlation between pairs of negative emotions (N,N), negative and positive emotions (N,P), and pairs of positive emotions (P,P) on (**a**) Twitter, (**b**) Facebook, and (**c**) YouTube during negative (red cross), positive (green dot), and polarizing (yellow star) events

4.2   User Behavior

For the purposes of this paper, OSN user behavior is defined as all user actions that result in sending or forwarding a public message/comment as well as user actions related to appreciating ("liking") a public message/comment. Moreover, in our analysis we also consider the number of messages per user and the speed of message generation (i.e., the number of messages per time unit).

User Behavior on Twitter As shown in Table 2, positive events trigger the highest number of retweets and likes. This shows a tendency of users to prefer engaging in positive discussions rather than negative (which confirms the *Pollyanna hypothesis*, see also [8, 12]). Moreover, we found that users tend to engage in a one-to-one communication (via @*username*) more frequently during positive events than during negative or polarizing ones. However, the results also indicate that users tend to send comparatively more tweets during negative events (2.86 tweets per user) than during polarizing (1.92 tweets per user) or positive (1.62 tweets per user) events. This finding corresponds to the ones discussed in [6], which suggests that emotions of a high arousal (such as anger) increase the social transmission of information. Interestingly, in our data set polarizing events exhibited the highest tweeting rate per minute (49.42 tweets/minute).

The results of the Welch's t-test (with a 95% significance level) indicate that there is a significant difference in how users respond to tweets conveying expected emotions and those containing shifted emotions. Apart from one exception in the like count ($p > 0.05$), all other tweeting behaviors that we considered exhibit a clear pattern: expected emotions receive more retweets. Moreover, for each of the 24 events that we analyzed, OSN users tend to send more tweets per minute that convey an expected emotion. Another interesting insight can be observed in the one-to-one communication (social sharing) of expected emotions between OSN

Table 2 Twitter user behavior in positive, negative, and polarizing events (confidence interval 95%; the highest value for each category is highlighted in bold font respectively)

	Negative	Positive	Polarizing
Retweet count	1600.10	**5677.63**	4821.90
	$t = 1.98, p < 0.05$	$t = 243.511, p < 0.05$	
Like count	0.98	**1.49**	1.22
	$t = -0.97, p > 0.05$	$t = 0.98, p > 0.05$	
Time rate	37.58	42.48	**49.42**
	$t = 25.94, p < 0.05$	$t = 57.47, p < 0.05$	
Tweet per user	**2.86**	1.62	1.92
	$t = 13.33, p < 0.05$	$t = 26.04, p < 0.05$	
@ count	1.02	**1.19**	1.02
	$t = 25.77, p < 0.05$	$t = 69.93, p < 0.05$	

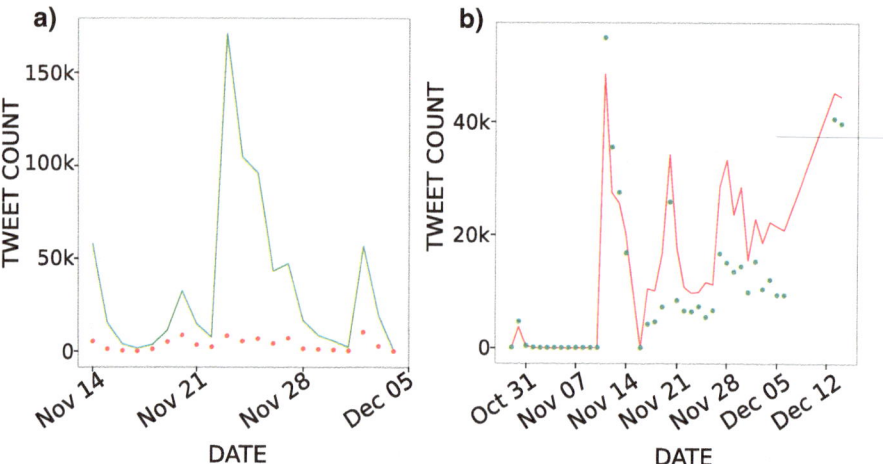

Fig. 7 Occurrences of negative messages during positive events on Twitter and vice versa. Positive messages are depicted in green and negative messages in red. (**a**) Positive events and (**b**) negative events

users. During positive events, users tend to engage in a one-to-one communication by sharing predominantly positive emotions. Analogously, negative events exhibit a comparable pattern (see Table 2).

Figure 7a shows the time series of tweets separated into those that carry a predominantly positive emotion and those that carry a negative emotion. In particular, there are a noticeable smaller number of tweets that convey negative (i.e., shifted) emotions during positive events. However, our data also shows that, although small in size, negative tweets occurred consistently throughout the extraction period (*mean(set difference) = 36668.11, sd(set difference) = 45844.64*).[7]

In contrast, we found that during negative events events a considerable number of tweets conveying positive (i.e., shifted) emotions occur (*mean(set difference) = 4231.67, sd(set difference) = 5603.162*). This observation was consistent over the entire extraction period (see Fig. 7b). Interestingly, our data set also revealed unexpected cases where the positive tweets (i.e., the shifted emotions) even exceed the (expected) negative tweets (the largest difference between the two subsets is 6403 tweets).

User Behavior on Facebook Table 3 shows that Facebook users also slightly prefer replying to and liking Facebook posts that have a positive emotion score, while in polarizing events we again found the highest average number of comments per unit of time.

---

[7]Set difference refers to the difference between the count of the expected emotions and shifted emotions, while *sd* stands for standard deviation.

Table 3 Facebook user behavior in positive, negative, and polarizing events (confidence interval 95%; the highest value for each category is highlighted in bold font respectively)

	Negative	Positive	Polarizing
Reply counts	0.17	**0.25**	0.09
	$t = 2.39, p < 0.05$	$t = 0.83, p > 0.05$	
Like count	2.78	**2.89**	1.79
	$t = 1.93, p > 0.05$	$t = 0.61, p > 0.05$	
Time rate (daily)	505.93	713.21	**4012.23**
	$t = 2.69, p < 0.05$	$t = 1.04, p > 0.05$	
Comment per user	1.19	1.31	**2.94**
	$t = 31.29, p < 0.05$	$t = 18.32, p < 0.05$	

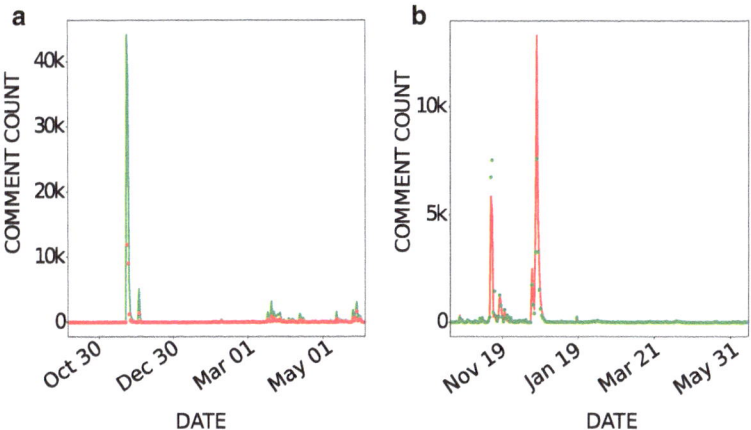

Fig. 8 Occurrences of negative messages during positive events on Facebook and vice versa. Positive messages are depicted in green and negative messages in red. (**a**) Positive events and (**b**) negative events

In particular, the results of the Welch's t-test indicate a significant difference in the effects of expected vs. shifted emotions in each data set (see Table 3). For negative events, we found that users tend to reply and comment predominantly on negative posts and also send more messages that convey negative emotions per day, as compared to positive posts (replies $t = 2.39$, $p < 0.05$; comments $t = 1.19$, $p < 0.05$; time rate $t = 2.69$, $p < 0.05$). For positive events, we found one statistically significant result for the comment rate per user ($t = 18.32$; $p < 0.05$), which indicates that users tend to comment more on positive posts during positive events rather than on negative posts.

By observing the time series plots in Fig. 8b, we can see that the temporal patterns of expected and shifted emotions during negative events resemble those we found on Twitter. In particular, a considerable number of messages conveying positive emotions are sent during negative events. The positive (shifted) emotions even dominate the negative emotions at certain dates (see the green dots in Fig. 8b).

With respect to the temporal patterns of negative messages sent during positive events, Fig. 8a shows that positive emotions dominate over the negative ones throughout the entire data extraction period. Again, this observation is analogous to the temporal patterns observed on Twitter (see Fig. 7a).

User Behavior on YouTube Similar to Facebook and Twitter, YouTube users also prefer to "like" comments on YouTube videos relating to positive events (see Table 4), as compared to comments on YouTube videos relating to polarizing or negative events.

However, unlike Facebook and Twitter users, YouTube users exhibit higher reply counts to comments on YouTube videos that are depicting a polarizing event (e.g., political campaigning, such as TV debates). Moreover, we also observed that YouTube users exhibit the highest rate of comments per time unit for videos on positive events, while Facebook users exhibited this behavior for polarizing events and Twitter users for negative events.

Analogously to the results for Facebook and Twitter, Table 4 shows that YouTube users tend to comply with the base mood of an event by replying more to negative messages during negative events ($t = 3.55$, $p < 0.05$) and positive messages during positive events ($t = 4.16$, $p < 0.05$). In the same way, YouTube users also tend to "like" positive messages during positive events ($t = 2.13$, $p < 0.05$) and send more negative comments per time unit during negative events ($t = 2.15$, $p < 0.05$).

For our YouTube data set, Fig. 9b shows that during negative events, we again found a considerable number of messages with a positive (i.e., shifted) emotion score. Similar to our findings for Facebook and Twitter, positive messages even dominate over negative messages on certain dates.

In positive events though, we again predominantly found messages conveying positive emotions (see Fig. 9a).

Table 4 YouTube user behavior in positive, negative, and polarizing events (confidence interval 95%; the highest value for each category is highlighted in bold font respectively)

	Negative	Positive	Polarizing
Reply counts	0.69	0.54	**0.99**
	$t = 3.55$, $p < 0.05$	$t = 4.16$, $p < 0.05$	
Like count	4.59	**7.24**	5.3
	$t = -0.36$, $p > 0.05$	$t = 2.13$, $p < 0.05$	
Time rate (daily)	958.94	**4097.81**	1782.85
	$t = 2.15$, $p < 0.05$	$t = 1.052$, $p > 0.05$	
Comment per user	1.81	1.67	**2.34**
	$t = 0.33$, $p > 0.05$	$t = 0.43$, $p > 0.05$	

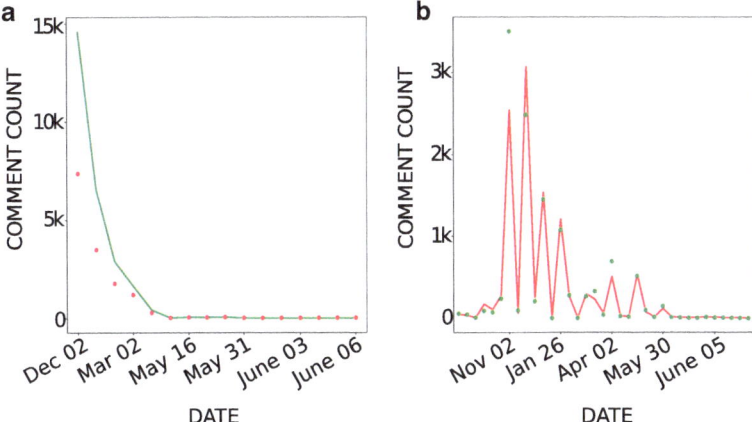

Fig. 9 Occurrences of negative messages during positive events on YouTube and vice versa. Positive messages are depicted in green and negative messages in red. (**a**) Positive events and (**b**) negative events

5 Discussion

Our results bring forth interesting insights into how OSN users behave during positive, negative, and polarizing events when faced with shifted emotions. In our study, we considered OSN user behavior in terms of retweets and one-to-one communication (on Twitter), replies (on YouTube and Facebook), as well as likes, the number of messages per user, and the speed of message generation (time rate) (on all three OSNs). Consistent with previous work from the field of psychology, we found that to a considerable extent, positive emotions also occur during negative events. An explanation for the observed phenomenon can be attributed to *social connection* [3, 14] as one of the fundamental human needs. In fact, previous studies indicated that even in the times of sorrow and anxiety, people tend to eventually be supportive and positive toward one another (see, e.g., [34]).

In our data set, we found examples of people explicitly calling for social bonding during emotionally tough events (e.g., after the 2016 earthquake in central Italy, people posted: *please join us as we #PrayforItaly*) and a public and explicit expression of vulnerability that triggers compassion (e.g., *Oh dear world, I am crying tonight*, during Aleppo bombings). Moreover, our data set indicates that people tend to show appreciation and love for a person they care about or admire (e.g., a deceased singer, such as Leonard Cohen) or even comfort each other and send messages of hope during natural disasters (e.g., earthquake in Italy) or war (e.g., Aleppo bombing). Thus, we found empirical evidence that supports the *undoing hypothesis* [13], which states that people tend to use positive emotions as an antidote to undo the effects of negative emotions.

For Twitter, our results further indicate that expected emotions result in more retweets. We thereby confirm findings from [17], which suggested that people prefer sharing messages that correspond to the emotional valence of the respective event (i.e., users tend to pass along negative tweets during negative events). This might be attributed to the human tendency to conform to the situation. However, we were also able to observe a similar phenomenon on Facebook and YouTube. Beyond the mere sharing of existing messages, we also observed that users in general prefer replying to and liking messages that convey emotions which correspond to the base emotion of an event. The same holds for the message generation time rate and message per user rate on all three OSN platforms we considered in our study.

Other studies bring an additional interesting insight into the interpersonal interactions over social media, which might explain our observations of users to conform to the base emotion. According to [45], emotional messages tend to influence the emotions conveyed in other users' messages. This phenomenon, called *emotion contagion* in [45], emerges from the social connections of OSN users (or their position in the network). In this context, we observed that messages sent by "fans" (we follow an assumption that fans follow their idols on OSNs with a high probability) tend to be congruent with the messages sent by their idols. For example, a tweet posted by Pentatonix in which they announce the release of their new album triggered positive reactions from their fans. Note, however, that considering structural network properties alone might not be sufficient to study emotional contagion. For example, OSN users might form a connection (e.g., "follow") with an influential user (e.g., a politician) even though they do not actually agree with the person's ideology or point of view. Thus, the emotions passed by an influential user might also be shifted by his/her followers due to disagreement or sarcasm [15]. We leave the study of this issue for our future work.

6 Conclusion

In this paper, we presented a systematic study concerning the influence of emotional valence shifts on the messaging behavior of OSN users on Twitter, Facebook, and YouTube. Our study is based on a data set including 5.6 million messages belonging to 24 real-world events. The events have been subdivided into positive, negative, and polarizing, and for each of these event categories, we analyzed the intensity of Plutchik's eight basic emotions (sadness, fear, anger, disgust, joy, trust, surprise, anticipation). Thereby, our paper complements existing studies by not only considering polarizing emotion scores (positive vs. negative) but also the influence of eight basic emotions according to Plutchik's wheel of emotions. In order to study the impact of the eight emotions on user behavior in OSNs, we considered user reactions to emotionally charged messages.

Our findings indicate that people generally prefer sharing messages that correspond to the emotional valence of the respective event. Furthermore, we conducted a time series analysis and found a clear distinction between positive and negative events, with respect to shifted emotions. In particular, we found that positive events trigger a comparatively smaller number of negative messages. However, while negative events exhibit predominantly negative messages, they are accompanied by a surprisingly large number of positive messages. In fact, our analysis shows that in negative events positive messages may even exceed the negative ones on all three OSN platforms. To the best of our knowledge, this is the first study which found empirical evidence that supports the *undoing hypothesis* in online social networks.

In our future work, we plan to extend our analysis to studying messages written in languages other than English. In addition, we plan to investigate how sarcasm is related to shifts in the emotional valence.

Acknowledgements Mauro Conti is supported by a Marie Curie Fellowship funded by the European Commission (agreement PCIG11-GA-2012-321980). This work is also partially supported by the EU TagItSmart! Project (agreement H2020-ICT30-2015-688061), the EU-India REACH Project (agreement ICI+/2014/342-896), the project CNR-MOST/Taiwan 2016-17 "Verifiable Data Structure Streaming," the grant n. 2017-166478 (3696) from Cisco University Research Program Fund and Silicon Valley Community Foundation, and the grant "Scalable IoT Management and Key security aspects in 5G systems" from Intel.

References

1. A. Agarwal, B. Xie, I. Vovsha, O. Rambow, R. Passonneau, Sentiment analysis of twitter data, in *Proceedings of the Workshop on Languages in Social Media* (Association for Computational Linguistics, Stroudsburg, 2011), pp. 30–38
2. M. Alarid, Recruitment and Radicalization: The Role of Social Media and New Technology. CCO Publications (2016)
3. R.F. Baumeister, M.R. Leary, The need to belong: desire for interpersonal attachments as a fundamental human motivation. Psychol. Bull. **117**, 497–529 (1995)
4. M. Bayer, W. Sommer, A. Schacht, Font size matters—emotion and attention in cortical responses to written words. PLoS One **7**(05), 1–6 (2012)
5. BBC.com, Study: social networks like Facebook can spread moods (2014), http://www.bbc.com/news/technology-26556295
6. J. Berger, Arousal increases social transmission of information. Psychol. Sci. **22**(7), 891–893 (2011)
7. A. Bessi, E. Ferrara, Social bots distort the 2016 U.S. Presidential election online discussion. First Monday **21**(11) (2016). http://firstmonday.org/ojs/index.php/fm/article/view/7090
8. J. Boucher, C.E. Osgood, The Pollyanna hypothesis. J. Verbal Learn. Verbal Behav. **8**(1), 1–8 (1969)
9. L. Coviello, Y. Sohn, A.D.I. Kramer, C. Marlow, M. Franceschetti, N.A. Christakis, J.H. Fowler, Detecting emotional contagion in massive social networks. PLoS One **9**, 1–6 (2014)
10. M. Faraon, G. Stenberg, M. Kaipainen, Political campaigning 2.0: the influence of online news and social networking sites on attitudes and behavior. eJ. eDemocr. Open Gov. **6**(3), 231–247 (2014)
11. E. Ferrara, Z. Yang, Measuring emotional contagion in social media. PLoS One **10**(11), 1–14 (2015)
12. E. Ferrara, Z. Yang, Quantifying the effect of sentiment on information diffusion in social media. PeerJ Comput. Sci. **1**, 1–15 (2015)

13. B.L. Fredrickson, The role of positive emotions in positive psychology: the broaden-and-build theory of positive emotions. Am. Psychol. **56**, 218–226 (2001)
14. J.J. Freyd, In the wake of terrorist attack, hatred may mask fear. Anal. Soc. Issues Public Policy **2**(1), 5–8 (2002)
15. R. González-Ibáñez, S. Muresan, N. Wacholder, Identifying sarcasm in twitter: a closer look, in *Proceedings of the 49th Annual Meeting of the Association for Computational Linguistics: Human Language Technologies: Short Papers - Volume 2* (2011), pp. 581–586
16. A. Gruzd, S. Doiron, P. Mai, Is happiness contagious online? a case of twitter and the 2010 winter olympics, in *Proceedings of the 44th Hawaii International Conference on System Sciences* (IEEE Computer Society, Washington, 2011), pp. 1–9
17. C. Heath, Do people prefer to pass along good or bad news? valence and relevance of news as predictors of transmission propensity. Organ. Behav. Hum. Decis. Process. **68**(2), 79–94 (1996)
18. I. Heimbach, O. Hinz, The impact of content sentiment and emotionality on content virality. Int. J. Res. Mark. **33**(3), 695–701 (2016)
19. Y. Hu, J. Zhao, J. Wu, Emoticon-based ambivalent expression: a hidden indicator for unusual behaviors in Weibo. PLoS One **11**(1), 1–14 (2016)
20. H.S. Kim, S. Lee, J.N. Cappella, L. Vera, S. Emery, Content characteristics driving the diffusion of antismoking messages: implications for cancer prevention in the emerging public communication environment. J. Natl. Cancer Inst. Monogr. **47**, 182–187 (2013)
21. A.D.I. Kramer, J.E. Guillory, J.T. Hancock, Experimental evidence of massive-scale emotional contagion through social networks. Proc. Natl. Acad. Sci. **111**(24), 8788–8790 (2014)
22. E. Kušen, G. Cascavilla, K. Figl, M. Conti, M. Strembeck, Identifying emotions in social media: comparison of word-emotion lexicons, in *Proceedings of the 4th International Symposium on Social Networks Analysis, Management and Security (SNAMS)*, August 2017 (IEEE, Piscataway, 2017)
23. E. Kušen, M. Strembeck, G. Cascavilla, M. Conti, On the influence of emotional valence shifts on the spread of information in social networks, in *Proceedings of the 2017 IEEE/ACM International Conference on Advances in Social Networks Analysis and Mining (ASONAM)* (ACM, New York, 2017), pp. 321–324
24. H. Kwak, C. Lee, H. Park, S. Moon, What is Twitter, a social network or a news media?, in *Proceedings of the 19th International Conference on World Wide Web* (2010), pp. 591–600
25. R. Lin, S. Utz, The emotional responses of browsing Facebook: happiness, envy, and the role of tie strength. Comput. Hum. Behav. **52**(Suppl. C), 29–38 (2015)
26. B. Mcmanus, An expert explains how social media can lead to the 'self-radicalisation' of terrorists (2015), https://www.vice.com/en_uk/article/we-asked-an-expert-how-social-media-can-help-radicalize-terrorists
27. S.M. Mohammad, P.D. Turney, Crowdsourcing a word-emotion association lexicon. Comput. Intell. **29**(3), 436–465 (2013)
28. J.G. Myrick, Emotion regulation, procrastination, and watching cat videos online: who watches Internet cats, why, and to what effect? Comput. Hum. Behav. **52**(Suppl. C), 168–176 (2015)
29. R.L. Nabi, Exploring the framing effects of emotion. Commun. Res. **30**(2), 224–247 (2003)
30. N. Naveed, T. Gottron, J. Kunegis, A.C. Alhadi, Bad news travel fast: a content-based analysis of interestingness on twitter, in *Proceedings of the 3rd International Web Science Conference* (ACM, New York, 2011), pp. 8:1–8:7
31. F.Å. Nielsen, Afinn (2011), http://www2.imm.dtu.dk/pubdb/p.php?6010
32. R. Plutchik, The nature of emotions. Am. Sci. **89**(4), 344 (2001)
33. M.G. Rordriguez, J. Leskovec, D. Balduzzi, B. Scholkopf, Uncovering the structure and temporal dynamics of information propagation. Netw. Sci. **2**(1), 26–65 (2014)
34. D.A. Savage, B. Torgler, The emergence of emotions and religious sentiments during the September 11 disaster. Motiv. Emot. **37**(3), 586–599 (2013)
35. C. St Louis, G. Zorlu, Can Twitter predict disease outbreaks? Br. Med. J. **344**, 1–3 (2012)

36. M. Steinbach, ISIL Online: Countering Terrorist Radicalization and Recruitment on the Internet and Social Media (2016), https://www.fbi.gov/news/testimony/isil-online-countering-terrorist-radicalization-and-recruitment-on-the-internet-and-social-media-

37. S. Stieglitz, D.X. Linh, Emotions and information diffusion in social media- sentiment of microblogs and sharing behavior. J. Manag. Inf. Syst. **29**(4), 217–247 (2013)

38. S. Stuart, Why do we pay more attention to negative news than to positive news? (2015), http://blogs.lse.ac.uk/politicsandpolicy/why-is-there-no-good-news/

39. B. Suh, L. Hong, P. Pirolli, E.H. Chi, Want to be retweeted? Large scale analytics on factors impacting retweet in Twitter network, in *Proceedings of the 2010 IEEE Second International Conference on Social Computing* (2010), pp. 177–184

40. M. Thelwall, K. Buckley, G. Paltoglou, D. Cai, A. Kappas, Sentiment strength detection in short informal text. J. Am. Soc. Inf. Sci. Technol. **61**, 2544–2558 (2010)

41. D.N. Trung, T.T. Nguyen, J.J. Jung, D. Choi, Understanding effect of sentiment content toward information diffusion pattern in online social networks: a case study on TweetScope, in *Context-Aware Systems and Applications: Second International Conference, ICCASA 2013* (2014), pp. 349–358

42. S. Tsugawa, H. Ohsaki, Negative messages spread rapidly and widely on social media, in *Proceedings of the ACM on Conference on Online Social Networks* (ACM, New York, 2015), pp. 151–160

43. S. Vieweg, A.L. Hughes, K. Starbird, L. Palen, Microblogging during two natural hazards events: what Twitter may contribute to situational awareness, in *Proceedings of the SIGCHI Conference on Human Factors in Computing Systems* (2010), pp. 1079–1088

44. G. Weimann, Terror on Facebook, Twitter, and Youtube. Brown J. World Affairs **16**(2), 45–54 (2010)

45. Y. Yang, J. Jia, B. Wu, J. Tang, Social role-aware emotion contagion in image social networks, in *Proceedings of the Thirtieth AAAI Conference on Artificial Intelligence* (2016), pp. 65–71

46. Z. Zhang, S.Y. Zhang, How do explicitly expressed emotions influence interpersonal communication and information dissemination? A field study of emoji's effects on commenting and retweeting on a microblog platform, in *20th Pacific Asia Conference on Information Systems* (2016), pp. 1–14

Diffusion Algorithms in Multimedia Social Networks: A Novel Model

Flora Amato, Vincenzo Moscato, Antonio Picariello, and Giancarlo Sperlí

1 Introduction

Several *online social networks* (OSNs) actually represent natural environments where a huge number of multimedia data, such as text, images, video, audio, and so on, are generated and shared among users: just to make an example, recent statistics reports that in 2017 there are about 2 billion monthly active users in Facebook, generating 4 new petabytes of data per day and posting about 350 million photos per day. A user usually interacts with other "friends" by means of images, video, or audio, thus creating special "social links," particularly interesting for analyzing the users' behaviors. It is the authors' opinion that in addition to social information (e.g., tags, opinions, insights, evaluations, perspectives, ratings, and user profiles), these user-generated multimedia contents are important especially from the perspective of *social network analysis* (SNA), for predicting user behavior, analyzing users' influence, modeling the evolution of the networks, and eventually detecting "interest-based" user communities.

However, only a few works have analyzed the role of multimedia data in social networks, despite the large number of research done in the field: we think that the definition of a data model for social networks that consider both multimedia content and relationships among users could be of crucial interest for effective SNA algorithms.

F. Amato · V. Moscato · A. Picariello · G. Sperlí (✉)
Department of Electrical Engineering and Information Technology, University of Naples "Federico II", Naples, Italy

CINI - ITEM National Lab Complesso Universitario Monte Santangelo, Naples, Italy
e-mail: flora.amato@unina.it; vincenzo.moscato@unina.it; antonio.picariello@unina.it; giancarlo.sperli@unina.it

© Springer Nature Switzerland AG 2019
M. Kaya, R. Alhajj (eds.), *Influence and Behavior Analysis in Social Networks and Social Media*, Lecture Notes in Social Networks,
https://doi.org/10.1007/978-3-030-02592-2_5

In this paper, we focus our attention on *influence analysis* issue where OSNs seem to provide the basis to find the most suitable solution, especially concerning the information *diffusion* and *maximizations* problems.

The study of influence spreading and diffusion over a SNA is useful for understanding trends and innovation strategies and for marketing campaigns: as reported in tradition marketing strategies, a few users, sometimes called *influentials*, can "influence" the behaviors of other users, although in a more modern view, one should consider interpersonal relationships that are often mediated by multimedia content; just to make an example, in SNA, the influence of a user is surely related to a "popularity" measure, linked to *user-to-user* relationships. In this paper, we address the following main questions:

- May we use the *similarity* related to multimedia data for mining hidden social links?
- May we use annotations such as tags, comments, reviews, and so on, for a more detailed SN analytics?
- What is the best data model that contains the different kinds of relationships within a SN?

The most simple manner to model a standard OSN is to adopt a *graph* constituted by a set of *vertices*, which represent the users of a community network, and a set of *edges*, which represent the different relationships established by the users. All the relationships generated within the social network create particular homogeneous graphs that can support SNA with a great number of applications such as lurker identification, expert finding, influence analysis, community detection, and so on.

In accordance with the novel communication theories and literature trend, a more effective way to model OSNs is to consider both the different kinds of entities typical of the discussed social environments: *users* and *multimedia* content. We take also into account the fact that relationships among the above entities can be not only dyadic (e.g., a friendship or a multimedia similarity) but "n-ary" relations involving more than two entity occurrences (e.g., a user tags another one within a picture).

To this goal, we decided to leverage the *hypergraph* formalism to model any kind of OSNs and better capture the different types of social entities and relationships that can be instantiated. In addition, we defined a novel information diffusion model on the top of the introduced data structure to support influence maximization task.

We explicitly note not that this paper represents an extension of our previous work by Amato et al.[1] and, to the best of our knowledge, is one of the first attempt to propose a novel OSN model having as primary aim the management and analysis of user-generated multimedia content within a unique framework for SNA applications.

The rest of this paper is organized as follows. Section 2 describes the main related work on OSN modeling and influence analysis problems. Section 3 details the proposed data model, while Sect. 4 is focused on the influence analysis methodology leveraging multimedia content, presenting the diffusion model and the maximization algorithms within the proposed framework. Section 5 illustrates experimental results. Conclusions and discussions are reported in Sect. 6.

2   Related Works

In the last decade, the continuous technological development has allowed online social networks to develop new features for sharing, commenting, and interacting with multimedia objects. Thus, multimedia objects, such as photo, video, audio, and image, play a key role representing a novel means to spread new ideas or technology among users. This facets led to define novel environments, namely, *multimedia social networks* (MSNs)[1, 2], whose features can be used to develop new approaches for properly supporting several applications such as viral marketing, community detection, social recommendation, and so on. *MultiComm*[3] is an example of a framework for finding groups of users who interact significantly on particular kinds of multimedia objects by evaluating the related *affinity*. Another approach, namely, *Nodal Attribute-based Temporal Exponential Random Graph Model* (NATERGM)[4], examines how the nodal attributes of a dynamic multimedia network affect the order in which the network ties are developed.

Those new features of MSNs led to the increase of new opportunities and challenges in viral marketing fields, whose main topic is the influence analysis and, in particular, the *influence maximization* problem. The influence maximization problem has been firstly introduced by Richardson and Domingos[5], which examines a specific market as a social network composed by different interconnecting entities and models it as a Markov Random Field in order to identify a subset of users to convince adopting a new technology for maximizing the adoption of this technology.

More in details, influence analysis problem facets into two following subproblems: firstly an influence model is defined for describing how the influence spreads over the networks and successively a NP-hard optimization problem, namely, *influence maximization*, is addressed for identifying a small set of users for maximizing the spread in a network.

Concerning the first problem, different models have been proposed in literature, which can be classified into the following two categories: progressive and nonprogressive models. The main difference between them concerns the facts that the nonprogressive models make the assumption that nodes's states can change indefinitely, while in the progressive ones, when a node is active, it cannot switch its status. For both the described categories, it's possible to classify the proposed models into the following six groups.

The first group is composed of stochastic models [6] in which the influence spread process is based on probabilistic effect of marketing actions on the initial activation of nodes.

The epidemic models[7] represent the second family, which describes the influence spread process as a disease among biological population by a given *infection rate*. Each individual could appear in one of the following states *susceptible (S)*, corresponding to healthy user-bearer of disease; *infected (I)*, infected node, or *recovered (R)*, node that was *infected*.

In the third family, a user's opinion can be changed based on its neighbors' behavior according to *voter model*[8]. A voter model on signed networks has been proposed in [9] for analyzing the dynamics of influence diffusion of two opposite opinions.

Markov Random Field models[5] represent the fourth group of influence diffusion models to analyze customer's network value.

The fifth group is based on *heat models*[10] that describe the influence spread as a heat diffusion process by assigning a diffusion probability to each node.

Finally, some authors model the influence diffusion problem as a particular case of *bond percolation* [11, 12], where the edges are configured as "bonds" and nodes as "sites." This approaches may be considered as a special case of the *Independent Cascade* (IC) model.

The second problem, namely, *influence maximization* (IM), of influence analysis concerns choosing the most influential nodes that have been proven to be NP-hard by Kempe et al.[6]. Moreover the authors addressed this complexity issue using *hill-climbing* greedy algorithm based on sub-modular influence function guaranteeing that the obtained solution is no worse than $(1 - \frac{1}{e})$ of optimal solution. Finally, a Monte Carlo simulation has been used for improving the accuracy of obtained solutions.

The main issue of this greedy approach concerns the running time for computing the expected spread that is equal to $O(kn)$ (where n is the number of nodes). For this reason, a number of methods have been developed in order to estimate the influence spread: *simulation based*, *heuristic based*, and *sketch based*.

The first group of methods, [13–15], try to improve the accuracy of the influence' processes repeating the simulation algorithms. The second and the third groups are also called *heuristic-based* methods [16, 17], which exploit communities or linear systems for restricting the influence spread, and *sketch-based* techniques [18, 19], which build a family of vertex sets exploiting a reverse simulation.

Concerning the IM problem, several approaches have been proposed in the literature that it is possible to classify in the following five categories.

Stochastic model approaches based on probabilistic theory for estimating the influential seed set compose the first family. Several algorithms, such as TIM [20] and IMM [21], have been proposed to reduce the number of iterations required by Monte Carlo [6]-based method.

The second family is composed of biologically inspired algorithm that has the aim to improve the initial seed set through an optimization process inspired by animal behaviors, such as bee waggle dance[22] and ant colony[23].

In the third group, there are approaches based on game theory to model the IM problem in oligopolistic market [24], to improve the knowledge of the network, or to deal with the problem of initial lack of information due to privacy problems leveraging the multi-armed bandit theory[25].

The fourth group is composed of genetic algorithms [26, 27] that have the aim to reduce the required time for obtaining the required solution, which is comparable with the other computed by other families, reducing the assumption on underlying graph.

Finally, the last group is built on algorithm based on community detection methods. In particular these approaches led to maximize the spread in the community verifying how it propagates intra-community [28, 29].

In this paper we leverage the multimedia content in a social network, proposing a certain greedy strategy. Differently from other authors, we define an original multimedia data model for OSN and a special influence operator, thus reducing the required samples for influence maximization and improving the effectiveness of the process.

3   The Data Model

3.1   Definitions

In this paper, we want to describe a general model for representing the concepts of relationships in a general-purpose OSN: we will successively focus on multimedia-generated content.

In our proposed model, we define three main OSN entities.

Users—it is the set of people (or organizations) that are part of one or more networks. We take into account the general profile, preferences, interests, and so on.

Objects—it is the set of user-generated items within a certain network. In some OSN, such as Flickr, YouTube, Last.fm, and Instagram, for example, the objects are multimedia information formed by image, video, audio, and text as well.

Topics—it is the set of the main named entities or general terms of one or more domains, used to describe objects.[1]

Among the main entities, different relationships may be established: for example, a user can post an image, two users (that are also "friend") can write a comment on the same object, a user can tag another user in a picture, a user can share some videos or can listen an audio, and so on.

We explicitly notice that the relationships are generally complex and heterogeneous: we thus use an OSN model using a *hypergraph*. In this framework, an OSN is a weighted and undirected hypergraph; in addition, using the relationships, different hyperpaths—or social paths—"connect" the previously discussed entities.

The following definitions will better clarify our ideas.

Definition 3.1 (OSN) An *online social network* OSN is a triple $(HV; HE = \{he_i : i \in I\}; \omega)$, HV being a finite set of *vertices*, HE a set of *hyperedges* with a finite set of indexes I and $\omega : HE \to [0, 1]$ a weight function. The set of vertices is defined as $HV = U \cup O \cup T$, U being the set of OSN users, O the set of objects, and T the set of topics. Each hyperedge $he_i \in HE$ is in turn defined by a ordered pair

---

[1]Sometimes, they are generated by automatic analysis of annotations, tags, keywords, comments, reviews, and so on. Of course, they are not always available for every kind of application.

$he_i = (he_i^+ = (HV_{he_i}^+, i); he_i^- = (i, HV_{he_i}^-))$. The element he_i^+ is called the *tail* of the hyperarc he_i, whereas he_i^- is its *head*, $HV_{he_i}^+ \subseteq HV$ being the set of vertices of he_i^+, $HV_{he_i}^- \subseteq HV$ the set of vertices of he_i^-, and $HV_{he_i} = HV_{he_i}^+ \cup HV_{he_i}^-$ the subset of vertices constituting the whole hyperedge.

Actually, vertices and hyperedges are particular *abstract data types* with a set of properties (attributes and methods) that allow to model several social networks, at the same time supporting different applications. For this reason, we use the "dot notation" to identify the attributes of a given vertex or hyperedge: as an example, he_i.id, he_i.name, he_i.time, he_i.source, and he_i.type represent the ID, name, time stamp, source (social network), and type of the hyperedge he_i, respectively. We note that several attributes are common to any kind of vertices/hyperdges, in turn, other ones are typical of specific vertices/hyperdges. Eventually, the weight function can be used to define the "confidence" of a given relationship.

Definition 3.2 (Social Path) A *social path* between two vertices v_{s_1} and v_{s_k} of an OSN is a sequence of distinct vertices and hyperedges $sp(v_{s_1}, v_{s_k}) = v_{s_1}, he_{s_1}, v_{s_2}, \dots, he_{s_{k-1}}, v_{s_k}$ such that $\{v_{s_i}, v_{s_{i+1}}\} \subseteq HV_{he_{s_i}}$ for $1 \leq i \leq k - 1$. The *length* γ of the hyperpath is $\alpha \cdot \sum_{i=1}^{k-1} \frac{1}{\omega(he_{s_i})}$, α being a normalizing factor. We say that a social path *contains* a vertex v_h if $\exists he_{s_i} : v_h \in he_{s_i}$.

Social paths between two nodes leverage the different kinds of relationships: a given path can "directly" connect two users because they are "friends" or members of the same group, or "indirectly", as they have commented the same picture.

Among the different types of social paths that can be instantiated in an OSN, the *relevant social paths*—i.e., particular hyperpaths that present certain properties—assume a particular importance for the social network analysis purposes.

Definition 3.3 (Relevant Social Path) Let Θ be a set of conditions defined over the attributes of vertices and hyperedges; a *relevant social path* is a social path satisfying Θ.

For our aims, we explicitly use a particular social path that connects two users, the *influential path* used to model the "influence" among users. In Flickr, for example, u_i influences u_j, if u_j adds to the list of favorites a pictures posted by u_i or if u_j gives good comments to a picture that u_i has just posed. In this case, note that the influential paths have the form $u_1, he_1, o_1, he_2, u_2$, where he_1.type = "*publishing*" $\wedge$ he_2.type = "*add_favorite*" $\wedge$ $(he_2$.time $- he_1$.time$) \leq \Delta t$ constitutes the set of conditions Θ, being Δt a given time. In other OSN, such as Twitter, influence is related to other actions, such as re-tweets, and we could observe that u_i influences u_j, if u_j has re-tweeted a tweet posted by u_i.

We put in evidence three different categories of relationships that can be retrieved in OSNs:

- **User-to-user** relationships, i. e., actions of a user with respect to other users
- **Similarity** relationships, i.e., the similarity between two objects, users, or topics
- **User-to-object** relationships, i.e., the actions of a user on objects

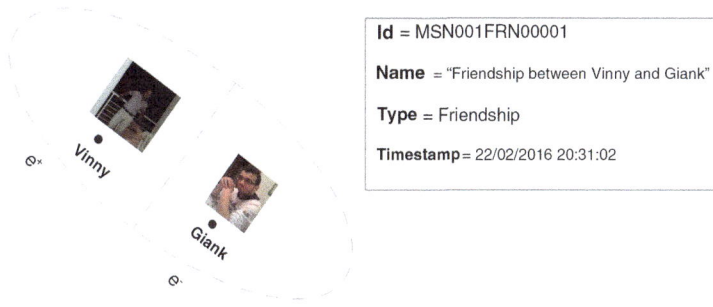

Id	= MSN001FRN00001
Name	= "Friendship between Vinny and Giank"
Type	= Friendship
Timestamp	= 22/02/2016 20:31:02

Fig. 1 Friendship relationship

Formally speaking, we define the following kind of relationships:

Definition 3.4 (User-to-User Relationship) Let $\widehat{U} \subseteq U$ a subset of users in an OSN; we define *user-to-user relationship* of each hyperedge he_i with the following properties:

1. $HV^+_{he_i} = u_k$ such that $u_k \in \widehat{U}$
2. $HV^-_{he_i} \subseteq \widehat{U} - u_k$

Examples of "user-to-user" relationships are properly represented by *friendship*, *following*, or *membership* of some online social networks (see Fig. 1). For this kind of relationships, we can set $\omega(he_i)$ to a value in [0,1] that is a function of the specific relationship and depends on the particular supported application. In the opposite, a general strategy can assign the value 1 to each user-to-user relationship.

Definition 3.5 (Similarity Relationship) Let $v_k, v_j \in V$ ($k \neq j$) two vertices of the same type of an OSN; we define *similarity relationship* each hyperedge he_i with $HV^+_{he_i} = v_k$ and $HV^-_{he_i} = v_j$. The weight function for this relationship returns similarity value between the two vertices.

We extract a similarity value between two users, considering different types of features (interests, profile information, preferences, etc.), between two objects (by means of high- and low-level features and the metrics proposed in the literature), and between two topics (using specific metrics based on vocabularies or ontologies). In the proposed model, a similarity hyperedge is effectively generated if $\omega(\boldsymbol{he_i}) \geq \eta$, η being a given threshold (see Fig. 2).

Definition 3.6 (User-to-Object Relationship) Let $\widehat{U} \subseteq U$ a set of users, $\widehat{T} \subseteq T$ a set of topics, and $\widehat{O} \subseteq O$ a set of objects in a OSN; we define *user-to-object relationship* each hyperedge he_i with the following properties:

1. $HV^+_{he_i} = u_k$ such that $u_k \in \widehat{U}$
2. $HV^-_{he_i} \subseteq \widehat{O} \cup \widehat{T} \cup \widehat{U}$

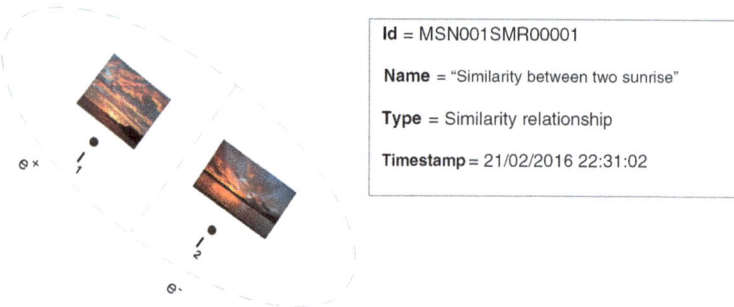

| Id = MSN001SMR00001 |
| Name = "Similarity between two sunrise" |
| Type = Similarity relationship |
| Timestamp = 21/02/2016 22:31:02 |

Fig. 2 Multimedia similarity relationship

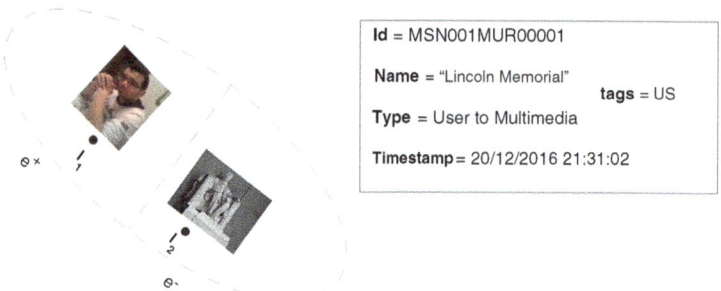

| Id = MSN001MUR00001 |
| Name = "Lincoln Memorial" |
| tags = US |
| Type = User to Multimedia |
| Timestamp = 20/12/2016 21:31:02 |

Fig. 3 Multimedia tagging relationship

Examples of "user-to-object" relationships (see Fig. 3) are represented by *publishing, reaction, annotation, review, comment* (in tfang2014topiche last three cases the set $HV_{e_i}^-$ can also contains one or more topics), or *user-tagging* (involving also one or more users) activities. For this kind of relationship, we set $\omega(he_i)$ to a value in [0,1] that is a function of the specific relationship and depend on the particular supported application. In the opposite, a general strategy can assign the value 1 to each user-to-object relationship.

3.2 Hypergraph Building and Computation

The proposed hypergraph building process is in part inspired by the methodology proposed in [30]. It consists of three different stages: hypergraph structure construction, topic detection, and item similarity computation. First, extracted data related to relationships are initially used to construct the hypergraph structure in terms of nodes and hyperedges. For the user-to-object relationships, textual annotations are then analyzed by a LDA approach to learn the most important topics and to infer relations between topics and textual annotations. From the other hand, similarity of values between users, objects, and topics can be eventually determined using proper strategies.

Generally, hypergraphs are very complex data structures to manage, and for computational reasons, different approaches have been introduced to deal with their intrinsic complexity, especially for large graphs. In this work, we have chosen to adopt a problem-oriented methodology that transforms the OSN hypergraph into a homogeneous graph depending on the particular application (i.e., influence analysis) on the basis of considered relevant social paths as we are detailing in the following.

4 Influence Diffusion and Maximization in OSNs

For the influence analysis goals, we deal with a homogeneous graph (*influence graph*) $IG = (V; E; \tau)$ whose vertices are specific users of an OSN; in particular, there exists an edge e between two vertices v_i and v_j for all influential paths connecting v_i and v_j. For each edge the related weight will be determined as in the following:

$$\tau(e_{i,j}) = \frac{\sum_{k=1}^{M} \gamma(sp_k(v_i, v_j))}{N_j} \tag{1}$$

M being the number of distinct influential paths between v_i and v_j and N_j the number of influential paths having a destination vertex v_j.

On the influence graph, it is then possible to apply all the most diffused models and techniques for influence maximization.

In this paper, we propose an approach that extensively uses multimedia contents, for estimating the influence or for retrieving communities of users, by means of *relevant paths* and *influence graph*.

Our approach can be seen an extension of sketch-based methods [20, 21], in which several samples are computed for identifying the nodes's set covering a large number of samples to infer an approximation of solution. Each sample is the set of nodes reachable from a given vertex on the influence graph, obtained by removing an edge with a given probability.

Our idea is to reduce the required number of samples exploiting relevant paths. In particular, we define the following three matrices.

Definition 4.1 (User-Relevant Path Matrix) Let U and P be, respectively, the sets of users and relevant influential paths of OSN; we define the *user-relevant path matrix* as:

$$\mathbf{UP} = \{up_{ij}\} = \begin{cases} \tau & u_i \text{ belongs to path } sp_j \\ 0 & \text{else} \end{cases}$$

Definition 4.2 (Relevant Path-Object Matrix) Let O and P be, respectively, the sets of multimedia objects and relevant influential paths of OSN; we define the *relevant path-object matrix* as:

$$\mathbf{PO} = \{po_{ij}\} = \begin{cases} 1 & o_j \text{ belongs to the path } sp_i \\ 0 & \text{else} \end{cases}$$

The above defined matrices may be then used to compute a *user-object matrix* that takes into account the total number of influential paths among graph vertices with respect to objects.

Definition 4.3 (User-Object Matrix) Let U, M, $\mathbf{UP}$, and $\mathbf{PO}$ be, respectively, the sets of users, objects, and user-relevant path and relevant path-object matrices; we define the *user-object matrix* as:

$$\mathbf{UO} = \{uo_{i,j}\} = \sum_{u \in U} \left(\prod_{p \in P} up_{ij} \cdot po_{ij} \right)$$

In other words, we want to reduce the amount of required samples choosing the minimum number of relevant multimedia objects that allow us to identify an appropriate number of samples. Eventually, we compute the seed set as vertices collection that maximize the fraction of samples covered from each node.

We choose the τ^* value to prune the sequences of actions on which the influence among users is less than τ^*. In the Algorithm 1, we focus our attention on the relevance of multimedia objects involved in the more relevant paths through *compute_sum* function. In this way, we identify a set of vertices from which we generate the samples that are exploited by the *Sample_generation* and *Node_covering* functions to find the desired subset.

5   Experimental Results

In order to evaluate the proposed methodology with regard to other techniques, we exploit the TIM and IMM[19] algorithms that are based on the *sketch* method.

TIM is a two-phase influence maximization algorithm: in the first phase, called sampling phase, the algorithm estimates the number of random reverse reachable sets, each one corresponding to a set of nodes that can reach a given node v; in the second step, called "node selection," the algorithm identifies a size-k node set that covers a large number of reverse random (RR) sets.

Algorithm 1 τ-Diffusion algorithm

1: **procedure** τ-DIFFUSION ALGORITHM(MSN, τ^*, θ,k)
2:   - - Input: OSN (the considered social network)
3:   - - Input: IG (the influence graph)
4:   - - Input: τ^* (the influence threshold)
5:   - - Input: θ (the relevance threshold)
6:   - - Input: k (the desired size of seed set)
7:   - - Output: S (the seed set)
8:   - - Temp: **UP** (the U-RP matrix)
9:   - - Temp: **PO** (the RP-O matrix)
10:   - - Temp: **UO** (the U-O matrix)
11:   - - Temp : sum (the relevance of given MO)
12:   - - Temp : E (the set of examined relevant paths)
13:   - - Temp : SS (the set of samples)
14:   - - Temp : T (the vertices set for sampling generation)
15:   **UP** $\leftarrow$ compute_matrix_UP(OSN,IG,τ_s)
16:   **PO** $\leftarrow$ compute_matrix_PO(OSN,IG,τ_s)
17:   **UO** $\leftarrow$ compute_matrix_UO(OSN,IG,τ_s)
18:   E $\leftarrow$ 0
19:   T $\leftarrow$ 0
20:   SS $\leftarrow$ 0
21:   j $\leftarrow$ argmax$_{u_i}\{\sum_{o_j} um_{ij}\}$
22:   sum $\leftarrow$ compute_sum(UO,j)
23:   **if** $(sum \geq \theta)$ **then**
24:     E $\leftarrow \{p_i : po_{ij} = 1\}$
25:     T $\leftarrow \{\forall e \in E, u_i : up_{ij(e)} \neq 0\}$
26:   SS $\leftarrow$ Sample_generation (T,**UP**)
27:   S $\leftarrow$ Node_covering(SS,k)

IMM is based on a similar approach, leveraging estimation probabilistic techniques [31] for reducing the required number of samples.

More in details, we use two versions of TIM and of IMM, one based on the classic TIM and IMM and the other ones, $TIM^\star$ and $IMM^\star$, based on our approach.

The experimental protocol is based on the following three different steps:

– We compare the effectiveness of the proposed approach varying the threshold θ;
– We analyze the effectiveness of the proposed method varying ϵ and κ, which represent the solution tolerance and the seed set size,
– We provide an efficiency evaluation in terms of running times.

Table 1 Dataset characterization

	Publishing	Comment	Favorites	Avg action per user
YFCC100M	641.630	189.174	109.146	4604

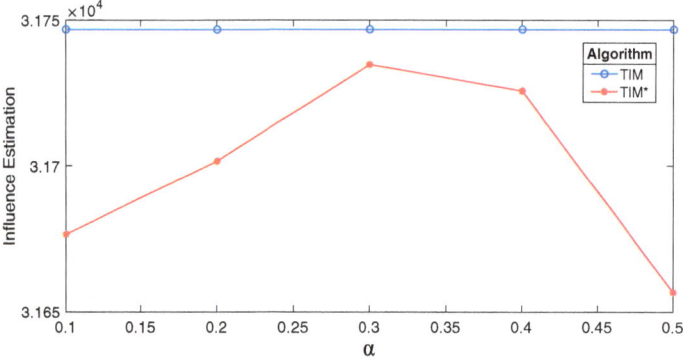

Fig. 4 TIM: influence estimation varying threshold α

A subset of Yahoo Flickr Creative Commons 100 Million (YFCC100M) dataset[2] has been used to perform this evaluation. More in details YFCC100M contains metadata of around 99.2 million photos and 0.8 million videos from Flickr shared under one of the different *Creative Commons license*. Moreover, we enrich this subset of photos crawling social data related to each photos through Flickr API to properly build user-to-user and user-to-content relationships of OSN.

In Table 1, the information related to the analyzed dataset is summarized.

The experiments have been carried out on Databricks platform,[3] a public cloud-based big data environment, using 3 computing nodes, each one composed by 4 core with 15 GB Ram, on which we installed Spark 2.1.11 and Hadoop 2.7.3.

In Figs. 4 and 5, it is possible to note how the diminishing of the threshold θ led to increase the performance of the method due to the increase of the samples. In particular this trend grow up to $\theta = 0.70$.

Figures 6 and 7 show the effectiveness of the proposed approach with respect to the normal version varying the tolerance threshold ϵ. It is easy to note that the proposed approach outperforms the normal version because it uses a small number of samples to identify the seed set. The same trend is shown also in Figs. 8 and 9, in which the analyses have been performed varying the size of seed set.

---

[2]https://webscope.sandbox.yahoo.com.

[3]https://www.databricks.com/.

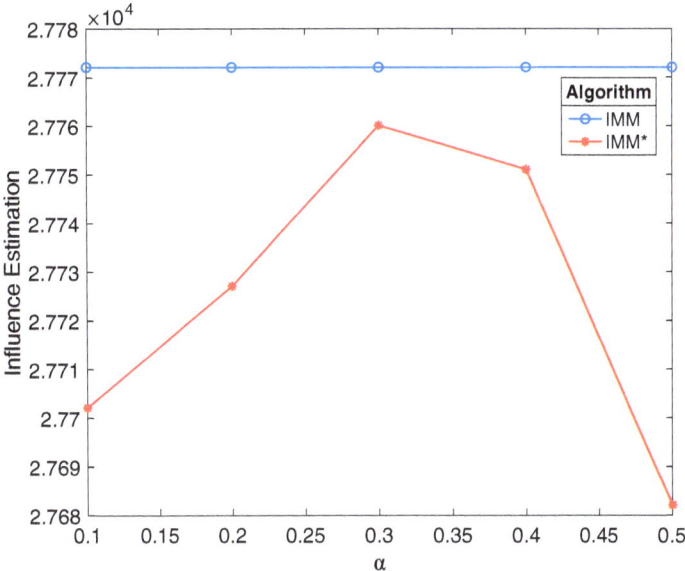

Fig. 5 IMM: influence estimation varying threshold α

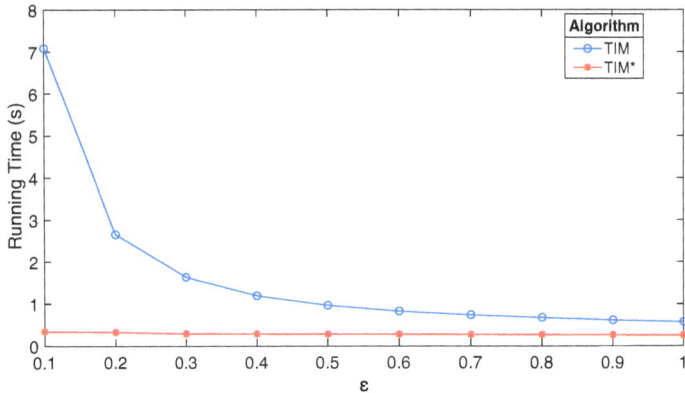

Fig. 6 TIM: running time varying epsilon

In Figs. 10 and 11, we show a running time comparison between the two versions of the analyzed algorithms, varying the tolerance of the algorithm, considering $k = 50$. Moreover, in Fig. 10 it is possible to note the same trend; in 11, the analysis have been obtained varying the seed set cardinality, considering $\epsilon = 0.1$ (Figs. 12 and 13).

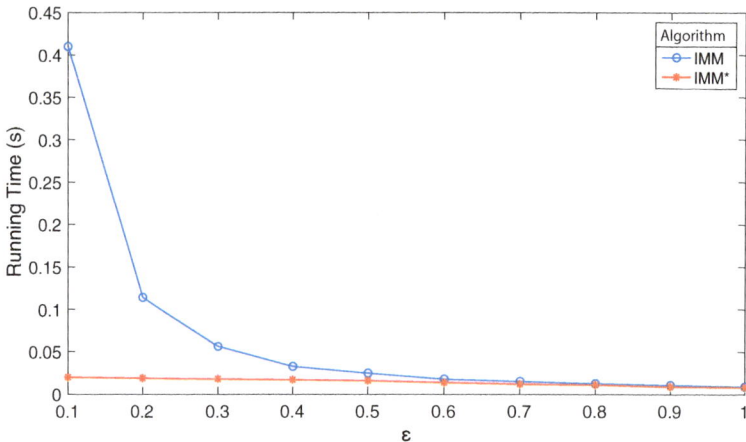

Fig. 7 IMM: running time varying epsilon

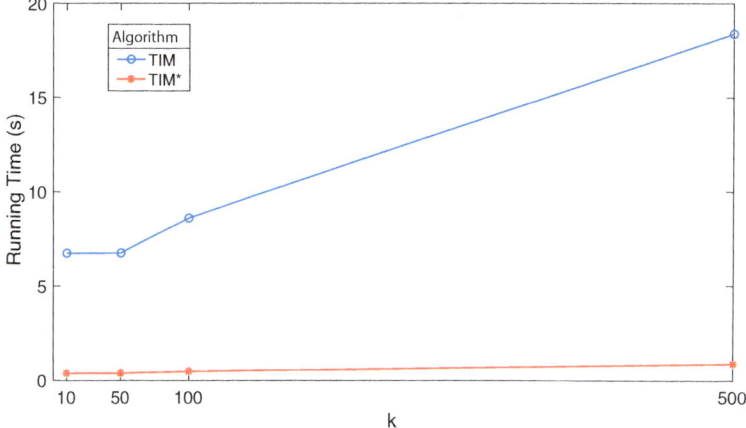

Fig. 8 TIM: running time varying kappa

In particular, it is possible to note that TIM (IMM) outperforms the, respectively, modified version because the proposed method uses a small number of required samples which leads to reduce the influence spread estimation. Furthermore, this trend occurs both varying ϵ and k because the choose of samples related to users involved in more important social paths allows to obtain good results in less time with respect to the normal version.

In conclusion, the interactions between user and multimedia contents contribute to properly identify a trade-off between number of required samples and running times of algorithm based on relevance of multimedia objects. These information

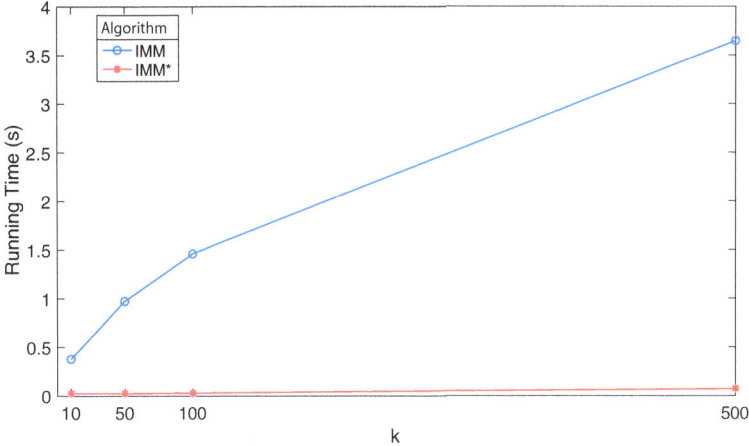

Fig. 9 IMM: running time varying kappa

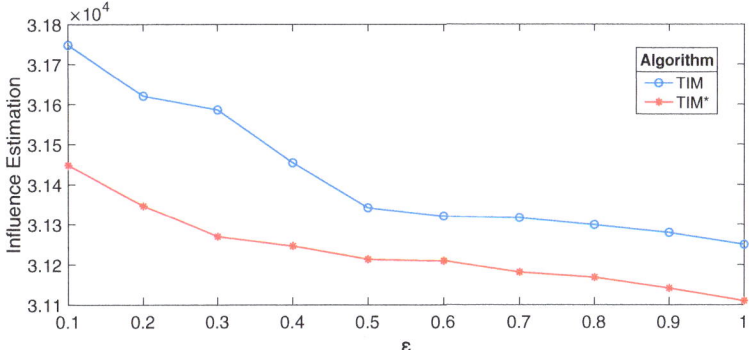

Fig. 10 TIM: influence estimation varying epsilon

are really relevant for viral marketing application in which the timeliness for recognizing the dynamic interactions between users can define innovative and effective business strategies, such as providing influential users discounts or gifts.

6 Conclusion and Discussions

In this paper, we have described a novel hypergraph data model for online social networks, which provides a simple mechanism for considering multimedia data as one of OSN's components. In addition, we have verified how classic algorithms such as influence analysis could be enhanced using our approach, defining a novel influence operator for a novel influence maximization algorithm. We have

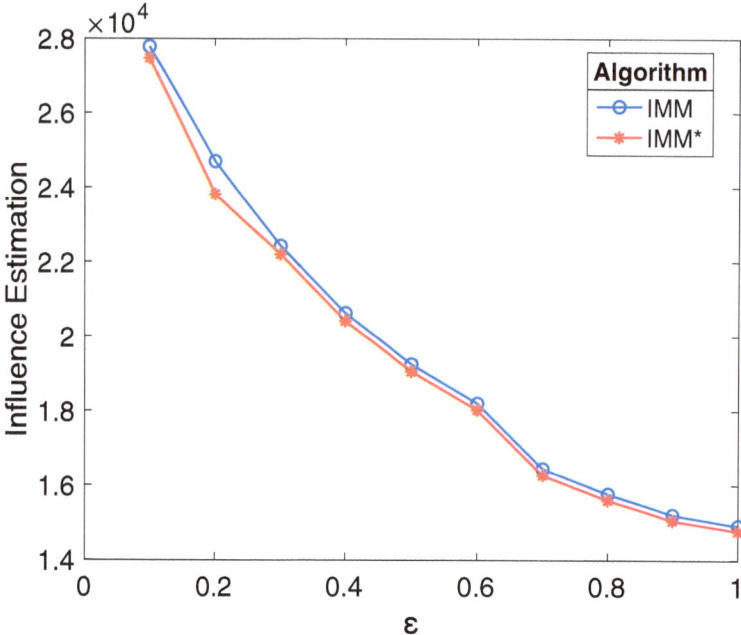

Fig. 11 IMM: influence estimation varying epsilon

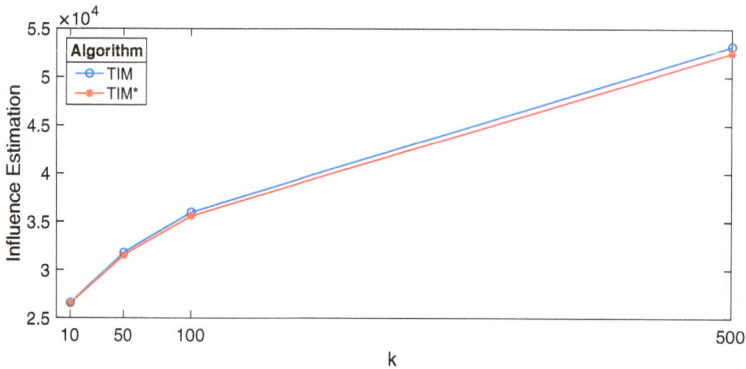

Fig. 12 TIM: influence estimation varying kappa

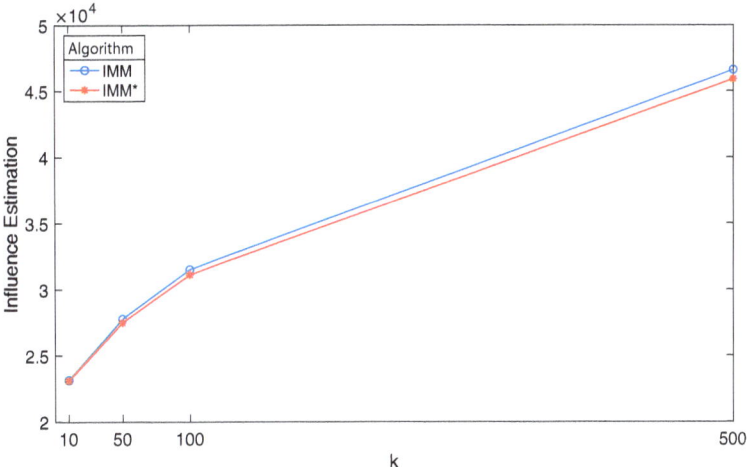

Fig. 13 IMM: influence estimation varying kappa

implemented a system on the top of a Spark platform, and several experiments have been carried out, using the Flicker YFCC100M dataset, showing encouraging preliminary results.

References

1. F. Amato, V. Moscato, A. Picariello, G. Sperlí, Multimedia social network modeling: a proposal, in *2016 IEEE Tenth International Conference on Semantic Computing (ICSC)* (IEEE, New York, 2016), pp. 448–453
2. G. Sperlì, F. Amato, V. Moscato, A. Picariello, Multimedia social network modeling using hypergraphs. Int. J. Multimed. Data Eng. Manage. **7**(3), 53–77 (2016)
3. X. Li, M. K. Ng, Y. Ye, Multicomm: finding community structure in multi-dimensional networks. IEEE Trans. Knowl. Data Eng. **26**(4), 929–941 (2014)
4. S. Jiang, H. Chen, NATERGM: a model for examining the role of nodal attributes in dynamic social media networks. IEEE Trans. Knowl. Data Eng. **28**(3), 729–740 (2016)
5. P. Domingos, M. Richardson, Mining the network value of customers, in *Proceedings of the Seventh ACM SIGKDD International Conference on Knowledge Discovery and Data Mining* (ACM, New York, 2001), pp. 57–66
6. D. Kempe, J. Kleinberg, É. Tardos, Maximizing the spread of influence through a social network, in *Proceedings of the Ninth ACM SIGKDD International Conference on Knowledge Discovery and Data Mining* (ACM, New York, 2003), pp. 137–146
7. S. Wen, J. Jiang, B. Liu, Y. Xiang, W. Zhou, Using epidemic betweenness to measure the influence of users in complex networks. J. Netw. Comput. Appl. **78**, 288–299 (2017)
8. V. Sood, S. Redner, Voter model on heterogeneous graphs. Phys. Rev. Lett. **94**(17), 178701 (2005)
9. Y. Li, W. Chen, Y. Wang, Z.-L. Zhang, Voter model on signed social networks. Internet Math. **11**(2), 93–133 (2015)

10. M. Doo, L. Liu, Probabilistic diffusion of social influence with incentives. IEEE Trans. Serv. Comput. **7**(3), 387–400 (2014)
11. Y. Hu, S. Havlin, H.A. Makse, Conditions for viral influence spreading through multiplex correlated social networks. Phys. Rev. X **4**(2), 021031 (2014)
12. Y. Jiang, J. Jiang, Diffusion in social networks: a multiagent perspective. IEEE Trans. Syst. Man Cybern. Syst. **45**(2), 198–213 (2015)
13. W. Chen, Y. Wang, S. Yang, Efficient influence maximization in social networks, in *Proceedings of the 15th ACM SIGKDD International Conference on Knowledge Discovery and Data Mining* (ACM, New York, 2009), pp. 199–208
14. J. Leskovec, A. Krause, C. Guestrin, C. Faloutsos, J. VanBriesen, N. Glance, Cost-effective outbreak detection in networks, in *Proceedings of the 13th ACM SIGKDD International Conference on Knowledge Discovery and Data Mining* (ACM, New York, 2007), pp. 420–429
15. N. Ohsaka, T. Akiba, Y. Yoshida, K.-I. Kawarabayashi, Fast and accurate influence maximization on large networks with pruned Monte-Carlo simulations, in *AAAI* (2014), pp. 138–144
16. K. Jung, W. Heo, W. Chen, IRIE: scalable and robust influence maximization in social networks, in *2012 IEEE 12th International Conference on Data Mining* (IEEE, New York, 2012), pp. 918–923
17. Y. Wang, G. Cong, G. Song, K. Xie, Community-based greedy algorithm for mining top-k influential nodes in mobile social networks, in *Proceedings of the 16th ACM SIGKDD International Conference on Knowledge Discovery and Data Mining* (ACM, New York, 2010), pp. 1039–1048
18. C. Borgs, M. Brautbar, J. Chayes, B. Lucier, Maximizing social influence in nearly optimal time, in *Proceedings of the Twenty-Fifth Annual ACM-SIAM Symposium on Discrete Algorithms* (Society for Industrial and Applied Mathematics, Philadelphia, 2014), pp. 946–957
19. Y. Tang, Y. Shi, X. Xiao, Influence maximization in near-linear time: a martingale approach, in *Proceedings of the 2015 ACM SIGMOD International Conference on Management of Data* (ACM, New York, 2015), pp. 1539–1554
20. Y. Tang, X. Xiao, Y. Shi, Influence maximization: near-optimal time complexity meets practical efficiency, in *Proceedings of the 2014 ACM SIGMOD International Conference on Management of Data* (ACM, New York, 2014), pp. 75–86
21. Y. Tang, Y. Shi, X. Xiao, Influence maximization in near-linear time: a martingale approach, in *Proceedings of the 2015 ACM SIGMOD International Conference on Management of Data*, ser. SIGMOD '15 (ACM, New York, 2015), pp. 1539–1554 [Online]. Available: http://doi.acm.org/10.1145/2723372.2723734
22. C.P. Sankar, S. Asharaf, K.S. Kumar, Learning from bees: an approach for influence maximization on viral campaigns. PloS One **11**(12), e0168125 (2016)
23. W.-S. Yang, S.-X. Weng, C. Guestrin, C. Faloutsos, J. VanBriesen, N. Glance, Application of the ant colony optimization algorithm to the influence-maximization problem. Int. J. Swarm Intell. Evolut. Comput. **1**(1), 1–8 (2012)
24. F. Zhou, R.J. Jiao, B. Lei, Bilevel game-theoretic optimization for product adoption maximization incorporating social network effects. IEEE Trans. Syst. Man Cybern. Syst. **46**(8), 1047–1060 (2016)
25. S. Vaswani, L. Lakshmanan, M. Schmidt, et al., Influence maximization with bandits (2015). arXiv preprint arXiv:1503.00024
26. D. Bucur, G. Iacca, Influence maximization in social networks with genetic algorithms, in *European Conference on the Applications of Evolutionary Computation* (Springer, New York, 2016), pp. 379–392
27. D. Bucur, G. Iacca, M. Gaudesi, G. Squillero, A. Tonda, Optimizing groups of colluding strong attackers in mobile urban communication networks with evolutionary algorithms. Appl. Soft Comput. **40**, 416–426 (2016)
28. J. Shang, S. Zhou, X. Li, L. Liu, H. Wu, Cofim: a community-based framework for influence maximization on large-scale networks. Knowl.-Based Syst. **117**, 88–100 (2017)

29. E. Bagheri, G. Dastghaibyfard, A. Hamzeh, An efficient and fast influence maximization algorithm based on community detection, in *2016 12th International Conference on Natural Computation, Fuzzy Systems and Knowledge Discovery (ICNC-FSKD)*, August 2016, pp. 1636–1641
30. Q. Fang, J. Sang, C. Xu, Y. Rui, Topic-sensitive influencer mining in interest-based social media networks via hypergraph learning. IEEE Trans. Multimed. **16**(3), 796–812 (2014)
31. D. Williams, *Probability with Martingales* (Cambridge University Press, Cambridge, 1991)

Detecting Canadian Internet Satisfaction by Analyzing Twitter Accounts of Shaw Communications

Analyzing Twitter Accounts of Shaw Communications

Satara Cressy, Brenda Pham, Hannah Wright, and Reda Alhajj

1 Introduction

While Internet service providers (ISPs) make their offered speeds available to the public, it is difficult to know the most reliable ISP to choose and whether or not they actually meet their claims. Currently, one of the best ways to gather this type of information is through word of mouth from others; this makes it difficult to know which ISP to choose when on the market for a new provider. While tools exist to measure outages over short periods of time, there is very little information about outage trends longer term.

On top of this, there is no clear way to measure overall customer satisfaction of ISP consumers. As Martin Pfaff puts it in his 1977 paper, "the maximization of consumer satisfaction is considered by most to be the ultimate goal of the market economy" (as cited in [4]). Considering this, it is valuable for all companies, including ISPs, to understand exactly how satisfied their customers are and where their services could be improved. This information would also be useful for consumers looking to switch their providers; choosing a company with a good reputation for satisfaction is more likely to guarantee satisfaction for themselves.

S. Cressy · B. Pham · H. Wright · R. Alhajj (✉)
Department of Computer Science, University of Calgary, Calgary, AB, Canada
e-mail: satara.cressy2@ucalgary.ca; brenda.pham@ucalgary.ca; hannah.wright@ucalgary.ca; alhajj@ucalgary.ca

© Springer Nature Switzerland AG 2019   105
M. Kaya, R. Alhajj (eds.), *Influence and Behavior Analysis in Social Networks and Social Media*, Lecture Notes in Social Networks,
https://doi.org/10.1007/978-3-030-02592-2_6

1.1 Problem Definition

Canadian consumers only have a choice from a handful of ISPs, with the largest providers being Bell, Rogers, Telus, and Shaw. These top four providers dominate the market in most areas of Canada [13]. Considering the fact that the Internet has become a crucial aspect of many Canadian lives, finding an ISP in your area that is reliable is especially important. Not only that, but choosing an ISP that has a good reputation is a factor as well; after all, Internet failures are inevitable, but how these failings are handled can vary. Considering the effect that communication can have on satisfaction [4], it is important to understand how other consumers feel about a company before making your choice.

This was the main goal of our project: to find out the true quality of our top tier Canadian ISPs. Do our top providers deserve their spot at the top? Or should we be demanding more out of our providers as consumers? While there are sites out there that delve into this information somewhat, we aimed to be more specific with what we look for. With this project, we intended to give consumers a better picture of how reliable and satisfying their ISP options truly are.

1.2 Motivation

Since customer satisfaction is such an important aspect of the market [4], it is important to understand exactly how satisfied ISP customers are. After all, positive customer satisfaction will not only encourage customers to stay with the same provider, but it also has the potential to recruit more customers to a specific provider overall. This information is not only valuable to consumers when choosing their ISP but also to the providers themselves as they consider whether or not their customers are satisfied with their services.

Currently, there is very little information out there regarding specifically ISP consumer satisfaction. Not only that, but there are limited resources for understanding long-term outage patterns and how these numbers affect customer satisfaction overall. Considering Internet outages and lag are inevitable for any ISP, it is important to understand exactly how much these factors influence their customer satisfaction as a whole. After all, the harmful effects of these issues could be mitigated through careful communication [4].

Hence, by trying to understand the patterns and trends in customer satisfaction of one of Canada's top ISPs, Shaw Communications, we hope to give ISPs in general the potential to improve their satisfaction levels through preparation and communication. Not only that, but we want to provide people searching for a new ISP the information they need to make a more informed decision than previously possible.

1.3 Summary

In order to get a better understanding of the customer satisfaction of various ISPs as a whole, we chose to focus on one of Canada's top ISPs, Shaw Communications. By analyzing their Twitter feed, we hoped to gather information regarding their outage numbers and the overall happiness of their customers; more specifically, we searched for keywords related to outage announcements by Shaw themselves as well as through analysis of customers via Tweets directed at them. While our conclusions are drawn from only this single firm, expanding these ideas to get a better understanding of the ISP market as a whole is considered future work.

By analyzing the Twitter feed of one of the top Canadian ISPs, Shaw Communications, we aimed to get a better understanding of their reliability and overall customer satisfaction. We found that, while Shaw's communication and customer service were handled well, they had a surprising amount of service problems. We also found that there did not seem to be a correlation between outages and sentiment.

In the remainder of this paper, we will delve into the details of previous work in this area, including a description of what makes our work different. We will then provide the methodology behind how we gathered our data, before we move on to the details of the results we found from our analysis of this information. A discussion of the limitations of our method, as well as possible improvements for future work, will also be included.

2 Related Work

2.1 Internet Issues

ISPs have existed as early as 1989 [3], and with that existence comes an expectation of good quality Internet service—an expectation whose standards have significantly increased, as the Internet becomes less a luxury and more a necessity in the modern world. The net is now a widely used space by large amounts of people, with over three billion users as of 2017 [8]. With that in mind, the problem of examining our country's Internet providers for good performance and excellent customer satisfaction is more important than ever before.

Not too surprisingly then, this is a problem that has been looked into already, at least in part, most notably by Ookla, which uses its *speedtest.net* site to gather speed tests from visitors in order to generate a variety of reports (including an overview of Canadian ISPs's speeds [12]). While Ookla does analyze the performance of various ISPs, namely, looking at speed, it fails to examine stability. Another site, Canadian Outages, does exactly this. It looks into reports of Internet outages using both Twitter comments and other sources [1].

Canadian Outages is the closest resource out there for finding out the reliability of a given ISP. However, it does not cover specific Internet issues beyond outages and fails to take customer satisfaction fully into account. To that end then, we aim to examine not just outages but Internet lag and customer satisfaction of a specific ISP in order to give a fuller picture. This is where our solution differs from existing research in this area. Besides just attempting to understand the outage patterns of Shaw Communications, we attempted to overlay this information with customer satisfaction measurements. With this, our goal was to understand how these two things are related, as well as to get an overall view of the satisfaction of ISP customers as a whole.

2.2 Sentiment Analysis

Most research on sentiment analysis is fairly outdated, with some of the latest papers we found having been written as far back as 2010. One such paper was written by Pak et al. [14] on using Twitter as a corpus for sentiment analysis and finding an effective method in doing so. This paper relates to our work in that it talks about sentiment analysis of Twitter posts, much like what our work entails. However, this research is more concerned about the use of sentiment analysis as a tool in general and does not actively use sentiment analysis with regard to a specific topic.

In their research, Pak et al. used linguistic analysis to find differences between collected texts of three classes: *positive*, *negative*, and *neutral* sentiment. They then used this linguistic information and a collection of texts to train a classifier that would sort different, arbitrary texts into the closest match of the three possible classes.

The main classifier used in this specific study was a *Naive Bayes Classifier*. Other classifiers were tried as well, namely, SVM and CRF, but Naive Bayes was considered the most effective. Once trained and used with various settings, Pak et al. produced results showing the *Naive Bayes Classifier* to be at its most effective with bigram features [14].

What their research reveals is what classifiers with specific features work best for sentiment analysis. This work was considered when choosing our own classifier for our own research. However, while ultimately a very thorough paper, Pak et al. fail to address the issue of detecting sarcasm and nuance in text which could alter sentiment analysis results. Furthermore, there is no mention of the use of images in Twitter posts, which is unfortunately likely due to its age.

In a research paper conducted by Chamlertwat et al. [2], the researchers instead focused on analyzing consumer behavior through Twitter, similar to our own research (although less specific). A system called the *Microblog Sentiment Analysis System* (MSAS) used a sentiment analysis approach to evaluate the public mood of smartphones. This MSAS collects Twitter data and outputs a visual summarization of the data. The result of this analysis showed statistics regarding the polarity of tweets and also compared keywords used in identifying how consumers viewed certain topics. Their research used data from 2010, from the months of March through June.

Similar to our own research, the MSAS gathered tweets containing specific hashtags and keywords. For their research, they collected 1 million tweets and selected 100,000 random tweets for their experiment. The design of the MSAS uses machine-learning approach when classifying a tweet as an opinion. A support vector machine is used for the opinion filtering module, where learning algorithms are used to analyze data for classification analysis. The tweets were categorized either as subjective or objective. The machine-learning approach requires initial tweets to be manually selected as subjective or objective for the opinion filtering module to learn from.

Each subjective tweet went through the *Polarity Detecting Module* (PDM). The PDM calculates the polarity score for each tweet, which is determined by averaging the scores of all *sentiment words* found in the tweet. *Stop words* (words that do not provide significant meaning) are removed. Words with sequences of the same character greater than two are shortened to be the original word (for instance, "heeeeelp" is now "help"). After these words are filtered from each Twitter post, each word in the tweet is compared to a dictionary of *sentiment words*, using the Python library `SentiWordNet`.

In `SentiWordNet`, a lexical English database called `WordNet` checks which *synset* (short for synonym set) a word belongs to. Each synset has three sentiment scores: positivity, negativity, and objectivity. Any word that is classified as "objective" is not used in calculating the final polarity score of the tweet. When calculating the sum of the polarity score of the tweet, the positive score is added to the final score, while the negative score subtracts from the final score. The tweets are also searched for *negation*, such as words like "not" and "no." These negation words will change a positive polarity score to one that is negative.

After all the subjective tweets have had their polarity scored, the *Feature Classification Module* (FCM) categorizes tweets by brand, model, and product feature. The final module is the *Summarization and Visualization Module* (SVLM), which provides a visual overview of the sentiment polarity of the tweets.

In comparison with the previous study by Pak et al., the researchers behind the MSAS have mentioned that it is difficult to identify sentiment in Twitter posts that contain sarcasm or irony. That is, "the language people speak today is complicated and full of slang, ambiguity, sarcasm, idiom, and irony" [2]. Such results can skew the results of sentiment analysis.

2.3 Consumer Satisfaction

While quite a bit of work has been done to measure outages of various ISPs [1, 13], there has been very little research in regard to customer satisfaction in this area. This is a gap that the 2003 paper by Erevelles et al. [4] hoped to fill. They performed a survey on ISP customers of various firms in the California area in an attempt to understand the needs and satisfaction models of ISP consumers as a whole. In their results, they looked at four different models of satisfaction: *expectations-disconfirmation*, *attribution*, *affective*, and *competitive positioning*.

The *expectations-disconfirmation* model measured whether the expectations of the consumers were met by the providers: going above and beyond results in *positive disconfirmation*, and not meeting expectations gives a *negative disconfirmation*. Unsurprisingly, most of the consumers felt more *negative disconfirmation* toward their previous ISPs; otherwise, they probably would not have switched. However, the researchers also noticed that, even with their current providers, most consumers felt only *neutral disconfirmation*; there were very few instances of *positive disconfirmation*. That is, "satisfaction levels of ISP consumers [were] relatively low" [4]. This was especially worrying, considering "consumer expectations of ISPs [were also] relatively low" [4] and, as a result, should have been easy to meet. This illustrated that there was a lot of room for improvement in the services and/or communication of the providers.

This was demonstrated using the *attribution* model, which measured how the placement of blame affects the consumer's response to a failure. In general, consumers tended to feel most negatively about failures that were deemed *external* (a result of the producer), *stable* (more likely to occur again), and *controllable* (preventable). Considering most consumers felt that the failures they experienced fell into these three categories, they tended to "perceive their dissatisfaction to be due to the negligence or indifference of the ISP" [4].

As a result, the researchers claimed that it was up to ISPs to improve their communication in order to let consumers know that the issues they were experiencing were *unstable* and/or *uncontrollable*, thereby reducing the impact such a failure had on customer satisfaction. After all, if providers "change consumer perceptions [through communication], their own service quality, or both" [4], then the inevitable failures would, hopefully, have less of an impact on consumer satisfaction.

Finally, the researchers used the *affective model* to measure the response of individual consumers to dissatisfaction, and the competitive positioning was used to measure the effectiveness of the ISPs marketing strategies. In conclusion, the researchers noticed that "ISPs have neglected the affective component, preferring instead to market their services like "commodities"" [4]. If an ISP chose to change this behavior, they argued that they "would have a tremendous advantage in the marketplace" [4] in comparison to those that did not.

This study illustrates why our research question is important: consumer expectations were not being met by ISPs, and, as a result, satisfaction was generally low. Considering how much of an impact *positive disconfirmation* can have on a company's success, it would be valuable for both the customer *and* the providers if the expectations of the consumers were better met. It is worth noting that this research is fairly outdated, so we wished to build on this with more recent data. In particular, we aimed to gain an understanding of whether or not these claims are still accurate today (at least in relation to Shaw Communications).

Since self-reported surveys, as was performed in this research, can suffer from biases, our results should also better represent the true feelings of consumers. Still, the models that Erevelles et al. put forward in order to measure satisfaction were useful as a guide to our own research, as well as their analysis of the benefits of communication.

3 Methodology

Shaw Communications has two different Twitter accounts: ShawHelp and ShawInfo. The first is most common for technical support and outage reports, whereas the latter tends to be used for marketing. As a result, most of our paper will focus on the communications from and to ShawHelp. However, we will still consider some ShawInfo tweets in our analysis when we believe it is relevant.

In order to perform our analysis, we used the Twitter API and a Python library called GetOldTweets [6] to gather just over a year's worth of data (from November 1st, 2016 to November 27th, 2017) from both ShawHelp, ShawInfo, and various hashtags. All results gathered in this paper are from these datasets in order to keep consistency, and we distinguish which datasets we used in each relevant section.

It is worth mentioning that Shaw Communications also provides television and phone services. While most of the collected data references Internet, it is possible that some of these other services are included in our analysis. While the focus of our paper is on Internet-related issues, we are also considering Shaw Communication's customer satisfaction as a whole; thus, including some of these other services in our analysis should not change our results overall.

3.1 Internet Issues

Reported Outages

In order to look for patterns in outage reports, we gathered two separate datasets based on who was reporting the outage: Shaw Communications own Twitter posts and their consumers tweeting at one of their official accounts. The data was collected based on finding the keyword of "outage" or "down" as a substring within each of the tweets.

However, while collecting tweets, it was noticed that many of the official reports had negation words denying rather than confirming the existence of an outage. For the sake of accuracy then, tweets in the official ShawHelp timeline were filtered out based on common words they used to negate such as "not" and "no." It was also noticed that the keyword "down" returned true if found in words such as "downtown," which may not have related to outages. To get around this, we had to search for "down" with a space after it as a substring instead. This unfortunately meant that if any tweet used punctuation after using the word "down," it was not considered in our analysis.

After collecting these tweets, we made comparisons between the two datasets: counting the number of reported outages of Shaw from their timeline versus their consumers. To account for the potential of customers reporting far more often than

Shaw, we only counted the days outages were mentioned. Thus if many customers reported an outage on a day, it would only count as a single report.

From there, we took our collected information and looked at which consumer reports were missed by the official Shaw reports. We then calculated the percentage of overall outages that were officially reported or missed by Shaw. This information gathered did not take into consideration whether the consumer reports were accurate, as it is possible that many users were reporting *internal* issues rather than *external* problems related to Shaw [4].

Common Internet Issues

Other common issues were searched for via keywords including "lag," "slow," "out," or "problem." In order to find these keywords, we once again looked for them as substrings in each individual tweet. Unfortunately, this meant words such as "about" counted toward our overall count of "out," for example. Unlike above, however, we could not search for "out" followed by a space, because we also wanted to include the word "outage" in our numbers. Hence, for "out" in particular, we separated it into looking for "out" and "outage" as strings rather than as substrings (but counted each toward our total for "out"). For the other keywords, we noticed they were not common substrings in irrelevant words, so we did not need this type of logic and simply looked for them as substrings in each tweet. Our overall counts measured both how many tweets each keyword appeared in and how many days out of our search period they appeared.

Average Sentiment on Outage Days

For a final look into outages, we took the dates where outages appeared, gathered the consumer tweets related to those dates, and then performed sentiment analysis to find how consumers felt, on average, during those days.

Initially when doing this, we used a list of dates including official outage reports from Shaw as well as dates that Shaw missed from the consumers' reports. However, after we performed our analysis, we found that consumers reported outages every day. This resulted in sentiment analysis statistics that were exactly the same as the statistics for our entire consumer tweets dataset.

In order to remedy this, we decided instead to look only at tweets that happened on the days of officially reported outages. This was done to get a better understanding of user sentiment in relation to outages to see if, for example, the percentage of negative tweets trended upward in response to an outage.

Locations

In order to see which provinces had the most complaints, we wanted to measure how many tweets @ShawHelp came from each province. Unfortunately, most of the tweets did not include geolocation information. As a result, it was difficult to get an understanding of where the tweets were coming from. So, instead of using this sparse information, we chose to count the occurrences of province names in the tweets themselves. If a province name occurred in a tweet, we counted it as a single occurrence (even if this name appeared multiple times in the text). This gave more information than using the geolocation data attached to the tweets; however, it also introduced some unreliabilities.

For example, we looked for both the abbreviations and the actual provinces names within each tweet. In reference to Prince Edward Island, we counted occurrences of both the actual abbreviation "PE" and the commonly used "PEI." We counted the abbreviations since it is a common practice to use these rather than the actual province name, especially when dealing with Twitter's character limit.

However, consider Ontario as an example: as a process of cleaning the tweets, we removed *stop words* such as "a," "an," "in," "the," etc. However, one of these stop words is "on," which happens to be the abbreviation for Ontario. As a result, many of the tweets that included "on" in reference to Ontario rather than as a stop word were filtered out. When we attempted to remove this word from being filtered, we instead received an inflated number that included every occurrence of the word "on" regardless of its intended usage.

Similarly, the abbreviation for British Columbia is "BC," which is commonly used as an abbreviation for "because." So, when we attempted to count occurrences of this province, we got inflated numbers when we included this abbreviation, but, when we excluded it, many of the tweets referencing British Columbia were unnecessarily excluded.

In order to get around these types of issues, we instead only counted occurrences of the abbreviations if they occurred in the text in capital letters. For example, we counted "ON" toward our Ontario count but did not include "on." For the actual province names, we included all possible uppercase/lowercase varieties. This excluded some occurrences in which the user was referencing a province abbreviation without the correct capitalization and also may have included tweets in which the user was using capital letters to express emotions rather than to indicate a province. However, this seemed to give the most consistent results in comparison to the methods discussed above.

3.2   Consumer Satisfaction

Sentiment

In order to measure sentiment in general, we used a pre-built Python library called TextBlob. This library determines sentiment using a Naive Bayes Classifier [10], which is a classifier technique based on Bayes Theorem [7]. Essentially, it "predicts membership probabilities for each class" [7] and classifies membership based on the class that is most likely (i.e., the one that has the highest probability). We chose TextBlob specifically for its use of this theorem and classifier, which was determined as the best choice in the research by Pak et al. [14].

In TextBlob, sentiment classification is done by first training the classifier on the polarity of a piece of text using a movie review database [10]. It then uses this training information to determine the probability that a piece of text falls into the "positive," "negative," or "neutral" category, and it classifies the text accordingly.

Unfortunately, sentiment analysis techniques (including those used by TextBlob) are still lacking when it comes to detecting more nuanced language, such as sarcasm [11]. Thus, if any of the Twitter posts that were mined have sarcasm, they will be read and labeled incorrectly by our classifier. It is best to keep this in mind when reviewing our results, as we noticed (from our testing) that many tweets using this type of language were incorrectly classified.

The main focus of this analysis was looking at the sentiment of tweets @ShawHelp. In order to measure this, we looked at both weekly and monthly trends in the Twitter posts to see if there were any noticeable patterns. Originally when we computed these values, we noticed a significant spike in the November numbers for the monthly analysis. However, upon further inspection, we noticed that this was due to the fact that we are essentially pulling *two* different Novembers: one from 2016 and one from 2017. In order to accommodate for this, we instead looked at the *average* number of tweets per day in each month. This was calculated by taking the total number of tweets (split by sentiment) and dividing it by the number of days in the relevant month. Since November was twice as large as the other months, we divided our total number of tweets by 57 rather than the expected 30. This helped to even out our results. For the weekly analysis, none of this consideration was necessary.

To give these trends more context, we also compared our results to those gathered in the Internet Issues section above. We wanted to see if there was any connection between unofficial/official outage reports and the overall sentiment and/or number of tweets. We did this by splitting up the outage reports in a similar fashion to the method used above in order to get a better understanding of the correlation between these two datasets (if it existed).

On top of this information, we also wanted to understand the sentiment of Shaw Communication's own Twitter accounts. Obviously, it is important (from a customer service stand point) to have these types of tweets fall into either the neutral or positive category, as the ShawHelp and ShawInfo Twitter accounts are a reflection of the Shaw Communications company as a whole. If a significant amount of the tweets were deemed negative, this could potentially negatively impact the satisfaction of customers who received responses to their concerns.

Word Usage

Considering sentiment analysis suffers from the issues mentioned above, we wanted to add to this information with various other measurements in an attempt to truly understand the satisfaction of Shaw Communication customers. For example, we wanted to know what kinds of words were being used when a user tweeted @ShawHelp. We measured this information in two different ways: we counted the ten most common words (and word combinations) used, and we searched for the number of occurrences of specific keywords. This gave us an understanding of the reasons users were tweeting @ShawHelp, which helped to give more context to the measured sentiment of tweets.

Before we began our analysis of word usage, we started by cleaning the text of each Twitter post. This included converting the text to lowercase, removing punctuation, and removing *stop words* such as "and," "or," and "the." As a result, the resulting bigrams/trigrams do not include these words in their consideration and, due to this, often were grammatically incorrect. However, in order to present these results, we manually added back punctuation and some capitalization based on context in order to make them easier to understand.

Hashtags

To add even more context, we wanted to see if there were any patterns to the use of hashtags in the Twitter posts. Part of the Tweet model in the GetOldTweets [6] library included the list of hashtags contained within each tweet. As a result, there was no need to manually parse for them; instead, we made a separate .csv file containing both the date each tweet was created and the hashtags in each tweet. For tweets that did not include any tags, this column was left blank. Once we had the necessary dataset, we simply filtered out the rows that included tweets with no hashtags and then counted the occurrence of each using Counter from the Python library collections.

Response Time

As noted by Ervelle et al., the *response time* of an ISP was an important consideration when consumers ranked their priorities. They found from their survey that, the more communication from providers regarding consumer concerns there was, the higher the overall reception was from customers. Further, as discussed in a 2009 paper by Jansen et al. [9], microblogging was shown to serve as a powerful "electronic word of mouth." That is, brands that utilize social media can increase their brand exposure by followers retweeting or mentioning the brand. Thus, companies that maintain a presence on social media can use this to boost customer loyalty. Because of this, we wanted to find the average time that it took for @ShawHelp and @ShawInfo to respond to a Twitter mention. If their average response time was fast, this would say they were both quick to respond to consumers and also actively communicating with them.

In order to do this, we had to gather all the tweets made by ShawHelp and ShawInfo using the previously mentioned Python library GetOldTweets that was used to gather all the other datasets. The most important part of this step was retrieving the attribute id of each tweet (which was not previously being recorded). However, this library did not include all the tweet attributes that were necessary in order to gather the replies to a tweet, which we needed in order to gather the first response.

In order to get around this limitation, we used the Twitter API through tweepy in order to find attributes we needed that the GetOldTweets library did not include, specifically, in_reply_to_status_id. This attribute gives the original tweet ID that the current ID replied to. In this case, the in_reply_to_status_id attribute corresponds to the customer's tweet.

The last step was to calculate the actual delta time between the initial customer's tweet and Shaw's response. This is simply the elapsed time between the two times, which is also the response time to a tweet. In order to find the *average* response time specifically, we needed to find the *mean delta time*. That is, we summed all the response times of tweets that contained a nonempty in_reply_to_status_id and divided that by the number of tweets Shaw replied to.

4   Results

4.1   Internet Issues

Reported Outages

When counting the number of days outages were reported, we found that, out of our search period of 392 days, outages were reported by users *every single day* of that period. This was an alarming discovery. However, considering the potential that some of these outages as claimed by consumers may have been mislabeled Internet problems or, as Ervelle's et al. puts it, *interal issues* [4], there is a good chance some of these reports are not accurate.

Looking instead at just the official reports from Shaw, however, shows that outages were reported on *225* days out of that same period. This means that over 392 days, Shaw had actual outages for 57% of those days—obviously, this is not a good sign for the reliability of their services.

Overall, since unofficial outages were reported every single day, Shaw potentially missed reporting on *167* outages. This would be about 43% of the total outage reports, assuming user-tweeted outages were accurate. However, once again, these missed outages were most likely not all legitimate *external* issues that Shaw was in control of.

Common Internet Issues

What we found when searching for common Internet issues was that, out of our search period of 392 days, "lag," "slow," or "problem" was mentioned on 376 of those days. While these mentions could also be suffering from the same mislabeling of problems that outage reports suffered, this does not explain away the large number of days these problems were noted. 376 days out of 392 (i.e., 92%) is an alarming number of days for Internet issues to be reported on, even if they are not all external problems.

When further looking into the number of tweets mentioning potential issues, we found the frequencies displayed in Table 1. The most common Internet issue mentioned was "out" in regard to outages. Given that consumers reported outages every day of our search period, this is unsurprising. The keywords "down" and "slow" were mentioned roughly the same number of times. While their frequencies are lower than "out," they are still relatively high. The word "lag" was rarely mentioned at only 89 times; however, this is likely due to a more common word like "slow" being used to describe the same problem.

Average Sentiment on Outage Days

The average sentiment of consumers on days of officially reported outages was mainly neutral overall at approximately 41% of the tweets. Positive tweets were at 33.89%, and negative fall in the remaining 24.3%. This corresponds to the overall sentiments shown in Fig. 1c, which will be discussed more later. While one might expect more negative sentiments to be present on official outage days, we attributed the majority neutral/positive results to Shaw's extensive communication in reporting those outages to their consumers—this is a sign of good faith.

Table 1 Frequency of Internet problem keywords

Word	Count
Down	546
Slow	557
Lag	89
Out	938

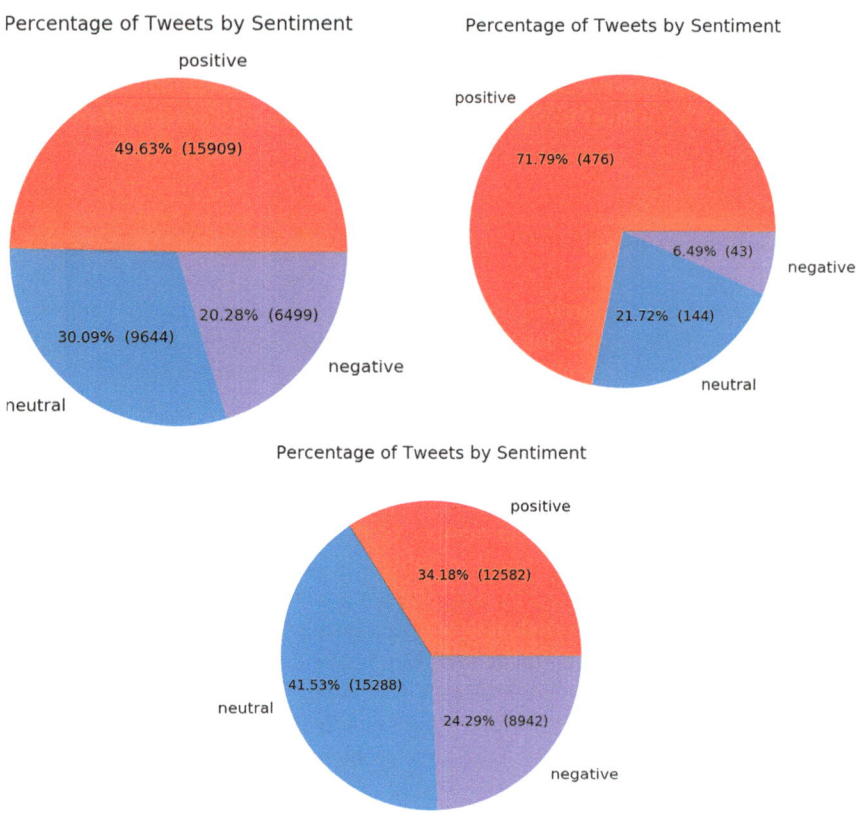

Fig. 1 Overall sentiment of tweets. (**a**) ShawHelp Timeline, (**b**) ShawInfo Timeline, (**c**) Customers @ShawHelp

Locations

Looking at the location counts in Table 2, we found that British Columbia had the most complaints in comparison to the other provinces. In second place was Alberta, which had a total of *226* tweets mentioning the province name. These line up with expected numbers; after all, British Columbia and Alberta are the top two provinces serviced by Shaw Communications [15]. Interestingly, Saskatechewan and Manitoba use Shaw's services in more locations than Ontario, despite them having less Twitter posts @ShawHelp. However, this is most likely due to the populations of each area rather than the actual service; considering the margin of difference is quite small. So, since no area seems to have a higher proportion of tweets (taking into account the service area and population), it does not seem as though one area is better served than another.

Interestingly, there are tweets that included location names for which Shaw does not provide services, specifically, Newfoundland and Labrador, New Brunswick,

Table 2 Province counts in tweets @ShawHelp

Province	Count
British Columbia (BC)	401
Alberta (AB)	226
Ontario (ON)	69
Manitoba (MB)	48
Saskatchewan (SK)	45
Newfoundland and Labrador (NL)	3
New Brunswick (NB)	3
Quebec (QC)	6
Nova Scotia (NS)	2
Prince Edward Island (PE)	0

Quebec, and Nova Scotia [5]. This could be due to limitations in the method used to determine location (as discussed in Sect. 3), but it could also refer to Shaw customers who are traveling or to something other than their current location (e.g., the location of a sporting event). After all, Shaw also provides television services, so these tweets are included in our analysis.

4.2 Consumer Satisfaction

Sentiment

Figure 1 shows the overall sentiment breakdown of each tweet dataset. From Fig. 1a and b, we can clearly see that the tweets from Shaw Communication's own Twitter accounts are overwhelmingly positive, with negative tweets being the lowest percentage in both cases. This is a positive reflection on their customer service, as it would be concerning if a majority (or even a higher percentage) of their tweets were negative. After all, receiving a potentially hostile or overwhelmingly negative response from a company has the potential to negatively impact how a customer feels toward that company.

It is worth mentioning that, in Fig. 1a, our sentiment analyzer labeled approximately 20% of ShawHelp tweets as negative. However, based on an understanding from working with smaller datasets, tweets including words like "sorry" and "no" were generally labeled as negative, even though this labeling is inaccurate in this setting. For example, as can be seen in Table 3b below, the bigram "sorry hear," which most likely corresponds to something along the lines of "sorry [to] hear [that]" including the removed stop words, is the second most common. However, most humans would not consider these types of responses as negative; in fact, this shows that Shaw tends to take ownership of user-reported issues, which should be interpreted as a positive according to the paper by Ervelle's et al.

As far as customer interaction with Shaw Communications, we looked specifically at Twitter mentions @ShawHelp. Figure 1c shows these results,

Table 3 Top 10 bigrams/trigrams

Rank	Bigrams	Trigrams	Rank	Bigrams	Trigrams
(a) Customers to @ShawHelp			*(b) @ShawHelp to customers*		
1	Customer service	Internet isn't working	1	DM us	Let us know
2	Last night	Since last night	2	Sorry hear	Follow DM us
3	Looks like	Shaw go wifi	3	Us know	DM us account
4	Shaw Internet	Blue sky TV	4	Let us	Take closer look
5	Internet service	NFL Sunday ticket	5	Follow DM	Please follow DM
6	What's going	Free range TV	6	Take look	Send us DM
7	Cable box	Thanks quick reply	7	Lance hi	Please DM us
8	Can't get	Signal lost detected	8	Closer look	Us know help
9	Blue sky	Thanks quick response	9	Please DM	DM account info
10	Isn't working	Shaw free range	10	Us account	Could follow DM

demonstrating that a majority of the mentions were deemed neutral by our sentiment analyzer. However, it is worth mentioning that, of the three datasets we are comparing, this specific set has the highest percentage of negative tweets (approximately 25%). This is fairly expected for similar reasons from above; a customer reporting an issue, even if they do so with a fairly neutral tone, was often interpreted as negative by our sentiment analyzer due to words such as "down" or "out." It is also likely that, when a user tweets @ShawHelp, they are experiencing an issue and thus are more likely to have a negative tone than a positive or neutral one.

In order to understand overall trends of sentiment of tweets, we divided our @ShawHelp datasets by both the day of the week in which it was created and the month. The day of the week graph includes the total number of tweets @ShawHelp that occurred in each week day, whereas the month graph shows the average number of tweets per day, per month.

When looking specifically at the day of the week tweets were posted, the first trend we noticed in Fig. 2 was that, while most days had a fairly uniform distribution of overall tweet numbers, Thursday's tended to have more. In order to diagnose this, we referred back to the outage reports from above (both official and unofficial).

Sorting the unreported outages dataset by number of tweets on a specific day gives us that, on April 27, 2017 (which is a Thursday), there was a staggering *618* tweets corresponding to some type of outage or lag. Considering the fact that the next highest date was on March 29, 2017 (a Wednesday) with only 49 unofficial outage/lag tweets, this seems to explain the spike we see. It is worth noting that there were *two* official Shaw-reported outages on this day, so it seems that this was a real issue and that Shaw was aware of it.

Despite this, the proportions of sentiment on this day remained fairly uniform to the overall distribution from Fig. 1c, with approximately 32% positive, 42% neutral, and 26% negative tweets. In fact, no day of the week seemed to stray far from the overall tweet sentiment percentages from Fig. 1c. This shows that, if issues

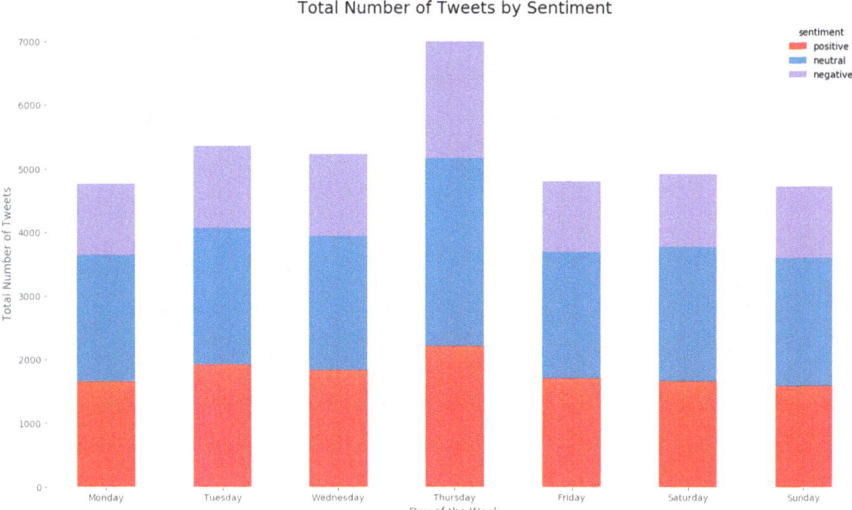

Fig. 2 Number of tweets @ShawHelp by sentiment

are indeed occurring, they did not correspond to an increase in negative tweets; otherwise, we would expect to see a spike in the percentage of negative tweets on Thursday, which includes the top two dates for most user-reported outages.

Thus, it seems that our assumption that a higher percentage of self-reported outage tweets being labeled as "negative" was wrong. This is clear from looking at Thursday: despite the top 2 outage days happening on Thursdays, there is no visible difference in the negative sentiment percentage as mentioned above. This could be due to limitations of our sentiment analyzer, or perhaps users are reporting their issues in a positive manner.

Now, when analyzing the trends on a month-by-month basis, Fig. 3 shows that only April had a significant spike in overall numbers, with approximately 52 positive, 71 neutral, and 44 negative tweets per day. This discrepancy is most likely due to the same increase in outages on Thursday in Fig. 2, corresponding to April 27, 2017. After all, so many complaints in a single day is going to up the average per day significantly.

In fact, 2 out of the top 10 official outage days were in April, so it seems as though this may be more than a onetime issue. Without a larger dataset, however, it is not a justifiable conclusion to make. After all, with only a single month's worth of data, it is possible that no previous April saw the same trend. That is, it may have been a onetime issue for this specific April. With respect to customer service, this is the ideal scenario; after all, according to Erevelles et al., this would indicate that it is an *unstable* issue and thus it would have less of an impact on satisfaction in comparison to a stable one [4].

After accommodating for the fact that we are measuring two different November counts, the spike that once occurred on November is significantly smaller than it was

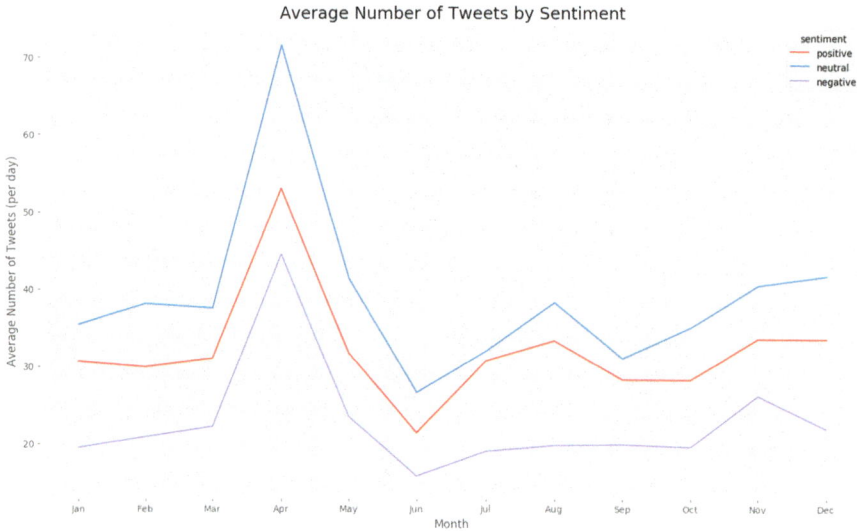

Fig. 3 Average number of tweets per day @ShawHelp by sentiment

at the start. However, November still has approximately 99 tweets per day, which is slightly more than any of the other months (excluding April). Even December, which has fairly similar positive and neutral counts to the previous month, saw a decrease in negative tweets resulting in only approximately 95 tweets per day. However, these 2 months in general seemed to have quite a number of issues.

It is worth mentioning that, of the top 10 official outage days, *3* of them are from November and *2* of them are from December: November 12th and 24th in 2016 and November 5th in 2017, as well as December 4th and 26th in 2016. This may explain why these 2 months see a slight increase in overall numbers. If we look at other months with uptrending averages, February also has 2 days in the top 10 official outages. In fact, February takes the top spot with *20* reported outages on February 9th. Interestingly, it still has fewer unofficial outage reports in comparison to other months with fewer official outages.

Similar to the week analysis above, it seems as though the percentage of each sentiment label remains fairly consistent through each month, even in the months with a higher average tweets per day overall. For example, of the average 169 outage complaints per day in April, 30% are positive, 45% are neutral, and 25% are negative. And similarly, in November, 32% are positive, 43% are neutral, and 25% are negative of the average 99 tweets per day. This stays consistent for every single month, regardless of the number of outages reported. That is, looking at both official and unofficial outage dates, there does not seem to be any correlation between the number of these reports and the sentiment.

In conclusion, looking at both Figs. 2 and 3 overall, there does not seem to be any discernible trend in the total number of tweets by day of the week nor by month nor in the sentiment of these tweets. It also seems that, when looking at these numbers in comparison to the measured outages, there is very little correlation. This is interesting, as it suggests that consumers seem to be fairly consistent in their satisfaction with Shaw. This lines up with Ervelle et al.'s findings, which suggested that consumers felt at most *neutral disconfirmation* with their current providers. After all, if a certain number of outages have become expected by customers, it makes sense that we would not see a huge variance in our sentiments when one occurs.

Word Usage

Looking at the most common (single) words used when tweeting @ShawHelp, the results were fairly unsurprising: the most common word tweeted to Shaw Communications' customer service account was "Internet," and the second was "Shaw." The third most common word was "thanks," which is a good indication that, when someone tweeted @ShawHelp, their issues were being resolved. However, it is worth mentioning that "thanks" can be used in a sarcastic context, so this may not necessarily be the case.

Looking at the bigrams (combinations of two consecutive words) and trigrams (combinations of three consecutive words), however, gives us more details. Referring to Table 3a, we can see that "customer service" is the top concern of customers tweeting @ShawHelp. In combination with this, there are a variety of bigrams that are negatives, such as "can't get" as number 8 and "isn't working" in last place. These suggest that the most common tweets at this account are from customers seeking technical support or reporting issues, which is unsurprising. The trigrams (combinations of three consecutive words) tell a similar story. However, it is interesting to see that "Internet isn't working" jumps to first place when considering three consecutive words rather than two. Numbers 7 and 8 indicate that customers tend to be satisfied with the response time, which, according to Ervelles et al., is an expectation of most ISP consumers. Hence, this should produce a *positive disconfirmation* in this area [4].

To see how Shaw Communications handled these types of issues, we looked out the most common bigrams/trigrams that were used by @ShawHelp in response to customer's concerns (Table 3b). The first place bigram is "[direct message] us," with number 5 and number 9 similarly referencing direct messaging. Number 2 shows that it is common for Shaw to apologize for the issues that a customer is experiencing. This is a good indication that they are taking ownership of issues, thus putting them in the *external* category [4] rather than internal. The trigrams tell a similar story, as well. This is positive, since it would be poor service if the issues were blamed on the customer's themselves. However, as described by Ervelles et al., external issues deemed *external*, *stable*, and *controllable* have the worst impact on customer satisfaction. Thus, by taking blame for the issues, it is up to Shaw to also communicate that these problems are unlikely to occur again and out of their control. Unfortunately, by looking at only word usage, it is difficult to decide whether or not Shaw's communication is enforcing these ideas.

Table 4 Top 10 hashtags
@ShawHelp

Rank	Hashtag	Count
1	#shaw	212
2	#yyc	141
3	#yeg	139
4	#vancouver	57
5	#yyj	45
6	#blueskytv	38
7	#fail	37
8	#shawcable	37
9	#hgohd	31
10	#winnipeg	29

Hashtags

Interestingly, many of the hashtags are used to reference specific cities (Table 4), which is something we did not look for in the Locations section above. However, the top tagged cities seem to align with the top two provinces we previously found: Calgary (number 2, #yyc) and Edmonton (number 3, #yeg) are from Alberta, and Vancouver (number 4) and Victoria (number 5, #yyj) are from British Columbia. Interestingly, the top two provinces from above corresponding to the hashtagged cities are in reverse order in this dataset: the two Albertan cities have the most tags, whereas British Columbian cities appear further down the list.

Other than the city hashtags, the top 7th hashtag directed to @ShawHelp is #fail, occurring exactly 37 times. As a result, this hashtags accounts for approximately 5% of the top 10 hashtags. It is worth mentioning that this is the *only* negative hashtag on the list; the other nine hashtags seem to be neutral, with five of them being the city names mentioned above. This data suggests that customers do not use hashtags to express their sentiment. Rather, it seems that hashtag usage is primarily used by customers only for the purpose of making it easier for other users to find tweets targeting their area.

Response Time

Using the data gathered via the methodology described above, we found that there was a total of *27,245* tweet replies with an average response time of *5 h, 51 min, and 32 s*. There were actually 31,221 replies from @ShawHelp; however, there were 3976 tweets that could no longer be accessed. This is due to the original tweets being deleted or not visible to the public. So, these were removed from our dataset in order to keep our results valid.

Upon further analysis, we found that the maximum time it took for @ShawHelp to reply to a tweet was nearly 194 days; this corresponds to a sent on September 21st, 2016, with Shaw's response occurring on April 3rd, 2017. However, it is worth mentioning that the response in April is *not* the first response, to the original tweet,

ShawHelp replied on the same day. They simply returned to this tweet in the future (for unclear reasons) and responded, despite the fact that the respective user had not revived the tweet.

For tweets that mentioned @ShawInfo, on the other hand, there was a total of 201 tweet replies with an average response time of *21 h, 32 min, and 48 s*. There was a total of 224 tweet replies from @ShawInfo, but, similar to the case above, there were 23 that were not accessible.

To explain the response time discrepancy between the two accounts, note that ShawHelp is the Twitter account responsible for technical support. Thus, it is expected that they receive more customer inquiries about technical difficulties and, as a result, should have a faster response time. Their other account ShawInfo, however, tends to be for promotional materials and therefore is less active.

The average response time from @ShawHelp is quite slow at just over 5 h for our total dataset. In order to understand whether this has improved over time, we investigated to see the average response time from the last *month* of the data instead. From October 27, 2017 to November 27, 2017, @ShawHelp responded to 1978 tweets and had an average response time of *52 min, 42 s*. In this same date range, @ShawInfo responded to two tweets with an average response time of *32 min, 41 s*.

This is a vast improvement in comparison to the previous average response times. We can conclude from this that it seems as though Shaw is trying to improve their customer communications for both of their official accounts, which is a positive. This is reflected by referencing Table 3a. Of the top ten tweeted phrases, the two trigrams from customers that mention @ShawHelp's fast responses are as follows:

"thanks quick reply" (number 7)
"thanks quick response" (number 9).

5   Conclusions and Future Work

When looking at Shaw as a whole, the ISP shows some reliability issues in terms of quality but otherwise appears to provide solid customer service. In terms of quality, the frequency of reported issues seems alarming, however, without information from other ISPs for comparison, it is hard to make conclusive statements about its impact on service. Even so, the number of outages was still exceptionally high. However, despite suffering several outages in a year, consumers remained largely neutral or positive. This is likely due to Shaw's quick and courteous responses to customer concerns, though it is also possible sarcastic texts may have skewed our results. Thus overall, the Shaw company looks to be handling their customers well but could potentially work on their service's actual quality.

As mentioned in the description of our methodology, drawing firm conclusions about the ISP market as a whole by looking at only a single provider is not ideal. As a result, we consider expanding the ideas in this paper to other ISPs, including both competing Canadian companies and those around the world, as future work. This has the potential to not only improve satisfaction worldwide but also to better understand how different regions compare in customer satisfaction overall.

Considering our small dataset (just over a year), there is also room for expanding our results to include Shaw's entire Twitter lifetime. As it is now, there are some anomalies in our results (such as the outage pattern in April mentioned above) which may or may not represent an actual pattern. With a larger dataset in comparison to our current one, these types of conclusions would be more justified when patterns appear. This could also lead to other interesting discussions, such as whether Shaw Communication's service and response time have improved over time.

Further future work could also be done to improve sentiment analysis tools currently on the market, especially in regard to considering sarcasm as well as image posts in order to get more precise information. This is due to the previously mentioned limitations of current tools, which most likely would have skewed our sentiment analysis and, therefore, our final conclusions.

References

1. S. BV, Canadian outages, http://canadianoutages.com/ [Online; Accessed 27 Sept 2017]
2. W. Chamlertwat, P. Bhattarakosol, T. Rungkasiri, C. Haruechaiyasak, Discovering consumer insight from twitter via sentiment analysis. J. Univ. Comput. Sci. **18**(8), 973–992 (2012)
3. R. Clarke, Roger clarke's web site, http://www.rogerclarke.com/II/OzI04.html#CIAP [Online; Accessed 23 Sept 2017]
4. S. Erevelles, S. Srinivasan, S. Rangel, Consumer satisfaction for internet service providers: an analysis of underlying processes. Inf. Technol. Manag. **4**(1), 69–89 (2003)
5. FindInternet.ca, Findinternet, https://www.findinternet.ca/en/shop [Online; Accessed 3 Dec 2017]
6. J. Henrique, Get old tweets, https://github.com/Jefferson-Henrique/GetOldTweets-python.git [Online; Accessed 3 Oct 2017]
7. How the Naive Bayes classifier works in machine learning (2017), http://dataaspirant.com/2017/02/06/naive-bayes-classifier-machine-learning/ [Online; Accessed 28 Nov 2017]
8. InternetLiveStats.com, Internet live stats, http://www.internetlivestats.com/ [Online; Accessed 23 Sept 2017]
9. B.J. Jansen, M. Zhang, K. Sobel, A. Chowdury, Twitter power: tweets as electronic word of mouth. J. Am. Soc. Inf. Sci. Technol. **60**(11), 2169–2188 (2009)
10. S. Loria, Textblob (2014), https://github.com/sloria/TextBlob
11. D. Maynard, M.A. Greenwood, Who cares about sarcastic tweets? Investigating the impact of sarcasm on sentiment analysis (2014), pp. 4238–4243
12. Ookla, Ookla: the definitive source for global Internet metrics, http://www.ookla.com/ [Online; Accessed 23 Sept 2017]
13. Ookla, Speedtest market report: Canada, http://www.speedtest.net/reports/canada/ [Online; Accessed 23 Sept 2017]
14. A. Pak, P. Paroubek, Twitter as a corpus for sentiment analysis and opinion mining, in *Proceedings of LREC* (2010), pp. 1320–1326
15. Shaw.ca, Hotspots - Shaw Go WiFi, https://www.shaw.ca/wifi/hotspots/ [Online; Accessed 3 Dec 2017]

Editing Behavior Analysis for Predicting Active and Inactive Users in Wikipedia

Harish Arelli, Francesca Spezzano, and Anu Shrestha

1 Introduction

Since the born of Web 2.0 in 2004, users evolved from simple readers of static Web pages to active creators of Web content via social media, question-answering Websites, crowd-sourced reviews, open collaboration systems, etc. Here, many users create, manipulate, and consume content every day, and the survival of these platforms strongly depends on the active and continuous contribution of their users. Thus, these platforms continuously face the problem of retaining the current users and finding new ways to welcome newcomers to grow the community. Also, because user-generated content platforms can be edited by anyone, malicious users take advantage of this open-editing mechanism to cause online harassment [6, 14, 20, 25] and vandalism [1, 9, 21, 26, 30].

One of the well-established and most studied open collaboration systems is Wikipedia, the free encyclopedia that anyone can edit. English Wikipedia is the biggest Wikipedia version and contains more than 5.5 million articles collaboratively written by volunteers around the world. More than 300K editors, from expert scholars to casual readers, edit Wikipedia every month. However, just a small part of them keep actively contributing. For instance, at the beginning of 2018, among a total of 389K editors who did at least one edit, only 5.2K of them had made more than 100 edits [36].

The number of active editors in Wikipedia grew until March of 2007 when a period of decline stated. One of the main motivations was the introduction of anti-vandalism tools [7, 28] to maintain the trustworthiness, legitimacy, and integrity

H. Arelli · F. Spezzano (✉) · A. Shrestha
Computer Science Department, Boise State University, Boise, ID, USA
e-mail: harisharelli@u.boisestate.edu; francescaspezzano@boisestate.edu; anushrestha@u.boisestate.edu

© Springer Nature Switzerland AG 2019 127
M. Kaya, R. Alhajj (eds.), *Influence and Behavior Analysis in Social Networks and Social Media*, Lecture Notes in Social Networks,
https://doi.org/10.1007/978-3-030-02592-2_7

of the encyclopedia content. However, one big side effect was that veteran editors started to suspiciously look at newcomers as potential vandals and rapidly and unexpectedly deleted contributions even from good-faith editors. Since then, many newcomers started to face many social barriers [27] preventing them from the integration in the editor community, with the consequence of stop editing after a certain period of time [3, 16]. As Halfaker et al. [12] have pointed out, "Wikipedia has changed from the encyclopedia that anyone can edit to the encyclopedia that anyone who understands the norms, socializes himself or herself, dodges the impersonal wall of semi-automated rejection, and still wants to voluntarily contribute his or her time and energy can edit."

The loss of active contributors from any user-generated content community may affect quantity and quality of content provision not only on the specific community but also on the Web in general. Thus, being able to early predict whether or not a user will become inactive is very valuable for any user-generated content community to perform engaging actions on time to keep these users contributing longer. For instance, the Wikipedia community considers several steps that can be taken to increase the retention rate such as (1) do a survey to newly registered users to capture user's interests and use them for making relevant editing recommendations and (2) connect editors with similar interests to form meaningful contribution teams. They also developed and deployed a tool, called Snuggle [13], to support newcomers socialization.

In this paper, we focus on English Wikipedia and study the editing behavior of active and inactive editors on a large scale to early predict if a user will become inactive and stop contributing to Wikipedia.

Our contributions are as follows:

– We investigate differences in the editing behavior of active vs. inactive users according to users' involvement in edit wars, reverted edits, meta-pages editing, and categories edited.
– We propose a machine learning-based model that leverages frequent patterns appearing in user's editing behavior as features to predict active vs. inactive Wikipedia users.
– We experimentally show that our model reaches an excellent area under the ROC curve of 0.98 and a precision of 0.99 in predicting editors who will become inactive. Moreover, we show that the proposed model can early predict inactive editors much more efficiently than competitors. For instance, by looking at the first three edits, we can predict inactive users with an AUROC of 0.73 vs. 0.56 for the baseline.
– We also show that our model is stable with an AUROC of at least 0.97 and outperforms the competitor even when we vary the threshold to differentiate between active and inactive users.

The paper is organized as follows. Section 2 discusses related work. Section 3 introduces the dataset we used in the paper. Section 4 studies differences in editing behavior of inactive vs. active users according to involvement in edit wars, reverted edits, meta-pages editing, and categories edited. Section 5 describes our behavior-based approach for predicting inactive users. Section 6 reports on our experiments and compares our approach with the state of the art. Finally, conclusions are drawn in Sect. 7.

This paper extends and refines the paper *"Who Will Stop Contributing? Predicting Inactive Editors in Wikipedia"* presented at the 2017 IEEE/ACM International Conference on Advances in Social Networks Analysis and Mining [2].

2   Related Work

Many studies have examined user-generated content communities and, in particular, the reasons that motivate users to become contributors, to continue contributing, and to increase contribution [4, 5, 23]. However, many users stop editing after a certain period of time.

Jian and MacKie-Mason [16] discuss their hypothesis about why some editors stop contributing on Wikipedia. They considered editor roles such as creator, preserver, and destroyer, and variables like the proportion of creations, the proportion of reversions, and proportion of damages as possible features that correlate with the leaving behavior. Based on two variables, namely, *Ontime* (number of minutes that an edit persists) and *Deled* (number of times an edit gets deleted), they hypothesize that the probability of leaving decreases according to the variation of *Ontime* (between the last week of edits and all other weeks) and, symmetrically, increases according to the variation of *Deled*. They also hypothesize that the higher the editor work intensity, the more likely they will leave. Based on the article stability, they hypothesize that the more stable the articles that an editor cares about, the more likely this editor will stop contributing.

Asadi et al. [3] addressed a research about discovering motivations for writing and editing in Persian Wikipedia, discouraging factors toward contribution, and reasons for contributing or giving up participating in Wikipedia. They concluded that to understand whether an editor is active or not, it is necessary to know how often they edit and how many edits they make as well as how recent their last contribution is. After they interviewed 15 Persian Wikipedia active editors, they concluded that personal motivations such as knowledge and experience sharing, receiving help from other users, and becoming more familiar with the structure of Wikipedia are also significant motivations for continuing to contribute. Also, they mentioned that cognitive motives and personal satisfaction are necessary to maintain ongoing participation in Persian Wikipedia. Other encouraging factors they found in their study are enriching Persian Web content, starting new topics and content production, as well as competition with Wikipedia in different languages. They also found that personal beliefs and concerns may be a motivation to start writing and editing, but it is also more likely to lead to edit wars and, as a result, frustration and discontinuation. The reasons they individuated for not continuing in Wikipedia are (1) lack of time to contribute to Wikipedia, (2) finding other Web-based entertainment, and (3) being impatient and lacking tolerance for criticism. Note that this is only a case study on a small group of 15 members of the community.

Lai and Yang [22] investigated the underlying reasons that drive individuals to edit Wikipedia content. They considered Wikipedia as a platform that allows individuals to show their expertise. Based on expectation-confirmation theory and expectancy-value theory for achievement motivations, they proposed an integrated model that incorporates psychological and contextual perspectives. They picked English-language Wikipedia for their survey. Analytical results, they indicated, confirmed that subjective task value, commitment, and procedural justice were significant to satisfaction of Wikipedia users, and satisfaction significantly influenced continuance intention to edit Wikipedia content. This work discusses individuals' interest in continuing edits of Wikipedia content, which is quite the opposite to our problem.

Takashi et al. [15] analyzed the editing patterns of Wikipedia contributors using dynamic social network analysis. They have developed a tool that converts the edit flow among contributors into a temporal social network. They used this approach to identify the most creative Wikipedia editors among the few thousand contributors who make most of the edits among the millions of active Wikipedia editors. In particular, they recognize the key category of "coolfarmers," the prolific authors starting and building new articles of high quality. As the second category of editors, they look at the "ego-boosters," i.e., people who use Wikipedia mostly to showcase themselves. They said that understanding these different patterns of behavior gives important insights into the cultural norms of online creators.

Suin et al. [19] studied multilingualism by collecting and analyzing a large dataset of the content written by multilingual editors of the English, German, and Spanish editions of Wikipedia. This dataset contains over two million paragraphs edited by over 15,000 multilingual users from July 8 to August 9, 2013. The authors analyzed these multilingual editors regarding their engagement, interests, and language proficiency in their primary and non-primary (secondary) languages and found that the English edition of Wikipedia displays different dynamics from the Spanish and German editions. Users primarily editing the Spanish and German versions make more complex edits than users who edit these editions as a second language. In contrast, users editing the English edition as a second language make edits that are just as complex as the edits by users who primarily edit the English edition. In this way, English serves a special role in bringing together content written by multilingual users from many language editions. Also, they found that multilingual users are less engaged and show lower levels of language proficiency in their second languages. They also examine the topical interests of multilingual editors and found that there is no significant difference between primary and non-primary editors in each language. The dataset they used for their study is also very small.

Other works have studied Wikipedia users' editing behavior to check how long they will keep active [34, 37], what their roles are [15, 32], and why they contribute [17, 19, 22].

In 2011, Wikimedia Foundation, Kaggle, and IEEE ICDM organized a competition about developing a model to predict the number of edits an editor will make in 5 months after the end date of the training dataset they provided (see the contest at [33]). The dataset, which was open to all contestants, was randomly sampled from English Wikipedia. The time period of this dataset was from January 2001 to August 2010. The team prognoZit, who won the first prize in the WikiChallenge contest, developed their algorithm to solve the problem. They used 13 features to predict the future editing activity: number of edits in 9 different time periods, number of reverted edits in 2 different time periods, and number of deltas in another 2 different time slots. Their Wikipedia page is available at [34]. Another team, zeditor, won third place in the contest [37]. They solved this problem by using features such as the number of edits, the number of edited articles, and the length of time between the first edit and last edit in ten different exponentially long time intervals with Gradient Boosted Trees as the classifier. Their Wikipedia page is available at [35].

3   Dataset

To conduct our study, we used the UMDWikipedia dataset (available at [31]) that consists of edits made by both benign and vandal users. We considered benign users only. This dataset contains a list of 16K randomly selected benign users who registered between January 01, 2013 and July 31, 2014. For each user, their edit history is available for the given time period (up to 500 edits per users), for a total of 609K edits made by benign users. For each edit the available information includes author's username, edit ID, edit timestamp, page title, page type (Wikipedia article or meta-page[1]), page category, and if the edit was reverted and when. The information about edit reversion is extracted by the edit reversion dataset provided by Halfaker [10] which marks an edit as "reverted" if it has been reverted within the next 15 edits on the page. We will use reversion information to compute whether users are involved in edit wars.

The UMDWikipedia dataset also provides a *User Log Dataset* that consists, for each user u, of the chronological sequence of each consecutive pair (p_1, p_2) of pages edited by user u. For each pair (p_1, p_2), a description of the pair is provided, in the form of a five-character length string, by using the following features:

–   **r/n**: Whether p_2 is a page that has already been edited by the user before (p_2 is a reedit, **r**) or p_2 is a page edited for the first time by user u (p_2 is a new edit, **n**).
–   **m/n**: Whether p_2 is a meta-page (**m**) or a normal page (**n**).
–   If p_2 is a reedit:

---

[1]A *meta-page* is a page which is not a regular article, but it can be, for instance, a User page (where editors describe themselves) or an article Talk page (where editors discuss about the content of the associated Wikipedia article).

- **c/n**: Whether p_1 is equal to p_2, i.e., these are two consecutive edits (**c**) on the same page or not (**n**).
- **r/n**: Whether a previous edit of p_2 by the user u has been reverted (**r**) by any other Wikipedia user or not (**n**).

Otherwise (p_2 is a new edit):

- **t/m/u** Hop distance between pages p_1 and p_2 in the Wikipedia hyperlink graph: at most three hops (**t**), more than three hops (**m**), or unknown distance (**u**).
- **z/o/u** Common categories between pages p_1 and p_2: zero categories in common (**z**), at least one category in common (**o**), or info unavailable (**u**).

- **v/f/s**: Time difference between the two edits: less than 3 min (very fast edit, **v**), less than 15 min (fast edit, **f**), and more than 15 min (slow edit, **s**).

Given the benign users in the UMDWikipedia dataset, we divided them into active and inactive users by using the following rule: If a user does not make any edit for Γ months, then we considered this user as an *inactive user*, i.e., a user who performed some edits and then, at some point, stopped editing and left the community. If an inactive user started editing again after more than Γ months, then we considered this user as a new user. All other users who do not have a gap of more than Γ months in their edit history are considered *active users*.

In our experiments, we set $\Gamma = 2$ months, which corresponds to a total of 16,191 inactive and 305 active users. We extend our results for different values of Γ in Sect. 6.3.

4 Differences in Editing Behavior

In this section, we study the differences in the editing behavior of active vs. inactive users according to users' involvement in edit wars, reverted edits, meta-pages editing, and categories edited.

Involvement in Edit Wars Edit warring occurs when other users do not agree on the content of a page or revision made by another user [8]. We define an edit war as one user revising a page, followed by other users reverting that revision, and this pattern happens at least two consecutive times. We say that a user is involved in an edit war if their edit is reverted within an edit war.

By comparing how active vs. inactive users are involved in edit wars, we see that active users are highly involved in edit wars (85.9% of them are involved in at least one edit war), while the percentage is much smaller for inactive users (20.6%). The average number of edit wars a user is involved in is 4.28 for active users vs. 0.33 for inactive ones.

Moreover, we studied the number of edit wars a user is involved in over time. We computed a time series for each user as follows. Given a user u, we consider the

Table 1 Inactive users' involvement in edit wars

Weeks before leaving	10–9	8–7	6–5	4–3	2–1
Number of inactive users	112	124	162	242	1630

edits made by u in the latest 10 weeks before stopping edits, and we split this time interval into time frames of 2 weeks (last 2 weeks, second last 2 weeks, etc.). Then we computed the number of edit wars u is involved within each time frame. Each value in a time series is normalized by computing its corresponding z-score, i.e., the number of standard deviations the number is away from the mean of all points series. We observe that, within 10 weeks before the contribution stops, there is a significant peak (a rapid increment followed by a quick decrement) in the number of edit wars an inactive user is involved in for 68% inactive users involved in at least one edit war. Table 1 shows, for each time period considered, the number of inactive users having the peak in that time period.

As we can see, the majority of inactive users (1630) leave the community very soon (within 1 or 2 weeks) after reaching the maximum involvement in edit wars, while fewer users try to resist longer before leaving. We also observe that active users have these kinds of peaks in their edit history, but this seems not to effect their willingness to contribute. Active users seem to accept critiques from other people in the community positively.

Reverted Edits Regarding reverted edits, we observe that the edits made by inactive users are reverted more as compared to active users. On average, the percentage of reverted edits is 9.12% for inactive users vs. 5.25% for active ones. This is a typical motivation why users become inactive [11, 29].

Editing Meta-pages There are two different types of pages on Wikipedia: regular article pages and meta-pages. Examples of meta-pages are *User* pages (where editors describe themselves), article *Talk* pages (where editors discuss the content of the associated Wikipedia article), *User Talk* pages (talk pages related to user pages), and Wikipedia *Project* pages.

In studying how users are editing meta-pages, we observe that, on average, inactive users write more on meta-pages than article pages (63.3% of all their edits), while active users write less on meta-pages (30.3%). Also, inactive users write on a more diverse set of meta-pages: the percentage of unique meta-pages among all meta-pages edited by a user is, on average, 29% for inactive users vs. 10.3% for active ones.

Figure 1 shows the average number of meta-page edits by meta-page type. As we can see, both classes of users have the same trend: the most edited type of meta-pages is, on average, User page, followed by Talk pages, User Talk pages, and Project pages. Inactive users edit, on average, many more User pages than active ones (77% vs. 36%).

Categories of Edited Pages Active users edit many more pages from different categories than inactive users: the average number of different categories edited by active users during all their edit history is 868.5 vs. 48.9 for inactive users.

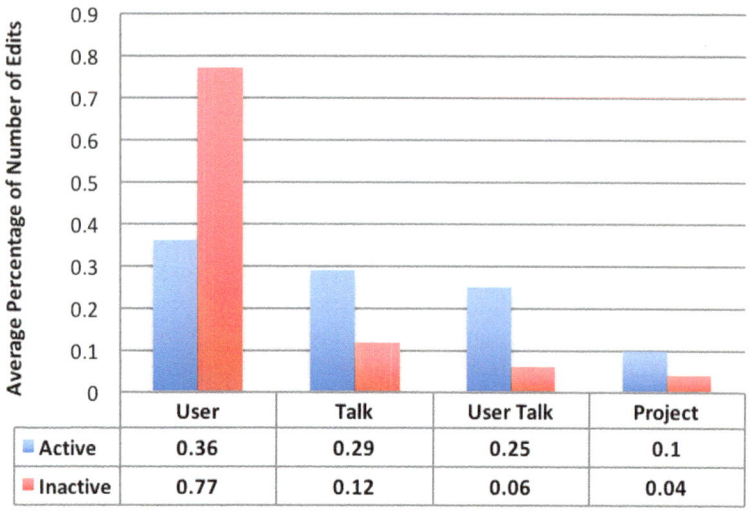

Fig. 1 Average percentage of number of edits on different types of Wikipedia meta-pages for active (blue) vs. inactive (red) users

When we look at pairs (p_1, p_2) of consecutive edits, we have that, when $p_1 \neq p_2$, active users consecutively edit pages that have much more categories in common (48 on average), while the corresponding number of inactive users is 4, on average. Thus, active users consecutively edit pages that are much more similar (regarding common categories) between them than inactive users.

5 Predicting Active and Inactive Users

In this section, we propose an editing behavior-based approach to predict which user will become inactive and leave the community. To find a set of features that differentiate the editing behavior of active vs. inactive users, we mined a set of features as follows [21].

First, we mined frequent patterns on the *User Log Dataset* for both active user logs and inactive logs by using the Prefix Span [24] algorithm. Each pattern represents a subsequence of a user's edit log and contains a sequence of pairs of pages consecutively edited by the user where each pair is described by using the features detailed in Sect. 3.

Second, for each frequent pattern f we mined, we computed the frequency of f for both the classes of active and inactive users. We found patterns that appear in both classes of users, while other patterns are exclusive for active users. We did not find any pattern that appears for the class of inactive users only.

Third, for each frequent pattern f we computed the absolute value $a(f)$ of the difference in frequency between the two classes and ordered these frequent patterns by $a(f)$ in descending order. Then, we selected as the set of features for classification the set of top-k patterns of length at most ℓ that appear for both active and inactive users and active users only. We used $k = 13$ and $\ell = 3$. The result was a total of 78 features. The value of each feature is a Boolean value indicating whether or not that pattern appears in the edit history of the user.

It is worth noting that, in predicting inactive users, we did not consider the duration of a user's edit history, from the first edit to their most recent edit, as this feature is biased toward inactive users who are short-lived because they stop editing Wikipedia. Moreover, our editing behavior-based features do not look at edited content, and, therefore, our resulting system has the advantage of being general and applicable not only for English but also for different other language versions of Wikipedia.

The complete list of 78 features is shown in Table 2. In the following, we discuss the top ten features that turned out to be the most important for the classification task.

5.1 Most Important Features

To compute the most important features, we used forests of 250 randomized trees. The relative importance (for the classification task) of a feature f in a set of features is given by the depth of f when it is used as a decision node in a tree. Features used at the top of the tree contribute to the final prediction decision of a larger fraction of the input samples. The expected fraction of the samples they contribute to can thus be used as an estimate of the relative importance of the features. Figure 2 shows the importance of the top ten features for the classification task. The green bars in the plot show the feature importance using the whole forest, while the blue bars represent the variability across the trees.

Figure 3 shows the frequency of the top ten most important features for the class of active (blue) and inactive (red) users. There is a significant gap in the frequency of these patterns for the two different classes of users. All the patterns are highly frequent for active users and less frequent for inactive users. As we will see in Sect. 6, our pattern-based features extracted from users' editing behavior will allow us to differentiate between active and inactive users with an area under the ROC curve of 0.981.

The top ten most important features are explained in detail here below.

1. **rnnnv**: there exists a pair of edits (p_1, p_2) s.t. p_2 is a reedit of a non-meta page, nonconsecutively ($p_1 \neq p_2$), not due to reversion, and very fast (p_2 is edited within less than 3 min from the edit on p_1). This pattern is frequent for 93% of active users vs. 12% of inactive users.

Table 2 Complete list of features used in our predictive model

Feature0-rnnnv	Feature39-"rncnf,nnuof"
Feture1-rnnnf	Feature40-"nnuos,rncnf,rnnns"
Feature2-nnuov	Feature41-"nnuos,rnnns,nnuos"
Feature3-nnuof	Feature42-"rncnv,nnuos,rnnns"
Feature4-rnnns	Feature43-"nnuos,nnuos,nnuof"
Feature5-"rncnv,rnnnf"	Feature44-"nnuos,nnuof,rncnv"
Feature6-"rncnv,rnnnv"	Feature45-rmcrf
Feature7-"nnuof,rncnf"	Feature46-rmnrv
Feature8-"rnnnf,rncnv"	Feature47-rncrs
Feature9-"nnuof,rnnns"	Feature48-rnnrf
Feature10-"nnuof,rncnv,nnuos"	Feature49-rnnrv
Feature11-"rncnv,nnuof,rncnv"	Feature50-"nnuos,rnnnv"
Feature12-"nnuof,nnuos,rncnv"	Feature51-"rnnnv,rncnv"
Feature13-"nnuof,rncnv,rncnv"	Feature52-"nnuof,rnnnv"
Feature14-"nnuof,nnuos,nnuos"	Feature53-"rnnnv,nnuos"
Feature15-nmuov	Feature54-"rnnnf,rnnns"
Feature16-nnuuv	Feature55-"nnuof,nnuof,nnuos"
Feature17-rnnrs	Feature56-"nnuof,nnuof,rncnv"
Feature18-rncrf	Feature57-"rncnv,rncnv,rnnnv"
Feature19-rmcrv	Feature58-"rncnv,rncnv,rnnnf"
Feature20-"nnuof,rnnnf"	Feature59-"nnuof,rncnv,rncnf"
Feature21-"rnnnf,nnuos"	Feature60-rncrv
Feature22-"rnnnf,rnnnf"	Feature61-nnuos
Feature23-"rnnnf,rncnf"	Feature62-rmnnf
Feature24-"rncnf,rnnnv"	Feature63-"nnuof,nnuos"
Feature25-"rncnv,rnnnf,rncnv"	Feature64-"nnuof,rncnv"
Feature26-"rncnv,rnnns,nnuos"	Feature65-"nnuof,nnuof"
Feature27-"rncnv,nnuof,nnuos"	Feature66-"rncnv,rnnns,rncnv"
Feature28-"rnnns,nnuos,rncnv"	Feature67-"rncnf,nnuos,rncnf"
Feature29-"nnuof,rncnv,rnnns"	Feature68-"nnuos,rncnv,rnnns"
Feature30-nmuof	Feature69-rmcrs
Feature31-rmnnv	Feature70-rmnrf
Feature32-nmuos	Feature71-rmnrs
Feature33-rncnf	Feature72-"rnnns,rnnnv"
Feature34-rncns	Feature73-"rnnns,nnuof"
Feature35-"rnnns,nnuos"	Feature74-"rnnnf,nnuof"
Feature36-"rncnf,rnnnf"	Feature75-"nnuos,rncnv,nnuof"
Feature37-"nnuos,rnnnf"	Feature76-"nnuof,rncnf,nnuos"
Feature38-"rncnv,nnuof"	Feature77-"nnuof,rncnf,rncnv"

2. **rnnnf**: same as the feature above but the pages are edited within less than 15 min (fast) one from the other. This pattern is frequent for 94% of active users vs. 14% of inactive users.

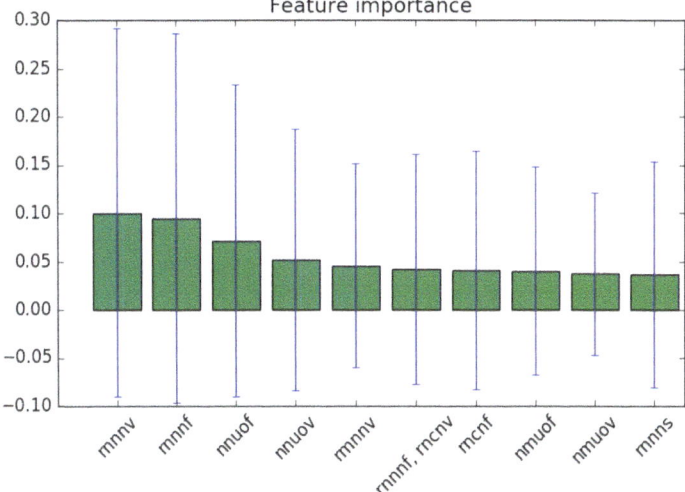

Fig. 2 Top ten most important features

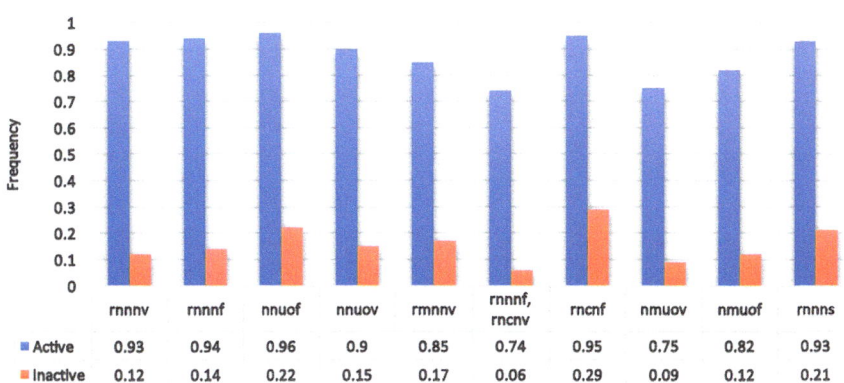

Fig. 3 Frequency of top ten most important features for active (blue) vs. inactive (red) users

3. **nnuof**: there exists a pair of edits (p_1, p_2) s.t. p_2 has never been edited before by the user u, p_2 is an article page (non-meta), a path does not exist between p_1 and p_2 in the hyperlink graph, the two pages have at least one category in common, and p_2 is edited within less than 15 min from the edit on p_1. This pattern is frequent for 96% of active users vs. 22% of inactive users.

4. **nnuov**: same as the feature above but the pages are edited within less than 3 min (very fast), one from the other. This pattern is frequent for 90% of active users vs. 15% of inactive users.

5. **rmnnv**: this pattern means that the user is reediting a meta-page, nonconsecutively ($p_1 \neq p_2$), not due to reversion, and very fast. This pattern is frequent for 85% of active users vs. 17% of inactive users.

6. **rnnnf, rncnv**: there exists a pair of edits as in pattern 2 (**rnnnf**) followed by another pair of edits (p_1, p_2) s.t. p_2 is a reedit of a non-meta page, consecutively ($p_1 = p_2$), not due to reversion, and the reedit happens very fast, i.e., within 3 min (**rncnv**). This pattern is frequent for 74% of active users vs. 6% of inactive users.

7. **rncnf**: this pattern means that the user is reediting an article page, consecutively, not due to reversion, and the reedit happens fast (within 15 min). This pattern is frequent for 95% of active users vs. 29% of inactive users.

8. **nmuov**: there exists a pair of edits (p_1, p_2) s.t. p_2 has been never edited before by the user u, p_2 is a meta-page, a path does not exist between p_1 and p_2 in the hyperlink graph, the two pages have at least one category in common, and p_2 is edited within less than 3 min from the edit on p_1. This pattern is frequent for 75% of active users vs. 9% of inactive users.

9. **nmuof**: same as the feature above but the pages are edited within less than 15 min (fast), one from the other. This pattern is frequent for 82% of active users vs. 12% of inactive users.

10. **rnnns**: there exists a pair of edits (p_1, p_2) s.t. p_2 is a reedit of a non-meta page, nonconsecutively ($p_1 \neq p_2$), not due to reversion, and the edit on p_2 happens slowly with respect to the edit on p_1 (more than 15 min after). This pattern is frequent for 93% of active users vs. 21% of inactive users.

6 Experimental Results

To test our proposed approach for inactive user prediction, we compared different classifiers, namely, logistic regression (LR), random forest (RF), and support vector machine (SVM). To speed up the SVM computation time, we used SVM bagging [18] instead of classical SVM. SVM bagging trains different SVMs on subsamples of the training dataset and then takes an ensemble of them. This also lead to improved results w.r.t. our short version of the paper [2]. To deal with class unbalance, we used class weighting. Class weighting is a way to learn from and unbalanced dataset where the classification imposes a penalty on the model for making classification mistakes on the minority class during training. To evaluate the performances, we performed tenfold cross-validation and measured the results according to precision, recall, area under the ROC curve (AUROC), and mean average precision (MAP).

The first three rows in Table 3 show classification performances for our approach when we consider the whole user's edit history. The best performing classifier in terms of AUROC (0.981) and MAP (0.620) is SVM. Precision and recall for the class of inactive users are also very high: 0.988 precision and 0.997 recall. The best precision for active users is also obtained by SVM (0.716), while the corresponding recall is 0.377, and a better value can be obtained with logistic regression (0.901).

Table 3 Performances of our features and comparison with prognoZit by considering the whole user's edit history according to precision, recall, area under the ROC curve (AUROC), and mean average precision (MAP)

	Precision		Recall			
	(Active users)	(Inactive users)	(Active users)	(Inactive users)	AUROC	MAP
Our features						
SVM	**0.716**	0.988	0.377	**0.997**	**0.981**	**0.620**
Logistic regression	0.257	**0.998**	**0.901**	0.950	0.973	0.559
Random forest	0.614	0.987	0.344	0.996	0.968	0.523
First prize winner						
SVM	**0.700**	0.984	0.174	**1.000**	**0.964**	0.650
Logistic regression	0.487	**0.998**	**0.943**	0.980	0.959	0.745
Random forest	0.631	0.993	0.647	0.989	**0.963**	**0.769**

The bold values represent the best values for our features and First prize winner

6.1 Comparison with Related Work

The closest related work to compare our results with is the method proposed by the prognoZit team [34], the first prize winner of the WikiChallenge competition [33]. The task they solved is very close to our problem, since predicting that a user will do zero or very few edits in the future is like saying that they will became inactive. To perform a fair comparison on our problem, we used the set of features proposed by prognoZit to learn a classifier for Wikipedia inactive user prediction.

PrognoZit proposed a set of features based on the number of edits and number of reverted edits during different time periods. Therefore, to compute features within the time frame of our dataset, i.e., from January 2013 to July 2014, we scaled the length of their time periods to be in our dataset dates and to have a length proportional to the ones used by prognoZit. The features we used are the following:

(re1) Number of reverted edits from 2013-01-01 to 2014-05-31 (73 weeks).
(re2) Number of reverted edits from 2014-05-31 to 2014-07-31 (8 weeks).
(e1) Number of edits from 2013-01-01 to 2013-10-01 (39 weeks).
(e2) Number of edits from 2013-10-01 to 2014-03-15 (23 weeks).
(e3) Number of edits from 2014-03-15 to 2014-06-01 (11 weeks).
(e4) Number of edits from 2014-06-01 to 2014-06-15 (2 weeks).
(e5) Number of edits from 2014-06-15 to 2014-07-01 (2 weeks).
(e6) Number of edits from 2014-07-01 to 2014-07-10 (1 week).
(e7) Number of edits from 2014-07-10 to 2014-07-20 (1 week).
(e8) Number of edits from 2014-07-20 to 2014-07-25 (5 days).
(e9) Number of edits from 2014-07-25 to 2014-07-31 (6 days).

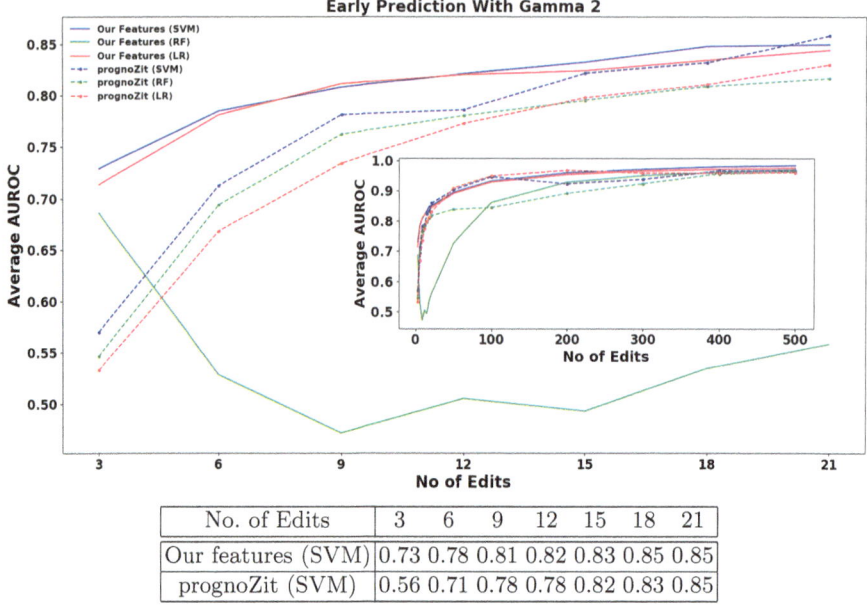

No. of Edits	3	6	9	12	15	18	21
Our features (SVM)	0.73	0.78	0.81	0.82	0.83	0.85	0.85
prognoZit (SVM)	0.56	0.71	0.78	0.78	0.82	0.83	0.85

Fig. 4 Average AUROC for early prediction of inactive users

The second three rows in Table 3 show classification performances of prognoZit according to three different classification algorithms and when we consider the whole users' edit history. In this case, the best performing classifier in terms of AUROC (0.963) and MAP (0.769) is random forest. They have a slightly worse AUROC in comparison with ours (0.981) but a better MAP (our best performing approach achieves 0.620). However, their features with SVM obtain the same AUROC as with random forest and, how we will see in the next section, it is better that random forest to early predict inactive users (see Fig. 4). Therefore, we chose SVM as the best classifier for prognoZit. SVM's results obtained for precision and recall are also comparable to ours.

Overall, when we consider the whole user edit history, the experimental results reported in this section show that our approach (with SVM) is better, according to AUROC, than the one proposed by the prognoZit team (with SVM) on the inactive user prediction task. The improvement is statistically significant with a p-value less than 0.001. The next experiment shows that our approach outperforms prognoZit on the *early prediction* of inactive users, as well.

6.2 Early Prediction of Inactive Users

Predicting inactive users as early as possible is more helpful than simply predicting who will become inactive. In fact, knowing while a user is still active that she/he is a user that can potentially leave the community can help administrators and other users to understand who to target with recovering actions on time to possibly avoid the loss of these contributors. Therefore, we performed an experiment where we computed the average AUROC on tenfold cross-validation by only using the first k edits of a user for feature computation. We compared both our features and the ones proposed by prognoZit and varied k from 3 to 500. Detailed results are shown in Fig. 4, where the main plot gives a close up for k up to 21 edits and the table reports the corresponding AUROC for SVM, the best classifier for both our and competitor's features; the subplot provides an overview of the classifiers' AUROC trend from 3 to 500 edits.

This experiment highlights that, when less user editing information is available, we can early predict inactive users more accurately than prognoZit. In fact, by considering only the first 3 edits a user performed, we can differentiate between inactive and active users with an AUROC of 0.73, while the corresponding AUROC for prognoZit is 0.56. Also, we need to look at the first 9 edits to have an AUROC of 0.81, while prognoZit needs 15 edits to reach the same result. In general, our curve is higher than the competitor's one, especially when we consider very few edits (from 3 to 15).

Moreover, we note that the features built by prognoZit have a bias toward the length of a user's edit history. In fact, before beginning to edit and after leaving the community, many features will be zero because the time periods used for the features are based on the global dataset dates. Considering edit history length is not helpful if we want to early predict inactive users to retain them in the Wikipedia community.

6.3 Varying the Threshold Γ

So far, we considered a threshold $\Gamma = 2$ to differentiate between active and inactive users in our dataset. In this section, we report on the experimental results when we vary the value of Γ. We build four new datasets corresponding to different Γ values in the set $\{3, 5, 7, 9\}$.

Table 4 shows our approach performances when considering the whole users' edit history in comparison with prognoZit and for different values of Γ. When $\Gamma > 2$, our solution always outperforms prognoZit according to AUROC, MAP, and both precision and recall for active users. Precision and recall results for inactive users are comparable.

Figures 5, 6, 7, and 8 show the AUROC comparison in the early prediction task. Also in this case, we significantly beat prognoZit.

Table 4 Performances of our features and comparison with prognoZit (by considering the whole user's edit history and different values for Γ) according to precision, recall, area under the ROC curve (AUROC), and mean average precision (MAP)

	Precision		Recall			
	(Active users)	(Inactive users)	(Active users)	(Inactive users)	AUROC	MAP
Our features (SVM)						
Γ = 3	0.642	0.988	0.432	0.995	0.990	0.664
Γ = 5	0.722	0.988	0.470	0.996	0.983	0.681
Γ = 7	0.682	0.987	0.458	0.995	0.977	0.669
Γ = 9	0.716	0.986	0.436	0.995	0.966	0.647
First prize winner (SVM)						
Γ = 3	0.6	0.983	0.178	1.000	0.983	0.634
Γ = 5	0.6	0.981	0.111	1.000	0.967	0.564
Γ = 7	0.3	0.978	0.016	1.000	0.947	0.449
Γ = 9	0.172	0.977	0.065	0.990	0.945	0.390

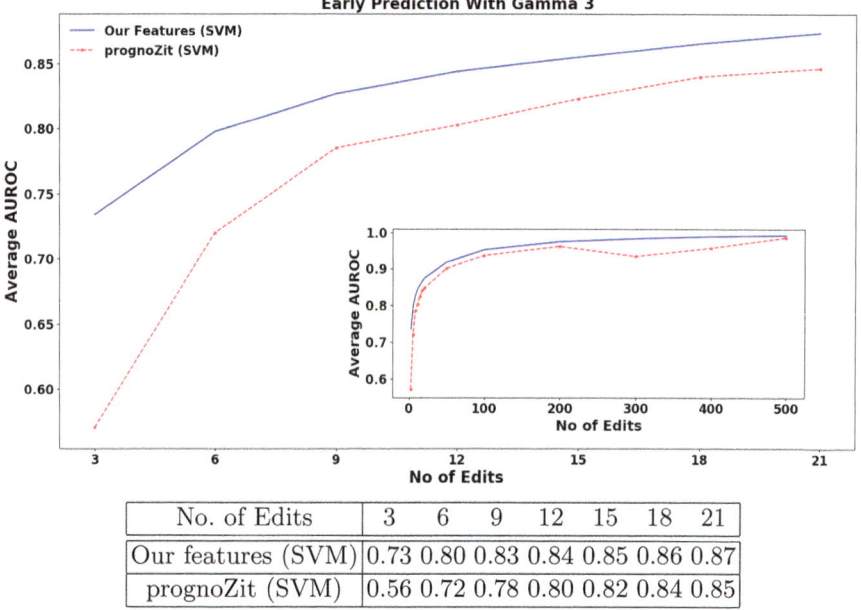

No. of Edits	3	6	9	12	15	18	21
Our features (SVM)	0.73	0.80	0.83	0.84	0.85	0.86	0.87
prognoZit (SVM)	0.56	0.72	0.78	0.80	0.82	0.84	0.85

Fig. 5 Average AUROC for early prediction of inactive users with Γ = 3. Blue line: our features + SVM. Red line: prognoZit's features + SVM

In summary, these results experimentally show that our model is stable and outperforms the competitor even when we vary the value of Γ.

We also computed the feature importance when Γ varies. When Γ > 2, the top ten most important features turned out to be the same and in the same order. Therefore, we show the feature importance only for Γ = 3 in Fig. 9. In comparison

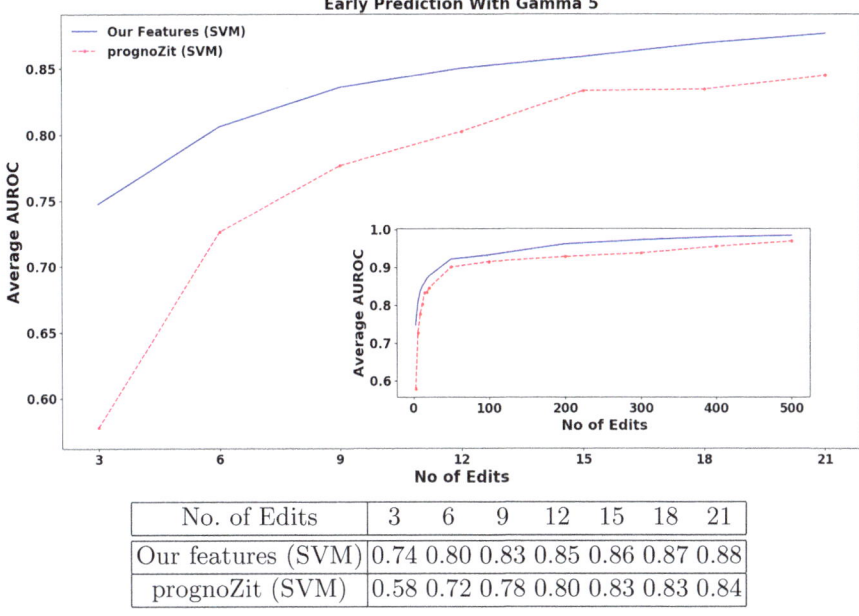

No. of Edits	3	6	9	12	15	18	21
Our features (SVM)	0.74	0.80	0.83	0.85	0.86	0.87	0.88
prognoZit (SVM)	0.58	0.72	0.78	0.80	0.83	0.83	0.84

Fig. 6 Average AUROC for early prediction of inactive users with $\Gamma = 5$. Blue line: our features + SVM. Red line: prognoZit's features + SVM

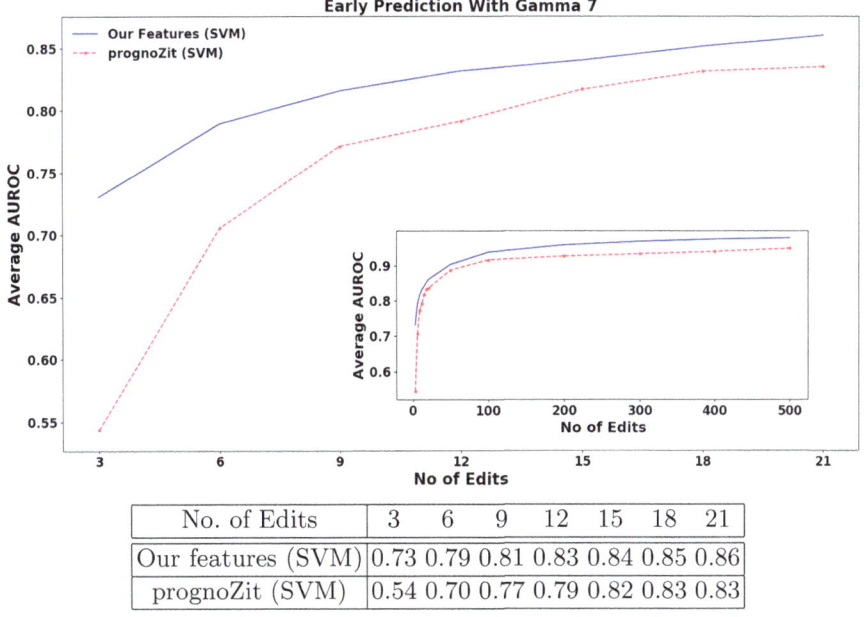

No. of Edits	3	6	9	12	15	18	21
Our features (SVM)	0.73	0.79	0.81	0.83	0.84	0.85	0.86
prognoZit (SVM)	0.54	0.70	0.77	0.79	0.82	0.83	0.83

Fig. 7 Average AUROC for early prediction of inactive users with $\Gamma = 7$. Blue line: our features + SVM. Red line: prognoZit's features + SVM

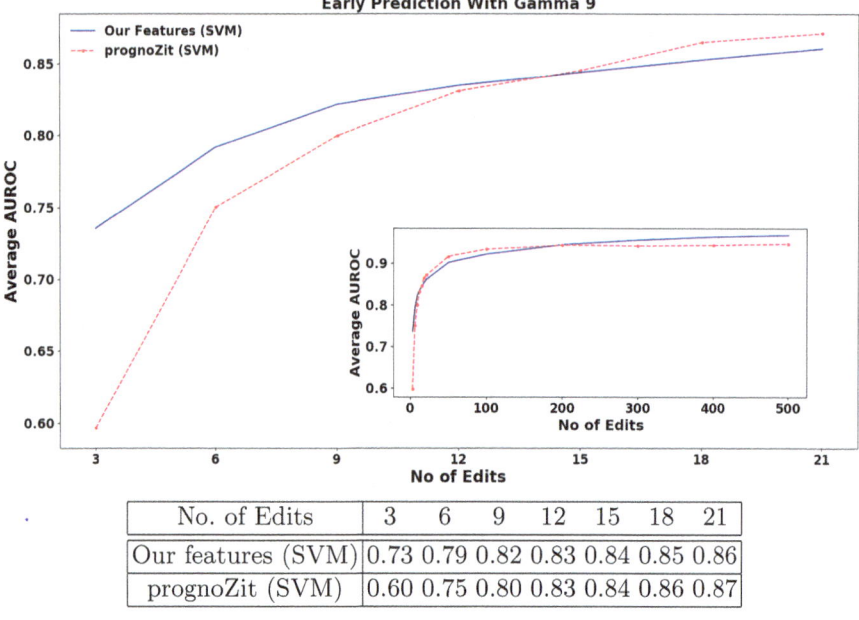

Fig. 8 Average AUROC for early prediction of inactive users with $\Gamma = 9$. Blue line: our features + SVM. Red line: prognoZit's features + SVM

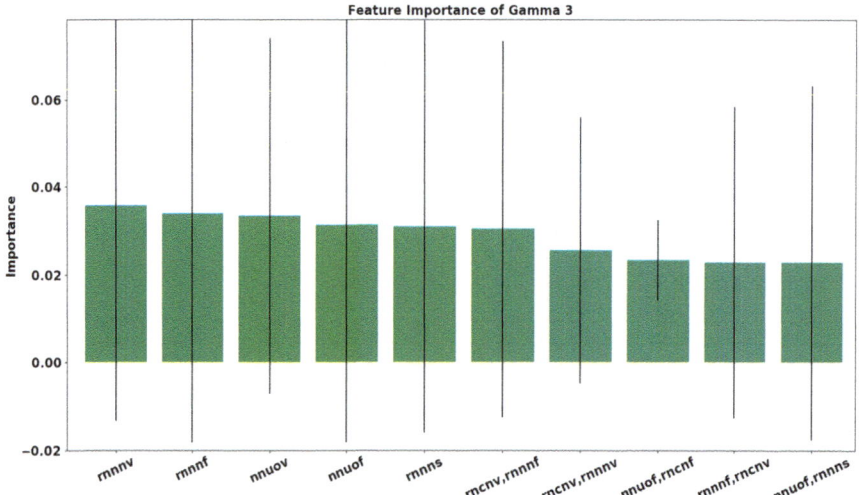

Fig. 9 Top ten most important features for $\Gamma = 3$. They are the same and in the same order also for $\Gamma \in \{5, 7, 9\}$

with the top ten most important features for $\Gamma = 2$ (shown in Fig. 2), we have that the top four most important features are the same, while in the cases $\Gamma > 2$, features corresponding to longer patterns are preferred.

7 Conclusions

The presence of anti-vandalism tools in Wikipedia helps to maintain the encyclopedia's content quality. However, the main drawback of these tools is that they increase the suspiciousness of veteran users toward newcomers, causing a low retention rate of new contributors. In this paper we addressed the problem of predicting whether or not a Wikipedia editor will become inactive and stop contributing. We proposed a predictive model based on users' editing behavior that achieves an AUROC of 0.98 and a precision of 0.99 in predicting inactive users. Moreover, we showed that our model significantly beats the baseline in the task of early prediction of inactive users, and it is stable even if we change the threshold discriminating between active and inactive editors. By comparing editing behavior of active vs. inactive users, we discovered that active users are more involved in edit wars and positively accept critiques and edit much more different categories of pages. On the other hand, inactive users have more edits reverted and edit more meta-pages (and in particular *User* pages). We believe that our proposed model is useful for the Wikipedia community to detect users who will become inactive early-on in order to perform recovery actions on time to try to keep them contributing longer.

References

1. B.T. Adler, L. de Alfaro, S.M. Mola-Velasco, P. Rosso, A.G. West, Wikipedia vandalism detection: combining natural language, metadata, and reputation features, in *Proceedings of 12th International Conference on Computational Linguistics and Intelligent Text Processing - Part II* (2011), pp. 277–288
2. H. Arelli, F. Spezzano, Who will stop contributing? Predicting inactive editors in wikipedia, in *Proceedings of the 2017 IEEE/ACM International Conference on Advances in Social Networks Analysis and Mining* (2017), pp. 355–358
3. S. Asadi, S. Ghafghazi, H.R. Jamali, Motivating and discouraging factors for wikipedians: the case study of persian wikipedia. Libr. Rev. 62(4/5), 237–252 (2013)
4. S.L. Bryant, A. Forte, A. Bruckman, Becoming wikipedian: transformation of participation in a collaborative online encyclopedia, in *Proceedings of the 2005 International ACM SIGGROUP Conference on Supporting Group Work* (2005), pp. 1–10
5. Y. Chen, F.M. Harper, J. Konstan, S.X. Li, Social comparisons and contributions to online communities: a field experiment on movielens. Am. Econ. Rev. 100(4), 1358–1398 (2010)
6. J. Cheng, M.S. Bernstein, C. Danescu-Niculescu-Mizil, J. Leskovec, Anyone can become a troll: Causes of trolling behavior in online discussions, in *Proceedings of the 2017 ACM Conference on Computer Supported Cooperative Work and Social Computing, CSCW* (2017), pp. 1217–1230
7. Cluebot_NG, http://bit.ly/ClueBotNG

8. Edit Warring, http://en.wikipedia.org/wiki/Wikipedia:Edit_warring
9. T. Green, F. Spezzano, Spam users identification in wikipedia via editing behavior, in *The 11th International AAAI Conference on Web and Social Media* (2017), pp. 532–535
10. A. Halfaker, http://datahub.io/dataset/english-wikipedia-reverts
11. A. Halfaker, A. Kittur, J. Riedl, Don't bite the newbies: how reverts affect the quantity and quality of wikipedia work, in *Proceedings of the 7th International Symposium on Wikis and Open Collaboration* (2011), pp. 163–172
12. A. Halfaker, R.S. Geiger, J.T. Morgan, J. Riedl, The rise and decline of an open collaboration system: How wikipedia's reaction to popularity is causing its decline. Am. Behav. Sci. **57**(5), 664–688 (2013)
13. A. Halfaker, R.S. Geiger, L.G. Terveen, Snuggle: designing for efficient socialization and ideological critique, in *CHI Conference on Human Factors in Computing Systems* (2014), pp. 311–320
14. H. Hosseinmardi, R.I. Rafiq, R. Han, Q. Lv, S. Mishra, Prediction of cyberbullying incidents in a media-based social network, in *2016 IEEE/ACM International Conference on Advances in Social Networks Analysis and Mining* (2016), pp. 186–192
15. T. Iba, K. Nemoto, B. Peters, P.A. Gloor, Analyzing the creative editing behavior of wikipedia editors: through dynamic social network analysis. Procedia Soc. Behav. Sci. **2**(4), 6441–6456 (2010)
16. L. Jian, J.K. MacKie-Mason, Why leave wikipedia? in *iConference* (2008)
17. L. Jian, J. MacKie-Mason, B. Chiao, A. Levchenko, A. Zellner, J. Kmenta, J. Dreze, W. Oberhofer, Incentive-centered design for user-contributed content, in *The Oxford Handbook of the Digital Economy*, ed. by M. Peitz, J. Waldfogel (Oxford University Press, Oxford, 2012), p. 399
18. H.C. Kim, S. Pang, H.-M. Je, D. Kim, S.Y. Bang, Support vector machine ensemble with bagging, in *Proceedings of the First International Workshop on Pattern Recognition with Support Vector Machines* (2002), pp. 397–407
19. S. Kim, S. Park, S.A. Hale, S. Kim, J. Byun, A.H. Oh, Understanding editing behaviors in multilingual wikipedia. PLoS One **11**(5), e0155305 (2016)
20. S. Kumar, F. Spezzano, V.S. Subrahmanian, Accurately detecting trolls in slashdot zoo via decluttering, in *2014 IEEE/ACM International Conference on Advances in Social Networks Analysis and Mining* (2014), pp. 188–195
21. S. Kumar, F. Spezzano, V.S. Subrahmanian, Vews: a wikipedia vandal early warning system, in *21st ACM SIGKDD International Conference on Knowledge Discovery and Data Mining* (2015), pp. 607–616
22. C.-Y. Lai, H.-L. Yang, The reasons why people continue editing wikipedia content–task value confirmation perspective. Behav. Inform. Technol. **33**(12), 1371–1382 (2014)
23. O. Nov, What motivates wikipedians? Commun. ACM **50**(11), 60–64 (2007)
24. J. Pei, J. Han, B. Mortazavi-Asl, H. Pinto, Q. Chen, U. Dayal, M. Hsu, Prefixspan: mining sequential patterns by prefix-projected growth, in *Proceedings of the 17th International Conference on Data Engineering* (2001), pp. 215–224
25. E. Raisi, B. Huang, Cyberbullying detection with weakly supervised machine learning, in *Proceedings of the 2017 IEEE/ACM International Conference on Advances in Social Networks Analysis and Mining* (2017), pp. 409–416
26. F. Spezzano, Ensuring the integrity of wikipedia: a data science approach, in *Proceedings of the 25th Italian Symposium on Advanced Database Systems* (2017), p. 98
27. I. Steinmacher, T. Conte, M.A. Gerosa, D.F. Redmiles, Social barriers faced by newcomers placing their first contribution in open source software projects, in *Proceedings of the 18th ACM Conference on Computer Supported Cooperative Work & Social Computing, CSCW* (2015), pp. 1379–1392
28. STiki, http://bit.ly/STiki_tool
29. B. Suh, G. Convertino, E.H. Chi, P. Pirolli, The singularity is not near: slowing growth of wikipedia, in *Proceedings of the 2009 International Symposium on Wikis* (2009)

30. K. Suyehira, F. Spezzano, Depp: a system for detecting pages to protect in wikipedia, in *Proceedings of the 25th ACM International Conference on Information and Knowledge Management* (2016), pp. 2081–2084

31. VEWS, http://www.cs.umd.edu/~vs/vews

32. H.T. Welser, D. Cosley, G. Kossinets, A. Lin, F. Dokshin, G. Gay, M. Smith, Finding social roles in wikipedia, in *Proceedings of the 2011 iConference* (2011), pp. 122–129

33. Wiki Challenge Competition, https://www.kaggle.com/c/wikichallenge

34. WikiChallenge First Prize Winner's Wikipedia Page, https://meta.wikimedia.org/wiki/Research:Wiki_Participation_Challenge_prognoZit

35. WikiChallenge Third Prize Winner's Wiki Page, https://meta.wikimedia.org/wiki/Research:Wiki_Participation_Challenge_zeditor

36. Wikipedia English Statistics, https://stats.wikimedia.org/v2/#/en.wikipedia.org/contributing/editors

37. D. Zhang, K. Prior, M. Levene, R. Mao, D. van Liere, Leave or stay: the departure dynamics of wikipedia editors, in *International Conference on Advanced Data Mining and Applications* (2012), pp. 1–14

Incentivized Social Sharing: Characteristics and Optimization

Joseph J. Pfeiffer III and Elena Zheleva

1 Introduction

Online social media and social networks have transformed the ways in which people communicate. Many companies have websites where millions of users can share information with one another, including photos, music, news, products, and services. These companies encourage sharing between individuals because social recommendations can increase traffic to their websites, resulting in higher engagement and revenue, in a process known as *viral marketing*. To further exploit the benefits of viral marketing, companies can *incentivize* users by giving them monetary rewards for adopting and sharing products and services.

There are two types of viral marketing, *direct viral marketing* and *mass-marketing sharing incentives*. *Direct viral marketing* aims at identifying a relatively small set of "influencers," i.e., individuals with high network centrality values, and then giving them a discounted or free product in the hope that they would influence many others to also adopt this product [1, 3, 7, 9, 13]. In contrast, *mass-marketing sharing incentives* reward *any* user who convinces their friend(s) to adopt a product but withhold the reward until the friend completes the *incentive goal*. There is research which suggests that methods for predicting influencers are generally unreliable and that targeting a wider range of users is a more cost-effective method for information diffusion [4, 22].

J. J. Pfeiffer III
Microsoft, Seattle, WA, USA
e-mail: joelpf@microsoft.com

E. Zheleva (✉)
University of Illinois at Chicago, Chicago, IL, USA
e-mail: ezheleva@uic.edu

© Springer Nature Switzerland AG 2019
M. Kaya, R. Alhajj (eds.), *Influence and Behavior Analysis in Social Networks and Social Media*, Lecture Notes in Social Networks,
https://doi.org/10.1007/978-3-030-02592-2_8

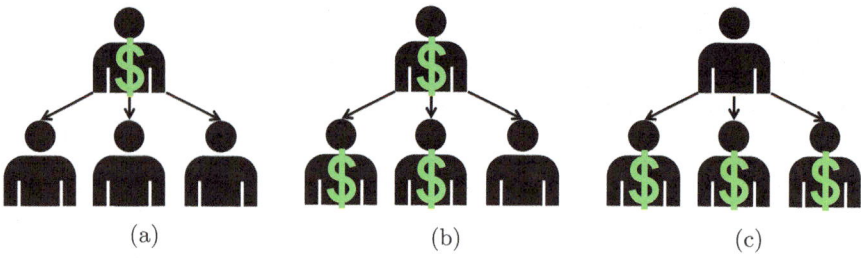

Fig. 1 Me+3 sharing process. (**a**) A user buys and shares a product with three of his friends. (**b**) If only two friends buy, the company receives the profits from all three purchases. (**c**) If three friends buy, the company refunds the purchase of the sharer

Many examples of mass-marketing sharing incentives can be found online. Lovefilm, an online movie rental company, gives £20 to any customer whose friend signs up for their service. In addition, the friend receives the first 1-month subscription for free. Fab, an online marketplace for designer items, gives a customer and her friend $25 each when the friend joins and makes his first purchase. At LivingSocial, an e-commerce company for online deals, when a user buys a deal and persuades three or more friends to purchase the same deal, the user is refunded the price of the deal (Fig. 1). With such incentives, successful recommenders self-select (or prove) themselves as influencers, and the company does not need to identify them explicitly or pay the reward to users whose sharing does not lead to increased adoption.

However, the profitability of mass-marketing sharing incentives remains largely unknown, partly due to the fact that real-world data on sharing incentives is difficult to obtain. The focus of our paper is to analyze such incentives and provide a framework for studying their effectiveness. In particular, we study a family of incentives, *Me+N*, in which after purchasing a product, a customer is offered a reward if she convinces N or more friends to purchase the same product. A number of *incentive parameters* can affect the incentive profitability, such as the value of N, the reward amount, the product price, and the profit margin. Moreover, this type of incentives has parameters over which the company has no direct control, such as the number of friends with whom a user would choose to share and her success rate. Thus, the effect of selected parameters on company's profits is often hard to predict without investing in expensive, large-scale controlled experiments.

The contributions of our work include:

– A thorough study of the characteristics of incentivized sharing using a real-world dataset
– The first study on *Me+N* incentives which reward all customers who convince N of their friends to adopt a recommended product or service
– An analysis and evaluation framework which provides guidance to companies for testing sharing incentives without incurring a prohibitive cost
– Proposing the first model which allows comparison between different *Me+N* incentive parameter values

In this chapter, we build upon our previous work [20, 21] with the goal of presenting a more comprehensive picture of the characteristics of incentivized sharing and modeling for incentivized sharing optimization, with their possibilities and limitations. First we motivate our problem (Sect. 2) and provide a formal problem definition (Sect. 3) and theoretical analysis of the expected benefits from incentivized sharing (Sect. 4). Then, we present the observed structural properties of sharing at an e-commerce company in Sect. 5, and propose a *Me+N graph evolution model* which generalizes incentivized sharing behavior in Sect. 6. Graph evolution models are widely used within the graph mining community for modeling social network behavior and giving informative answers to "what if" questions and scenarios [6]. We simulate the model with different incentive parameters and show the parameter values under which *Me+N* incentives can be successful in bringing additional profits in Sect. 7.

2 Incentivized Sharing: A Motivating Example and Evaluation Framework

The scenario which motivates our work is the following: a company is interested in tapping into the social network of its customers, in order to increase the adoption of its products or services. We assume that the company (1) is interested in implementing a *Me+N* sharing incentive only when it increases its profits (i.e., not investing in an incentive cost that is higher than the additional revenue coming from friends' adoption) and (2) has a limited budget for running controlled experiments. If the second assumption was not an obstacle, then it is best to run large-scale A/B tests, exploring the full parameter space and assessing profits directly. In most realistic scenarios, such experiments require a very large user base, they can be costly in terms of lost profits, software infrastructure to develop and maintain, as well as increased customer confusion and customer service cost. The key questions we would like to answer are:

Q1:   Should a company implement a *Me+N* sharing incentive?
Q2:   For what N would the company increase its profits?
Q3:   For what N would the company maximize its profits?

One simple way to analyze the effect of a *Me+N* incentive on profits is to assume *perfect sharing*, i.e., that all customers who share a purchased product do it because of the incentive and they can convince exactly N of their friends to buy that product (Fig. 1c). In this case, the most important incentive parameter is the cost of the reward. For example, if the reward is getting the original purchase for free, the company not only loses the revenue from the sharer's purchase but also incurs a cost for the free product. To illustrate this further, let us assume a company selling products with a profit margin of 50% (the company receives 50% of the sold item price as profit and the other 50% is the item cost). Implementing *Me+2* would mean that for any sharer, the revenue from the first friend's purchase (i.e., $50\% * price$)

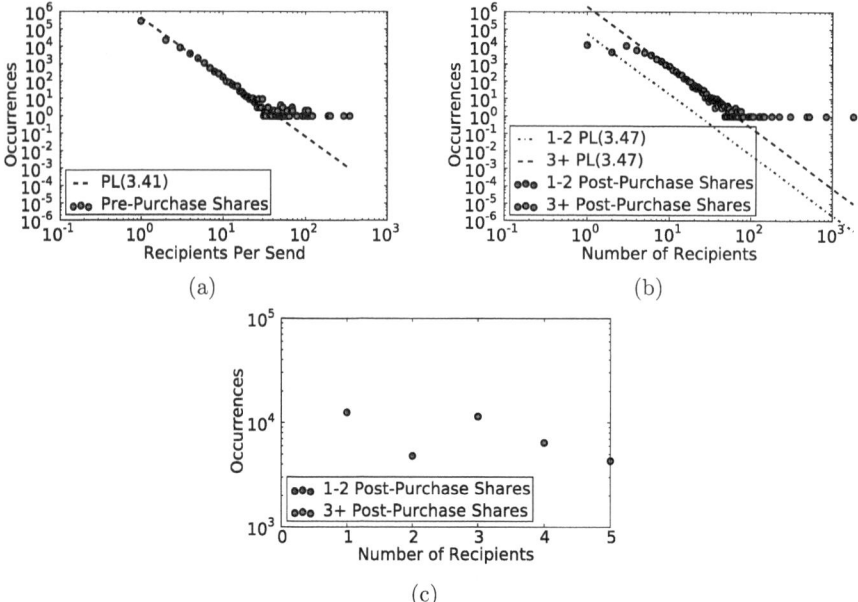

Fig. 2 Degree distribution of (**a**) non-incentivized sharing, (**b**) incentivized sharing, (**c**) closer view at degrees 1 through 5

would cover the cost of the sharer's reward (i.e., $(1–50\%) * price$) and the revenue from the second friend's purchase brings the only final profit for the company. This incentive is not attractive for the company because it does not bring any additional profits in comparison to the case where the company does not offer incentives and gets only the profit from the original sharer. However, implementing *Me+3* would be attractive because it is the equivalent of gaining one incremental purchase. For lower profit margins, N has to be higher to make it worthwhile for the company. For example, at a profit margin of 10% (i.e., cost of 90%), *Me+10* would mean no additional revenue was gained, while *Me+11* would gain one incremental purchase. In perfect sharing, the answer to $Q1$ is always "yes" for margins larger than 0%, the answer to $Q2$ depends on the profit margin, and the answer to $Q3$ is "as large as possible."

A perfect-sharing assumption has two main flaws. First, it disregards the fact that users share with different numbers of friends and have varying success rates. In fact, as we demonstrate later, shares follow a shifted power-law distribution (Fig. 2). The answer to $Q2$ under a perfect-sharing assumption is conservative and requiring higher N than necessary, while in fact lower N can increase profits due to the extra shares coming from users who successfully refer $M \neq N$ friends. At the same time, the answer to $Q3$ is overly optimistic because very few people would be able to reach an incentive goal with a large N, e.g., "if 100 of your friends buy this item, you will get it for free." Moreover, customers may be discouraged by such unattainable incentive goal and not share at all. The second flaw of the perfect-sharing assumption is that it does not take into account the fact that users share organically, even without monetary incentives. If the monetary incentive does not increase the volume of successful shares enough to cover the cost of the reward for both incentivized and organic sharing, the company would be incurring an unnecessary cost.

Therefore, assessing the *expected* number of additional shares due to an incentive is very important. The only reliable way to do that is through an A/B test which is costly, and picking which incentive(s) to test is not straightforward. Here, we limit the space of incentives that need to be A/B tested to a small set that have guarantees about their cost. To do that, we incorporate the additional shares as a parameter into our proposed probabilistic model of user behavior. The parameter represents the probability of a person to be incentivized to share. The model takes into account both the increase in sharing and adoption, and the increase in overall cost (incurred by the company) due to the incentive.

To answer the three key questions, we break down the incentive evaluation into finding the "optimal incentive" (Q3), "better than no incentive" (Q2), and "safe incentive." "Optimal incentive" is defined as the incentive which maximizes profits. Sometimes, having no incentive is the optimal option. "Better than no incentive" is defined as the incentive(s) which has higher profit than organic sharing profit, i.e., revenue from additional referred purchases due to the incentive is higher than the incurred cost. "Safe incentive" is defined as the incentive(s) in which revenue from referred purchases (from both organic and incentivized shares) is higher than the cost paid for rewards. This analysis allows a company to bound the cost of the incentive by the revenue from sharing.

Table 1 exemplifies the output from our experiments. Its entries are determined by simulating our proposed *Me+N model* under various profit margins and % additional shares due to the incentive. They show a very different picture when compared to the initial, perfect-sharing analysis. Recall that the conservative analysis of perfect sharing at a profit margin of 10% suggested that the incentive can lead to additional profits only if $N > 10$, while our model-enabled experiments show that even *Me+4* is a profitable incentive if it drives at least 5% of additional shares.

Table 1 Incentive comparison for different incentive parameters under *Me+N model*

	Margin = 10%			Margin = 50%		
	% additional shares due to incentive					
	0%	5%	50%	0%	5%	50%
Optimal incentive	No incentive	Maximum *N*		No incentive	Maximum *N*	
Better than no incentive	No incentive	*Me+4*, etc.	*Me+3*, etc.	No incentive	*Me+3*, etc.	*Me+2*, etc.
Safe incentive	Me+3, *Me+4*, etc.			Me+2, *Me+3*, etc.		

3   Notation and Problem Statement

Let $G = \langle U, D, P, S \rangle$ refer to a graph, where U refers to the users who participate in sharing (or recommending) items, D is the set of items that can be purchased and shared, $P = U \times D$ are the item purchases by users, and $S = \langle U \times U \times D \rangle$ are the item shares between users. Each 3-tuple s is ordered in terms of the share *sender* or *origin* (o) and *recipient* (r) of an item d. The set of all recipients with whom user o shared item d is $R(o, d) = \{r : \langle o, r, d \rangle \in S\}$, and the share *outdegree* is the set size, $outdegree(o, d) = |R(o, d)|$. The outdegree reflects the sharing behavior of a given sender over one given item, rather than aggregating across different shared items.

Every item d has a set of properties, such as price, $price_d$, and a profit margin, $margin_d$ (i.e., a percentage of the item price that the company keeps). Every user has a set of properties such as their arrival time into the network and purchasing and sharing preferences. Every incentive $i \in I$ is defined by two properties: a *goal* (i.e., an objective that a sharer has to reach) and a *reward* (i.e., the benefit to the sharer if he reaches the goal). The $cost_{u,d}(i)$ is the incentive cost to the company when a sharer o shares item d, achieves the incentive goal and must be given the reward. Ideally, the company picks an incentive $i^* \in I$ for an item d that maximizes profit over the set of users: $profit_d(i) = \sum_{u \in U(d)} profit_{u,d}(i)$ where

$$profit_{u,d}(i) = \begin{cases} -cost_{u,d}(i) & \text{if } u \text{ reached } goal_i \\ margin_d \cdot price_d & \text{else.} \end{cases}$$

In practice, a company must search for an optimal incentive that increases profits, limiting the search over incentives that are better than the non-incentivized baseline.

Consider two disjoint sets of sharing users: $A \subseteq U$ are *altruistic* users unaffected by an incentive i, and $V = U \setminus A$ are the set of *incentivized* users who share with more people with the hope of achieving the incentive goal. At a high level, the incentivized users are responsible for any additional profits that the company would receive from a given incentive through the encouragement of additional purchases of a product. In contrast, the altruistic users are unaffected by the incentive but could achieve the incentive goal anyways, in which case the company would incur a cost for organic sharing.

Let α_i represent the percentage of additional profits produced due to an incentive i. Our goal is to lower bound α_i for both the "better than no incentive" and "safe incentive" values. Let rev_i^V denote the additional revenue ($price_d * margin_d$) coming from a set of incentivized users V and their successful recommendations and $cost_i^V$ denote the total cost of the incentive reward for V. Similarly, rev^A refers to the revenue from altruistic users and purchases due to their recommendations (note that rev^A is independent of i), and $cost_i^A$ is the cost of the incentive reward for A. Then the respective bounds for α_i are:

Better than No Incentive   Safe Incentive

$$\alpha_i \geq \frac{\mathbb{E}[cost_i^A]}{\mathbb{E}[rev_i^V] - \mathbb{E}[cost_i^V]} \qquad\qquad \alpha_i \geq \frac{\mathbb{E}[cost_i^A] - \mathbb{E}[rev^A]}{\mathbb{E}[rev_i^V] - \mathbb{E}[cost_i^V]} \qquad (1)$$

The intuition is that as the difference between additional revenue from the incentive and the cost get higher (in the denominator), fewer incentivized users are needed. Additionally, the value for *safe incentive* is smaller due to the subtraction of the revenue attributed to the sharing by altruistic users. This implies that if the cost incurred due to the incentive on the altruistic users is less than the total revenue from altruistic users, the incentive is safe. We discuss how we derive these bounds in the next section.

4   Theoretical Analysis

In this section we consider the expected benefits from incentivized sharing the company receives under various sharing scenarios. Specifically, we want to know under what scenarios an incentive is expected to have higher profit than organic sharing, as well as whether one sharing incentive is expected to outperform another.

To start, we consider the set of users $u \in U(d, i)$ who purchased a product d under incentive i. Let $benefit_i(d)$ indicate the additional profits received under an incentivized scenario as compared to organic sharing for a product. To have a "better than no incentive" case, a company should have a positive benefit in expectation:

$$\mathbb{E}[benefit_i(d)] \geq 0$$

Let $benefit_i(d, u)$ indicate the amount of profit the company receives due to the incentivization scheme i for a user u, while $\mathbb{E}[benefit_i(d, u)]$ indicates the expected benefit due to the incentivized sharing. Thus, given a set of independently and identically distributed users $U(d, i)$ who purchased product d, the expected benefit the company receives from sharing for a product can be broken down into:

$$\mathbb{E}\left[benefit_i(d) \mid |u(d, i)|\right] = |u(d, i)| \cdot \mathbb{E}[benefit_i(d, u)]. \qquad (2)$$

It is reasonable to assume independence between the product and incentive. In this case, we can take the expectation over the number of purchasers of a product and apply Wald's equation [10]:

$$\mathbb{E}[benefit_i(d)] = \mathbb{E}[|u(d)|] \cdot \mathbb{E}[benefit_i(d, u)] \qquad (3)$$

Applying our previous inequality, we see that in order to benefit in expectation for a product, we must benefit in expectation *per user*:

$$\mathbb{E}[benefit_i(d, u)] \geq 0. \tag{4}$$

If an incentive does not meet this criterium, then the penalty for the incentive outweighs the incentivized purchases, and the incentive should not be used.

"Better Than No Incentive" Analysis We can reduce the expected benefit from incentivized shares into three terms and a scalar:

$$\mathbb{E}[benefit_i(d, u)] = \alpha_i \cdot \left(\mathbb{E}[rev_i^V] - \mathbb{E}[cost_i^V]\right) - \mathbb{E}[cost_i^A] \geq 0. \tag{5}$$

If $\alpha_i = 0$, then the incentive has attracted no new shares of the product, leaving only a penalty to pay altruistic users who attained the incentive $\mathbb{E}[cost_i^A]$ (without the need for the incentive). Solving for α_i, we see:

$$\alpha_i \geq \frac{\mathbb{E}[cost_i^A]}{\left(\mathbb{E}[rev_i^V] - \mathbb{E}[cost_i^V]\right)}. \tag{6}$$

In order to benefit from an incentive compared to organic sharing, percentage α_i of the additional shares needs to exceed this ratio. If the denominator is *negative*, there is no scenario where $\alpha_i \geq 0$ satisfies the equation, meaning the incentive should not be applied.

"Safe Incentive" Analysis Next, let $\mathbb{E}[share\,profit(i, u)]$ be the expected sharing profits under a given scenario:

$$\mathbb{E}[share\,profit(i, u)] = \alpha \cdot \left(\mathbb{E}[rev_i^V] - \mathbb{E}[cost_i^V]\right) + \mathbb{E}[rev^A] - \mathbb{E}[cost_i^A] \geq 0. \tag{7}$$

This is similar to the *benefit* criteria defined above, but with the additional term $\mathbb{E}[rev^A]$ to ensure the company can bound its losses by the sharing revenue. As above, we can reformulate to find:

$$\alpha \geq \frac{\mathbb{E}[cost_i^A] - \mathbb{E}[rev^A]}{\left(\mathbb{E}[rev_i^V] - \mathbb{E}[cost_i^V]\right)}, \tag{8}$$

a ratio which ensures a "safe bet" when testing. Note that when the denominator is negative in this case, there are situations where $\alpha \geq 0$, depending on the sign of the difference between the altruistic cost and revenue. More interestingly, we can have situations where the altruistic cost outweighs the altruistic revenue, but the benefits from the incentive are strong enough to overcome the discrepancy for large enough α. An example of this behavior is shown in Sect. 7.

Comparison of Incentives In order to determine the incentive i^* which maximizes profits, we need to determine which incentives perform best under different circumstances. For example, given the incentive $Me+1$, we may wish to compare it with $Me+2$, to determine under what conditions $Me+2$ will outperform $Me+1$. For incentive 2 to be better than incentive 1, the following must hold:

$$\alpha_2 \cdot \left(\mathbb{E}[rev_2^V] - \mathbb{E}[cost_2^V] \right) - \mathbb{E}[cost_2^A] - \alpha_1 \cdot \left(\mathbb{E}[rev_1^V] - \mathbb{E}[cost_1^V] \right) - \mathbb{E}[cost_1^A] \geq 0. \tag{9}$$

This is a generalization of the comparison to organic (Eq. (5)). Solving for α_2, we get:

$$\alpha_2 \geq \frac{\mathbb{E}[cost_2^A] + \mathbb{E}[cost_1^A] + \alpha_1 \cdot \left(\mathbb{E}[rev_1^V] - \mathbb{E}[cost_1^V] \right)}{\left(\mathbb{E}[rev_2^V] - \mathbb{E}[cost_2^V] \right)} \tag{10}$$

This formulation creates a lower *bound* on the percentage of incentivized shares α_2 necessary for incentive 2 to outperform incentive 1. We can also incorporate prior knowledge of sharing behavior to form an upper bound. For example, if $Me+3$ brings in additional shares α_3, it is unlikely for $Me+4$ to exceed that amount. Thus, we have an *upper* bound for $Me+4$'s corresponding α_4, in addition to the lower bound derived above. Using this analysis, companies with functioning sharing incentives can find the potential benefits of switching to other, new incentives.

Computation of Expected Values This analysis relies on the ability to compute the expected behavior of users under varying incentives. Some of these behaviors are easier to characterize, such as $\mathbb{E}[cost_i^A]$, which can be computed from the company's existing data. Other data may be less available, specifically for the behavior of users under the incentive. However, as shown in the next section, characteristics of user behavior, such as the power law of sharing, make it possible to make reasonable assumptions about behavior for incentivized users, given knowledge of organic users. The next section discusses how users behave under a $Me+3$ incentive, demonstrating that their actions can be accurately characterized under basic assumptions, while the subsequent section lays out a generative model for comparing incentives under this framework, as well expanding to domains where independence assumptions may not hold.

5 Characteristics of the Me+3 Incentive

Next, we discuss the characteristics of incentivized social sharing and analyze an e-commerce dataset obtained from LivingSocial. LivingSocial is an e-commerce company whose core business centers around connecting customers to local merchants, such as restaurants and beauty salons, through online deals. The deal price is lower than the regular price of merchants' products and services. It encourages customers to try a local business, while enabling merchants to reach new customers.

LivingSocial distributes deals through its website, email newsletters, mobile notifications, and social media. It also offers its users the ability to share deals. Moreover, it *incentivizes* them to share through the *Me+3* program. To participate in the program, a user must first purchase a deal and then share it with their friends through email, Facebook, or Twitter. The participant can obtain the purchased deal for free (through a refund) if she convinces *three* (or more) friends to purchase the same deal (Fig. 1).

As users send deals to each other and to prospective users, a directed social network is revealed with users acting as senders and receivers of recommended deals. Due to incentivization, we observe interesting and unusual structural properties in the network that distinguish the LivingSocial social network from other social networks. We analyze the sharing characteristics of users who emailed deals to each other through the LivingSocial website interface.[1] Here, we present the properties we discovered in [20], such as degree distribution and purchase probability, sharing behaviors at different price points, and the predictive power of the shared recommendations in terms of recipient preferences. We also overview properties such as the probability of getting a free deal conditional on the number of share recipients, the new user arrival distribution, and the time delay between subsequent user purchases [21].

5.1 Incentivized Sharing Degree Distribution

LivingSocial users can share any deal posted on the website through email, Facebook, or Twitter, even if they have not purchased it. If the user hasn't purchased the deal prior to sharing it, the share cannot be a part of the *Me+3* program, and it has no monetary incentive. This implies that these shares are inherently *altruistic*. We call these *pre-purchase (or non-incentivized) shares*. If a share occurs after a purchase, then we call it a *post-purchase (or incentivized) share*.

Figure 2a shows the outdegree distribution for a sample of 100, 000 pre-purchase shares. The non-incentivized sharing distribution was fitted to a power law using maximum likelihood [8]. A power-law distribution for a random variable X is one where:

$$P(X = x) \propto x^{-\alpha}.$$

The altruistic sharing distribution follows the power law quite well—such behavior mirrors the degree distributions found in many other social networks. The implication is that we have a large number of senders who share with a handful

---

[1]The work was performed while the authors worked at LivingSocial.

of recipients and far fewer senders that share with a large number of recipients. A notable exception of the LivingSocial share network compared to other networks is the *sharpness* or *steepness* of the distribution. The majority of networks typically have a power-law exponent α where $2 \leq \alpha \leq 3$ [8]; in contrast, the exponent for LivingSocial share data is nearly 3.5, which is considerably larger. This implies that users are emailing deals to subsets of their friends rather than all their friends. This is partly due to the time-sensitive nature of LivingSocial deals. All deals through LivingSocial are for a fixed amount of time, most for less than a week, which gives users considerably less opportunity to share links with friends. This contrasts with email and Facebook friendships, where the outgoing connections of users accrue over a long time period.

In contrast, the degree distribution of a sample of 100, 000 incentivized shares (Fig. 2b) has a noticeable "dip" at outdegrees 1, 2, and 3 (Fig. 2c). Beginning at around outdegree 3, the power law has nearly the same exponent as found in the non-incentivized case, around 3.5. Thus, we can assume the distribution of incentivized users has been *shifted* due to the incentive, resulting in approximately the same distribution with approximately 2–3 shares added to every point. Post-purchase share senders exhibit a mixed behavior: those who share with one or two people (*outdegree* $\in [1, 2]$) are clearly *altruistic* because they do not try to reach the incentive of *Me+3*, while users who share with three or more recipients can reach the incentive even if this was not their primary reason for sharing. The average outdegrees in the two sharing scenarios also differ widely. While the non-incentivized shares have an average outdegree of 1.3, the incentivized shares have an average outdegree of 4.1: this implies that the incentive drives a significant amount of additional shares.

We try to estimate the amount of additional shares due to the incentive. While we cannot determine directly whether a user shared because of the incentive, we can find a lower bound on the number of post-purchase shares that would have occurred without the incentive and find the difference with actual shares. For this, we use (a) the power law of the *altruistic* users, adjusted to go through the point at degree 2 (Fig. 2b) and (b) a power-law fit to the first two points only. In the first case, we estimate that at most 58% of shares are the additional incentivized shares and in the second at most 46%.

An interesting question is what is the effect of the incentivized shares on whether or not the recipient makes a purchase. Next, we analyze the behavior of recipients and their share *indegree*.

5.2 Social Pressure and Adoption

To assess the effect of social pressure on adoption, we next examine the probability of a user purchasing a deal given that a certain number of people recommended the deal to them. This can be found in Fig. 3a, while the share indegree distribution can

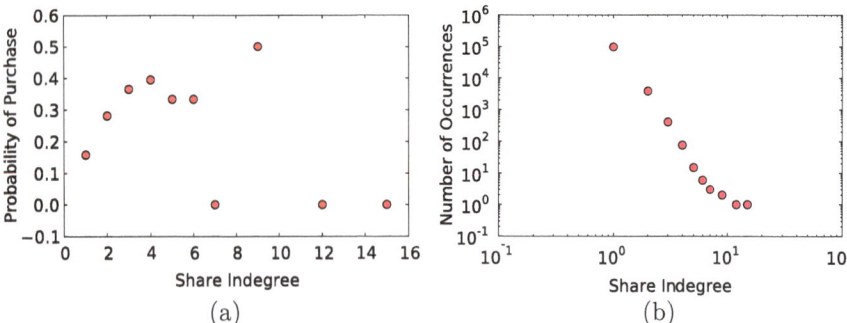

Fig. 3 (**a**) Probability of purchase given an incoming recommendation degree for a *single* product. (**b**) Number of instances with incoming degree for a single product

be found in Fig. 3b. This is performed on a sample of 100,000 $(recipient_j, deal_k)$ pairs, and indegree is the number of emails that were sent to $recipient_j$ for $deal_k$.

Notice the beginning part of Fig. 3a, where we can see that the higher the number of recommendations for a *particular* deal, the higher the probability of a user to purchase that deal, up to degree 4 which has the highest probability of 0.4. It appears that after this instance, we have little improvement as the number of recommendations increases, but this can be attributed to the low number of sample points for these higher degrees (e.g., only two sample points at 9). As Fig. 3b shows, the number of shares with more than *four* recommendations drops significantly. However, the points between 1 and 4 indicate that users send deals according to whether their friend is likely to buy the product, and a high volume of incoming recommendations for a product is a good predictor for whether the user is likely to purchase the product.

A complementary finding, based on Fig. 3b, is that unlike the incentivized share outdegree distribution, the indegree distribution does not have a dip at 2. This means that while the *outgoing* share distribution has been shifted for 3 and above, the effect on the incoming share distribution remains unclear. This can be explained by the fact that the $Me + 3$ incentive does not apply to the recipient; therefore, it does not shift the behavior of recipients in the same manner as the behavior of senders.

As the recipient purchase probability is correlated with the number of recommendations that user receives, a key question is which *type* of recommendation contributed to the purchase of the product. More specifically, did the sender recommend the deal to the recipient because they believed the recipient had an interest in the deal, or was the sender simply trying to get their own free deal and sending the deal at random in hopes of a fortunate purchase? We explore these questions next.

5.3 Purchase Probabilities and Free Deals

Here, we study the probability that the share recipient purchases the deal. Specifically, we are interested in the hypothesis that as the sender increases the number of recipients, he becomes less discriminative in choosing good recipients, and on average the recipients are less likely to purchase the shared deal. For this test we examine all $\{o, r, d\}$ tuples that occurred within a 1-year period at LivingSocial. Figure 4a shows the probability of a recipient purchasing the recommended deal given the outdegree of the recommendation, which confirms our hypothesis. Figure 4d examines this in more detail by showing the distribution of successful recommendations conditioned on the number of recipients. For example, if the sender shares a product with *four* friends, what is the probability no friends will purchase the product, *one* friend will purchase the product, and so on? A (truncated) χ^2 distribution provides the best fit for the observed distribution.

We also examine the probability of a sender receiving a free deal (Fig. 4b). As expected, the more the recipients, the higher the likelihood of a free deal, meaning

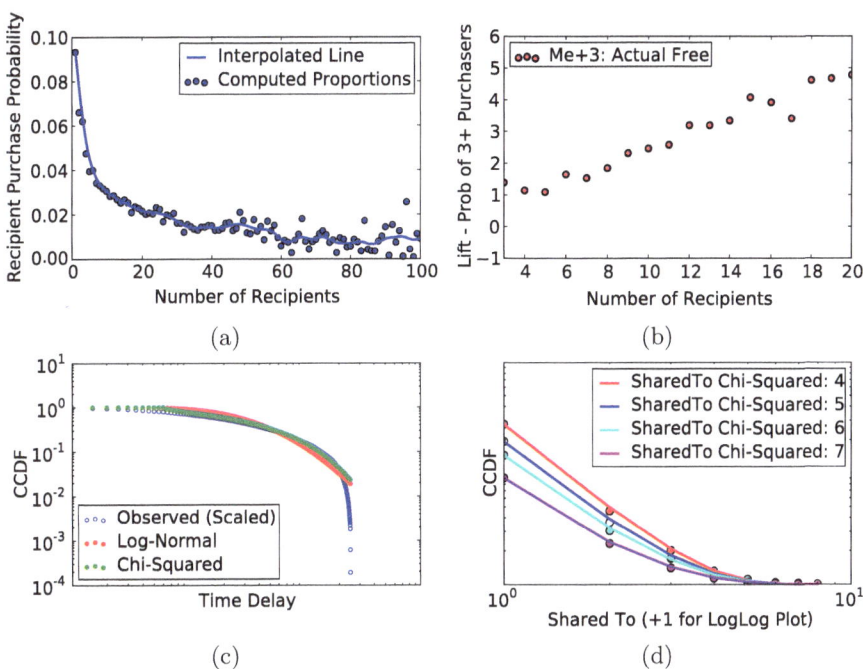

Fig. 4 Observed properties of Me+3: (**a**) Recipient purchase probabilities. (**b**) Free deal distributions given a share outdegree. (**c**) The awakening function. (**d**) Distribution of successful recommendations conditioned on the number of recipients

that while senders who send to many recipients choose them less carefully than those who send to fewer recipients, they are also more successful in obtaining free deals.

5.4 Shares and Recipient Purchase References

People have intrinsic motivations to share information online with others, and sharing deals is no exception. While certain users may only share deals with other users due to the monetary incentive, many users share LivingSocial deals without such an incentive, as discussed in Sect. 5.1. This type of behavior has been observed also in peer-to-peer network sharing where some users serve files to others because of the group's common welfare, while others respond only to monetary incentives [11].

The distribution of shares per sender showed that a large proportion of shared deals are shared *only* with one or two other individuals (Fig. 2b). As these deal shares can never reach the incentive, it is safe to assume that the sender has little interest in the incentive and believes the recipient truly has some interest in the recommended deal. We categorize this type of sharing as *altruistic*. In contrast, any sender who shares with three or more recipients has the potential to be sharing solely for the incentive or being an *incentivized* sender.

In order to learn whether low-volume senders are more accurate with their assessments on which friends might purchase a deal, we first examine how often a recipient of a deal will purchase the deal, based on the number of recipients the sender shared with. Here, we only consider *recipients who are registered* with LivingSocial with the email address that the sender used.

In Fig. 5a, we can see that senders who only send to a handful of users are considerably more accurate when choosing which friends may be interested in a deal. Here, the *probability of purchase* is the proportion of users who purchased the

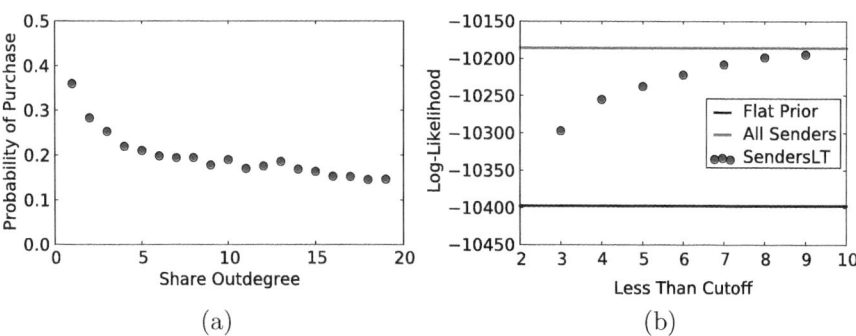

Fig. 5 (a) Probability of purchase when sender shares deals with varying numbers of recipients. (b) Predictive ability using various amounts of recipients per recommendation

recommended deal from a sender. This figure shows that if only a single person is sent the email, the probability of making that purchase is 36 percent, as compared to *five* or more friends, which tails down from 20 percent. However, as the probability of any user making any particular purchase at random is much lower than 20 percent, *there is still useful information provided by higher degree senders*. This implies that higher-volume senders, while less accurate than when sending to a low-volume number of recipients, are still being somewhat discriminative when determining which users might be interested in particular deals.

In addition to whether or not a deal recommendation results in a purchase given the volume of targeted recipients, we analyze whether senders know their friends well and whether shares reflect the recipient preferences. Every deal at LivingSocial is hand classified in a particular *category*: for example, a dentist visit may be placed in a category named Healthcare while a diner deal might be classified under Eateries. We pick a sample of 5000 users with whom at least 1 deal was shared in 1 year and who have bought at least 1 deal in following year. Using the recommendations sent across the second year, we build simple preference models which learn the multinomial distribution over the shared deal categories for *each recipient*. A uniform Dirichlet prior is then applied over the categories for each user to avoid category probabilities of 0 if a user has never been recommended a deal of that category. Then we check the log-likelihood of future purchases made in the second year, given the models.

The performance of the model which considers all incoming deal shares is shown as a red line in Fig. 5b. We can see that it performs better than a flat multinomial distribution which is shown as a black line.

An interesting question is whether the deals shared with a high number of recipients are too noisy to extract any meaningful recipient preference information and whether they can be excluded from the model. In other words, do the high-volume deal shares contain information about the recipients' categorical preferences that are not already present and available through the low-volume deal shares? If the high-volume deal shares are mostly noise, then at best they add little value to models which build categorical preferences of recipients, while at worst they could potentially *decrease* the models' performance by washing out the relevant information found from low-volume deal shares.

To test whether these high-volume deal shares interfere with our categorical model's ability to predict future deal purchases, we build models which include varying levels of share volumes (Fig. 5b). The x-axis indicates the model's "cutoff" point, that is, the maximum number of recipients per share which will be included in the recipient's categorical model. For example, the point corresponding to "3" on the x-axis indicates a model where only deals shared with *one*, *two*, or *three* recipients will be incorporated in the recipients' models, omitting all deal shares sent to *four* or more recipients from any recipient's model. We then gradually increase the volume of deal shares to be incorporated in the recipients' models, up to 9. We first observe that each of these points outperforms a "flat" distribution (the black line), meaning they never do worse than random. Furthermore, we can see that as the additional deal shares are included, the predictive power of the recipients' model increases, indicating better performance when the higher-volume deal shares are incorporated into the recipients' categorical models. Finally, we compare against the model which incorporates all deal shares sent, regardless of volume (the red line). As this line outperforms all the other various points, it shows that while a limited amount of information is available from these high-volume shares, the noisy data does not interfere with the lower-volume shares. Furthermore, it does add some additional performance, indicating slight amount of information can be gleaned from such high-volume shares.

This shows that the flat prior alone (black) performs worse than any of the recipient informations, indicating that senders are using some amount of discrimination when determining which users might be interested in a deal. When comparing the likelihoods between models as the number of recipients allowed per share is increased, we find that the amount of information found in the high-volume senders stagnates, indicating less discrimination by the sender as to whether the receiver has interest in the present deal. However, the information is not completely random, as the predictions continue to slowly increase in accuracy. High degree senders are likely highly motivated by the incentive, and they also target individuals they believe have a chance at purchasing the deal.

Next, we discuss the impact the deal price has on the sharing behavior, in particular whether the price can affect on how desirable the incentive is.

5.5 Impact of the Incentive Amount

So far, we discussed how the incentive and volume of sharing affect the behavior of both recipients and senders. An interesting question to explore next is the effect of the incentive amount. One hypothesis is that the higher the incentive, the more additional shares it drives. However, this turned out not to be the case.

To understand the effect price has on shares, we examine the shift in the share outdegree distribution for two distinct price ranges, [\$0–\$50] and [\$100–\$150]. We sample 100,000 ($sender_i, deal_k$) pairs from the corpus of data (50,000 per price range). Figure 6a shows the share outdegree distribution, i.e., the number of shares with a certain number of recipients. Part (a) shows the distribution of send volume, and part (b) shows the complementary cumulative distribution function (CCDF) of the distribution of send volume—at every point along the x-axis we see the number of points greater than this one in the distribution. Contrary to our initial intuition, when the price is higher, the sender typically shares with *fewer* people. As 100–150 remains below 0–50 in Fig. 6b, this shows that fewer senders are flooding the inboxes of their friends when the items are in a higher price range but are more comfortable asking around to see if a random friend may be interested in the cheaper deals.

This is further magnified in Fig. 6c. Here, we have focused on just the senders who send to *five* or fewer recipients. We note a pivot point at *three* shares—for low-priced items the senders more frequently send to *four* or *five* recipients. For

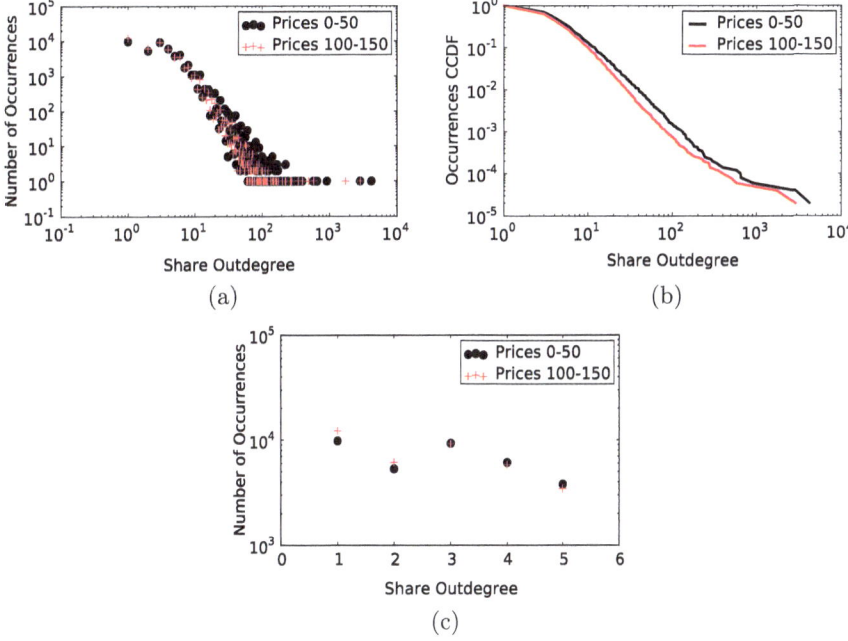

Fig. 6 (**a**) The distribution of the number of recipients per share for varying prices. (**b**) The complementary cumulative degree function for the number of recipients per share for varying prices. (**c**) Close view of the volume of senders who shared with one through five recipients

high-priced items the senders are more focused on the individuals they believe are interested in the items, sending more frequently to just one or two individuals. The volume of additional incentivized sharing appears to be lower at the higher price point.

5.6 Arrivals and Awakening

While the goal of sharing incentives is to convince customers' friends to make a purchase, it can only be useful when a subset of the users make an initial deal purchase. Here, we characterize this behavior through the usage of two processes: user *arrival* and user *awakening*. User *arrivals* to LivingSocial are users who have never purchased from LivingSocial previously, but for a particular deal on a particular day, they have enough interest in the offered deal to sign up for the service and purchase it. For simplicity and without loss of generality, here we assume that the date of the first purchase is when a user joins the service. For the LivingSocial data, the distribution is Gaussian.

In contrast to arrivals, user *awakenings* are the result of current LivingSocial users making a purchase from LivingSocial of a newly presented deal; consequently, we term the duration between purchases as the user *sleeping*. To study awakenings, we take a 2-month time period as our "starting" point: for each of the purchases which occur in this period, we determine the lag until the user's next purchase (Fig. 4c) (Note: values are scaled to remove proprietary information). To avoid "crop" effects or the removal of users with very large durations between purchases, we count subsequent purchases that occurred up to a year from the beginning of the 2-month period. Multiple distributions were fitted against the distribution, resulting in the χ^2 and log-normal distributions empirically matching the best.

The arrival and awakening distributions generate the *non-sharing* portion of the user purchase behavior. However, some of these users recommend deals to their friends and thus contribute to the sharing process.

6   Me+N: A Model for Incentivized Sharing Optimization

While incentivized sharing through the *Me+3* program leads to increased profits and a greater volume of shares than in the non-incentivized case, it is hard to gauge how other incentives would affect the company's profits. To solve this problem, we present our generalized *Me+N* graph evolution model which rewards users if *N* of their friends buy their shared item [21]. The model is designed to be *modular*, in order to test and compare different hypotheses with respect to incentivized sharing. Algorithm 1 lays out the model with input θ, the set of incentive parameters. The main *for loop* (Lines 3 through 12) captures the *daily* sharing behavior of customers through the following functions:

– *Arrival*: How new users *join* the network (make their first purchase)
– *Awakening*: How long users wait between purchases
– *Sharing*: How users share
– *Recipient Purchasing*: How recipients choose to purchase the shared item
– *Profits*: How the incentive affects the overall profits

These functions can have a significant impact on the profit, and there are many nuances to consider (see Sect. 2). To simplify this, we focus on the three main parameters: (1) $\theta.N$ (over which the company has control), (2) the percentage of additional profits $\theta.\alpha$ (which is governed by user behavior), and (3) the profit margin $\theta.margin$ (which can be supplied as input by the company). We briefly describe the rest.

Algorithm 1 DailyActivity(days,θ)

1: nodes = [], purchases=[], incent=[]
2: profit = 0
3: **for all** day **in** days **do**
4:     arr_n = $Arr(\theta)$, awake_n = $Awake(\theta)$
5:     **for all** node **in** arr_n **do**
6:         incent[node] = $Incent(\theta)$
7:     **end for**
8:     daily_n = arr_n + awake_n
9:     profit += θ.purch_profit * len(daily_n)
10:     sp, sl = Share(daily_n, incent, θ)
11:     profit += (sp - sl)
12: **end for**
13: **return** profit

Algorithm 2 Share(daily_n,incent,θ)

1: # Initialize
2: profit=0, loss = 0,purchases = []
3: # Determine sharing for each node
4: **for all** node **in** daily_n **do**
5:     r = $Share(\text{incent[node]}, \theta)$
6:     # Store purchases from shared
7:     $r_p = RPrch(\text{r}, \theta)$
8:     profit += θ.purchase_profit * len(r_p)
9:     loss += $Cost(r_p, \theta)$
10: **end for**
11: **return** profit, loss

6.1 Arrival and Awakening Functions

The *Arrival* and *Awakening* functions which we discussed in the previous section are explicitly incorporated in the graph model (line 4 of Algorithm 1). They determine the nodes which *choose to buy* from the site on a particular day.

Arrival functions in social networks can have from exponential to sub-linear growth [19]. Two other options are the Gaussian $(Arr(\theta) = \text{round}\,(\mathcal{N}(\theta.\mu, \theta.\sigma)))$, such as the LivingSocial case, or the Poisson $(Arr(\theta) = \text{Poisson}(\theta.\lambda))$, which are frequently used to model arrival rates [10]. Other options are to incorporate seasonal or day-of-week effects into the arrival function.

Equally important is the *awakening* function (*Awake*). As shown earlier, the awakening function of LivingSocial users follows a χ^2, making $Awake(\theta) = \chi^2(\theta.k)$. Another possibility for the awakening function would be to awake users who are likely to purchase an offered product: $Awake(u, d, \theta) = P(u|d, \theta)$. This function would be useful if we had a *preference model* for each user.

6.2   Creating a **Me+N** *Sharing Distribution*

We showed earlier that the *Me+3* incentive causes a shift in the degree distribution of user shares, resulting in nearly identical exponents for both the pre-purchase (non-incentivized) and post-purchase (incentivized) shares. Based on this, our model assumes that modifications of the incentive threshold N in *Me+N* will result in a similar distribution shift for the incentivized shares *while leaving the exponent intact*. Relaxing this assumption is left for future work.

While the shift can be characterized as a constant, it is unclear how large this shift (i.e., the proportion of incentivized users) becomes as the incentive parameters change. Nevertheless, it is safe to assume that as N increases (and thus the hurdle for attaining the reward gets higher), the overall percent of additional shares would decrease. For example, when given a *Me+100* incentive, it is highly likely that most users would find the incentive unattainable or not worth their effort.

Varying N Figure 7a shows one example of how N can change the sharing distribution. In it, we see the non-incentivized distribution laid out by the red dash-dot line. Correspondingly, we see various distributions as we alter the incentive threshold value of N in *Me+N*. Notice that as N increases, the distribution lies closer to the original non-incentivized line, until the two converge. We assume that the volume under the dashed line corresponds to the *altruistic* sharing of individuals, while the area above the dashed red line (but under the solid line) corresponds to the additional shares resulting from the incentive. Alternatively, Fig. 7b shows sharing that does not change the proportion of additional shares at each outdegree, as we increase N but the assumption of decrease in additional shares as N increases holds. It is also plausible that shares at outdegrees smaller than N shift downwards, meaning that users who were likely to share with $m < N$ users in a non-incentivized scenario are now more likely to share with $m \geq N$ given the incentive (the drawing of the graph for this scenario is left as an exercise to the reader). We provide an evaluation of different shift assumptions in Sect. 7.

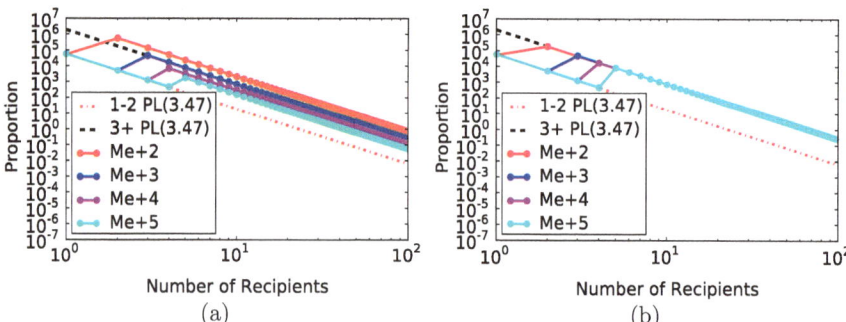

Fig. 7 Hypothetical distributions of incentivized sharing based on the assumption that sharing changes the proportion of additional shares at each outdegree (**a**), and that sharing does not change that proportion (**b**)

Generating For the sharing model, the remaining question is how to determine which users share because of the incentive and which ones share in an altruistic manner. Let $incent[node] \sim Bernoulli(\theta.p)$ (Algorithm 1 line 6) indicate whether a purchaser $node$ shares altruistically with other users, while $PL(\theta)$ indicates a known power-law distribution of sharing. The parameters of these distributions can be estimated from existing data. For each new user, we decide whether they are altruistic or not $incent[node] \sim Bernoulli(\theta.p)$, if $incent[node]$ is true we have an *altruistic* sharer and draw the number of users to share with r (Algorithm 2) from the corresponding power law. If $incent[node]$ is false, we then draw $will\_share \sim Bernoulli(\theta.\alpha)$ to determine if the incentive had convinced the person to share. If so, we draw from the power law and add the incentive threshold; if false, no sharing occurs.

6.3 Generated Purchase Probabilities

Based on the findings in Sect. 5.3 (Fig. 4d), the number of successful purchase recommendations is sampled from $RPrch(\theta) = \text{truncated}(\chi^2(\theta.k), \theta.outdegree)$. We estimate the free item probabilities for different N by examining the *Me+3* data. We plot the lift probabilities of free items (noting that the original N is 3), where Lift can be characterized as: $Lift(\theta.outdegree) = \frac{P(freeitem|\theta.outdegree)}{P(freeitem)}$. We can see the results of this analysis in Fig. 8, where the free item probabilities for varying incentives are calculated by looking at the number of people who have reached N successful recommendations in the data. We find a consistent behavior for each of the varying N values implying that the free item probabilities are independent of N. For example, if a user always picked their top 3 choices and the rest completely at random when filling up their outdegree, we would expect the *Me+2* line to lie nearly on top of *Me+3*, as all examples of acquiring 2 friends would also likely acquire 3. This is not the case, so this example can be ruled out.

Fig. 8 Free item distributions for varying outdegrees

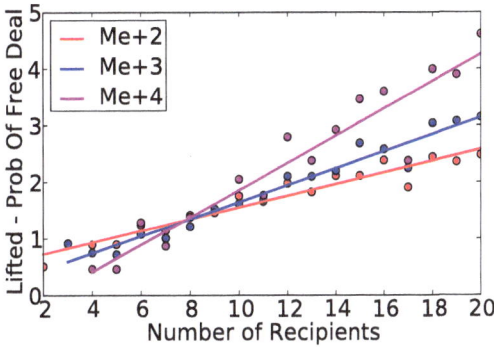

6.4   Cost of Sharing Incentives

As described in Sect. 3, the last piece that we need to define, in order to be able to calculate profits under different scenarios, is the cost to the company when a sharer achieves the incentive goal and must be given the reward. The cost depends on the reward, and it can be a percent of the item price: $cost_{u,d}(i) = \mathbb{I}[\|r_p\| \geq \theta.N] \cdot \$\theta.reward$, where $\mathbb{I}$ is the indicator and $\theta.N$ is the incentive threshold. The cost can also be fixed (e.g., \$10), such as the one used by the refer-a-friend program by Fab and LivingSocial for new user acquisition.

7   Experiments

We focus on determining which N performs well under various assumptions for the sharing percentage α and margin m. We use the *Me+N model* to generate different networks and measure the *benefit over organic* sharing: $profit_d(i) - rev^A$. When this measure is positive, the incentive is "Better Than No Incentive." We fix the price at \$50 and simulate 50 days with 1000 new customers arriving to the site each day. The awakening function is based on $\chi^2(50)$ distribution.

Variable Profit Margins To assess the effect of profit margins, we vary the proportion of additional shares α for different N. Figure 9a shows that for a *low* profit margin (i.e., a free product has a high cost), methods such as *Me+1* and *Me+2* are *worse* than not having incentives (*Me+1* is far negative and omitted from the plot). In higher margin areas, we see that *Me+2* generally does much better: for both margin = 0.5 (Fig. 9b) and margin = 0.9 (Fig. 9c), *Me+2* performs comparably to *Me+3* and *Me+4*. While *Me+1* improves, it does not become profitable, even for the high margin products.

Safe Incentives The profitability of $Me + N$ highly depends on α. Since true value of α for any given incentive is unknown, at least we would like to check whether it is

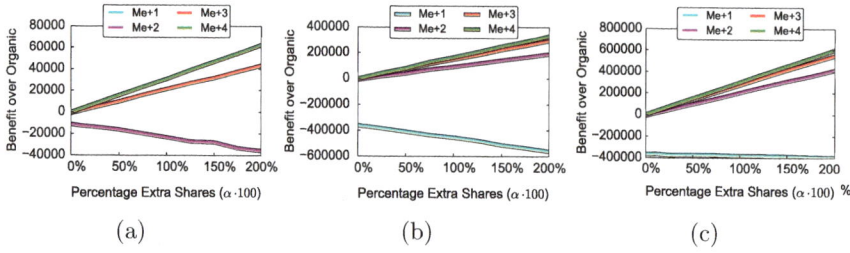

(a)   (b)   (c)

Fig. 9 Benefit over organic sharing for varying $Me+N$ with (**a**) Margin = 0.1, (**b**) Margin= 0.5 and (**c**) Margin = 0.9. When the margin is too small, the benefit of *Me+2* is negative. Further, there is never benefit for *Me+1*

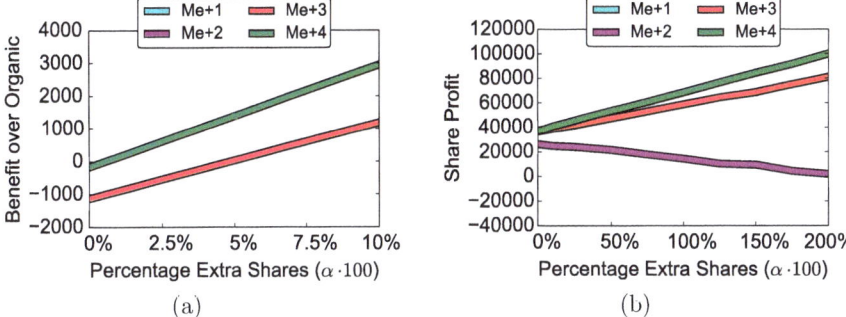

Fig. 10 (**a**) For small margins, *Me+3* can have a negative impact. (**b**) However, *Me+3* is a 'safe incentive'

a "Safe Incentive." For these experiments, we fix the profit margin at 0.1. Figure 10a shows that for $\alpha \geq 0.05$, *Me+3* is "Better Than No Incentive." Moreover, when we consider the organic sharing profits (Fig. 10b), we see that *Me+3* is above 0, making it a "Safe Incentive" at any level of $\alpha > 0$.

Performance of Me+3 So far, we assumed that different N models have the same α. However, due to the higher hurdle of higher N, it is more likely that $\alpha_N > \alpha_{N+1}$.

To examine these cases, we analyze the company's *benefit over organic* for different incentives by fixing α for one of the incentives. For example, if we fix $\alpha_3 = 0.5$, we ask how large should the extra percentage of shares α_N be in order to beat *Me+3*? In Fig. 11a, we compare *Me+2* and *Me+3* at margin 0.5. The red dashed line marks the benefit of *Me+3* for $\alpha_3 = 0.5$. It crosses the purple *Me+2* line at approximately $\alpha_2 = 0.78$. This means that *Me+2* would outperform *Me+3* only if $\alpha_2 > \alpha_3 + 28\%$. At a margin of 0.9, this will hold true only if $\alpha_2 > \alpha_3 + 19\%$ (Fig. 11b). Thus, lower N is more likely to be better under higher margins.

We also study how *Me+4* compares to *Me+3*. Figure 11c shows that for *Me+3*'s benefit at $\alpha_3 = 0.5$, any $\alpha_4 \leq 0.47$ is *less* than the benefit we receive from *Me+3*. Since $\alpha_4 \leq \alpha_3$, we see that $0.47 \leq \alpha_4 \leq 0.5$, meaning there is a very small window of percentage additional sharing where *Me+4* can outperform *Me+3*. Conversely, in Fig. 11d, the window widens when the margin is 0.1: $0.3 \leq \alpha_4 \leq 0.5$. Thus, for low margins, the larger N is more likely to provide higher benefit.

8 Related Work

Our work is closely related to work in graph mining and network science which study structural properties of social networks (e.g., degree distribution) and graph evolution models [5, 8, 16, 17, 25]. Graph evolution models mirror the behavior and properties of real-world networks, giving informative answers to "what if" questions

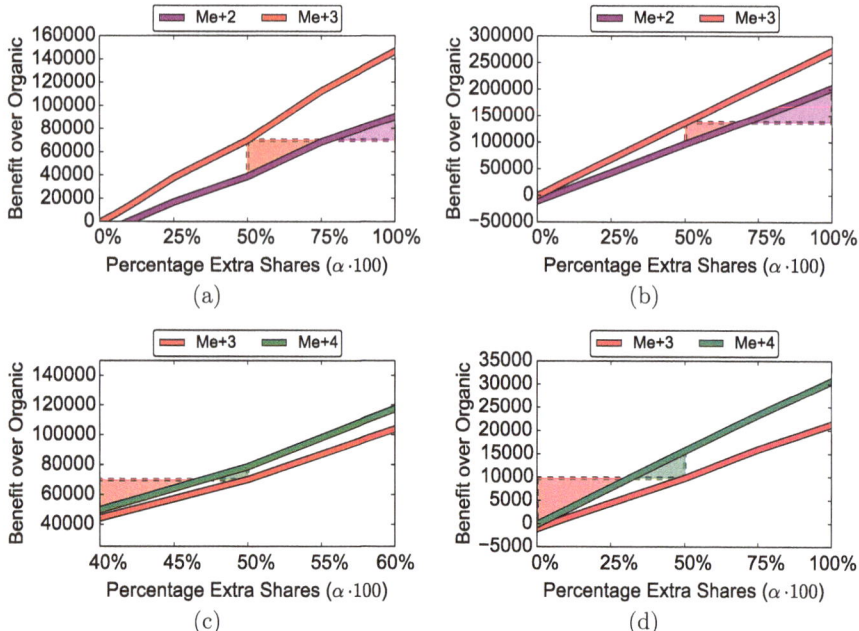

Fig. 11 Lower bound of *Me+2* with *Me+3* ($\alpha_3 = 0.5$), for (**a**) Margin = 0.5 and (**b**) Margin = 0.9. Bounding of *Me+4* with *Me+3* ($\alpha_3 = 0.5$) for (**c**) Margin = 0.5 (zoomed) and (**d**) Margin = 0.1

and scenarios [6]. Our graph evolution model is the first one to capture incentivized sharing patterns of users and to allow exploration of a wide range of incentives.

Our proposed model also complements work on viral marketing. Direct viral marketing incentivizes a subset of individuals to adopt a product, with the goal to maximize the diffusion of adoption through the network [1–3, 7, 9, 12, 13, 18]. In contrast, we consider mass-marketing sharing incentives, also known as referral programs [14], which are offered to *all* users, where a user receives the benefit *after* the goal is reached. This implies that only early adopters and good recommenders benefit from the incentive. Incentives for sharing can also inspire spamming behavior, leading some users to develop resistance to their friends' recommendations [23].

While the sharing incentives we cover can be applied outside the daily-deal domain, it is useful to place them in the context of daily deals. Some of the aspects that have been explored are the effects of deal scheduling on revenue maximization [15], and predicting the future popularity of a deal [24]. Additionally, because each deal expires after a limited amount of time, this leaves little room for longitudinal, cascading effects such as the ones observed in [17].

9 Conclusions

We proposed a novel problem for optimizing mass-marketing sharing incentives, and we introduced a framework for understanding when and why an incentive would be profitable to a company. We also presented empirical evidence of the value of such incentives by using data from an e-commerce company. We showed new characteristics of incentivized sharing, such as the "shifted" power law and how the user's probability of achieving the incentive goal increases as they share with more recipients, despite recipients' purchase probabilities decreasing for higher outdegrees. We also introduced a probabilistic, graph-evolution model to simulate how an incentivized network grows over time, which is flexible enough to accommodate multiple incentive types.

Our experiments show that while $Me+2$ is worse than no incentive for products with low profit margins, it may prove beneficial for higher margins. Additionally, while $Me+4$ has fairly tight bounds in comparison to $Me+3$, when profit margins are very low, these bounds become looser and $Me+4$ might be a better option. This is the result of an inherent tradeoff between the share volume increase caused by the incentive and the cost of the incentive itself. These findings can lead companies towards more informed decisions when they consider implementing sharing incentives.

Some potential areas of future research include estimating the exact α through controlled experiments, and studying the impact of item price, reward, product quality, geographical and seasonality on sharing and purchases. The reward recipients can vary as well, for example the sharer and recipients may share the reward. Another interesting direction is in attribution modeling, which determines which adoption behavior can be attributed to the monetary incentive and which one to altruistic motivation.

References

1. N. Agarwal, H. Liu, L. Tang, P.S. Yu, Identifying the influential bloggers in a community, in *WSDM* (2008)
2. A. Anagnostopoulos, G. Brova, E. Terzi, Peer and authority pressure in information-propagation models, in *PKDD* (2011)
3. S. Aral, D. Walker, Identifying influential and susceptible members of social networks. Science **337**, 337–341 (2012)
4. E. Bakshy, J.M. Hofman, W.A. Mason, D.J. Watts, Everyone's an influencer: quantifying influence on twitter, in *WSDM* (2011)
5. A. Barabasi, R. Albert, Emergence of scaling in random networks. Science **286**, 509–512 (1999)
6. D. Chakrabarti, C. Faloutsos, *Graph Mining: Laws, Tools, and Case Studies*. Synthesis Lectures on Data Mining and Knowledge Discovery (Morgan & Claypool Publishers, San Rafael, 2012)

7. W. Chen, Y. Wang, S. Yang, Efficient influence maximization in social networks, in *KDD* (2009)
8. A. Clauset, C. Shalizi, M. Newman, Power-law distributions in empirical data. SIAM **51**(4), 661–703 (2009)
9. P. Domingos, M. Richardson, Mining the network value of customers, in *KDD* (2001)
10. R. Durrett, *Essentials of Stochastic Processes*. Springer Texts in statistics (Springer, New York, 2012)
11. P. Golle, K. Leyton-Brown, I. Mironov, M. Lillibridge, Incentives for sharing in peer-to-peer networks. Electron. Commer. **2232**, 75–87 (2001)
12. N. Immorlica, V. Mirrokni, Tutorial: optimal marketing and pricing in social networks, in *WWW* (2010)
13. D. Kempe, J. Kleinberg, E. Tardos, Maximizing the spread of influence through a social network, in *KDD* (2003)
14. L. Kornish, Q. Li, Optimal referral bonuses with asymmetric information: Firm-offered and interpersonal incentives. Market. Sci. **29**(1), 108–121 (2010)
15. T. Lappas, E. Terzi, Daily-deal selection for revenue maximization, in *CIKM* (2012)
16. S. Lattanzi, D. Sivakumar, Affiliation networks, in *STOC* (June 2009)
17. J. Leskovec, J. Kleinberg, C. Faloutsos, Graphs over time: densification laws, shrinking diameters and possible explanations. Trans. Knowl. Discov. Data **3**(2), 177–187 (2005)
18. J. Leskovec, L.A. Adamic, B.A. Huberman, The dynamics of viral marketing. ACM Trans. Web **1**(1) (2007)
19. J. Leskovec, L. Backstrom, R. Kumar, A. Tomkins, Microscopic evolution of social networks, in *KDD* (2008)
20. J.J. Pfeiffer III, E. Zheleva, Incentivized sharing in social networks, in *VLDB Workshop on Online Social Systems (WOSS)* (2012)
21. J.J. Pfeiffer III, E. Zheleva, Optimizing the effectiveness of incentivized social sharing, in *ASONAM* (2017)
22. M. Salganik, P. Dodds, D. Watts, Experimental study of inequality and unpredictability in an artificial cultural market. Science **311**(5762), 854–856 (2006)
23. H. Sharara, W. Rand, L. Getoor, Differential adaptive diffusion: understanding diversity and learning whom to trust in viral marketing, in *ICWSM* (2011)
24. M. Ye, C. Wang, C. Aperjis, B.A. Huberman, T. Sandholm, Collective attention and the dynamics of group deals, in *WWW* (2012)
25. E. Zheleva, H. Sharara, L. Getoor, Co-evolution of social and affiliation networks, in *KDD* (2009)

Rumor Source Detection in Finite Graphs with Boundary Effects by Message-Passing Algorithms

Pei-Duo Yu, Chee Wei Tan, and Hung-Lin Fu

1 Introduction

Shah and Zaman in [1] formulated the problem of finding the culprit of a rumor spreading as a maximum likelihood estimation problem. In particular, a *rumor centrality* approach, a form of network centrality, solves this problem for degree-regular tree graphs *assuming that the underlying number of susceptible vertices is countably infinite*. This means that each infected vertex always has a susceptible vertex as its neighbor. The infected vertex with the most number of ways to spread to other vertices is the *rumor center* that coincides with the maximum likelihood estimate. This rumor centrality approach was subsequently extended to various problem settings, e.g., extension in [2–4] to random trees, extension in [4, 5] to constrained observations, extension in [6] to multiple source detection, and extension in [7] to detection with multiple snapshot observations. It is shown in [8, 9] that the rumor center is equivalent to the graph centroid.

There is however a key limitation in the rumor centrality approach. *A main modeling assumption is that the underlying graph (i.e., number of susceptible vertices) is countably infinite.* First, this does not accurately model practical real-world networks where the number of underlying susceptible vertices is countably finite. For example, the current world's population is about seven billion. Second, we can incorporate even more complex dynamical spreading model. The *vertices without susceptible neighbors*, i.e., end vertices, in the rumor graph can model users

P.-D. Yu (✉) · C. W. Tan
City University of Hong Kong, Kowloon Tong, Hong Kong
e-mail: peiduoyu2-c@my.cityu.edu.hk; cheewtan@cityu.edu.hk

H.-L. Fu
National Chiao Tung University, Hsinchu, Taiwan
e-mail: hlfu@math.nctu.edu.tw

© Springer Nature Switzerland AG 2019
M. Kaya, R. Alhajj (eds.), *Influence and Behavior Analysis in Social Networks and Social Media*, Lecture Notes in Social Networks,
https://doi.org/10.1007/978-3-030-02592-2_9

who are disinterested in passing on the rumor to their neighbors. The end vertices thus introduce non-trivial boundary effects that cannot be ignored and this makes the constrained maximum likelihood estimation problem a much harder problem. In essence, the boundary effects limit the span of the dynamical spreading process, and in fact may increase the likelihood that vertices near the boundary are the culprit. Hence, the number of boundary end vertices and their location can significantly shape spreading and therefore the probabilistic inference performance. To be exact, existing algorithms in the literature, e.g., [1, 2, 5–7], are no longer optimal *even with the presence of a single end vertex* in degree-regular rumor graphs with boundary effects. Rumor source detection over a graph with boundary effects is an open problem, but one that is more realistic and also significantly generalizes all previous work [1, 2, 5–7].

1.1 Our Contributions

The main contributions are summarized as follows:

- We propose a *generalized rumor centrality* to solve the maximum likelihood estimation problem by taking into account the boundary effects of spreading.
- For a finite *degree-regular tree graph* with a single end vertex at the boundary, we derive a key result to analytically characterize the optimal maximum likelihood estimator.
- We extend our analysis to degree-regular tree graphs with multiple end vertices and propose message-passing-based algorithms that narrow down the search and are near-optimal in performance.
- The message-passing algorithm gives enhanced and better performance as compared with a naive approach that merely uses the graph centroid for tree graphs.

2 Preliminaries of Rumor Centrality

We model an online social network of vertices by an undirected graph $G = (V, E)$, where the set of vertices V represents the vertices in the underlying network, and the set of edges E represents the links between the vertices. We shall assume that V is *countably finite* (this is the crucial departing point from the previous assumption of infinite graph in the literature [1, 2, 5–7]). Following [1], we use the susceptible-infectious (SI) model in [10] to model rumor spreading. Vertices that possess the rumor are called *infected vertices* and otherwise they are *susceptible vertices*. The spreading is initiated by a single vertex $v^\star \in V$ that we call the rumor source. Once a vertex is infected (i.e., possesses the rumor), it stays infected and can in turn infect its susceptible neighbors. A rumor is spread from vertex i to vertex j if and only if there is an edge between them (i.e., $(i, j) \in E$). Let τ_{ij} be the spreading time from i to j, which are random variables that are independently and exponentially distributed with parameter λ (without loss of generality, let $\lambda = 1$). Hence, we have a random spreading model over an underlying *finite graph*. Let G_n be a subgraph of order n of G that models a snapshot observation of the spreading when there are n infected vertices, i.e., $|G_n| = n$. Clearly, G_1 is the *actual rumor source*, i.e., $v^\star$. The rumor source detection problem is thus to find $v^\star$ given this observation of G_n.

First, we review the maximum likelihood estimation problem of the rumor source in a tree network. The maximum likelihood estimator for the rumor source is the vertex v with the maximum probability $P(G_n|v)$ [1]. Next, we focus on characterizing $P(G_n|v)$ for degree-regular tree networks.

Definition 1 For a given G_n over the underlying graph G, $\hat{v}$ is a maximum likelihood estimator for the source in G_n, i.e., $P(G_n|\hat{v}) = \max_{v_i \in G_n} P(G_n|v_i)$.

By Bayes' theorem, $P(G_n|v)$ is the probability that v is the *actual rumor source culprit* that leads to observing G_n. Now, let σ_i be the possible spreading order sequence starting from v, and let $M(v, G_n)$ be the collection of all σ_i when v is the source in G_n. Then, we have

$$P(G_n|v) = \sum_{\sigma_i \in M(v, G_n)} P(\sigma_i|v). \tag{1}$$

In particular, for a d-regular tree, we have [1]:

$$P(\sigma_i|v) = \prod_{k=1}^{n-1} \frac{1}{dk - 2(k-1)}. \tag{2}$$

Now, if the spreading has not reached the end vertices, then $P(\sigma_i|v) = P(\sigma_j|v)$ for all $\sigma_i, \sigma_j \in M(v, G_n)$. By combining (1) and (2), we have

$$P(G_n|v) = \sum_{\sigma_i \in M(v, G_n)} P(\sigma_i|v)$$

$$= |M(v, G_n)| \cdot P(\sigma|v) \quad \forall \sigma_i \in M(v, G_n)$$

$$= |M(v, G_n)| \cdot \prod_{k=1}^{n-1} \frac{1}{dk - 2(k-1)},$$

which means that $P(G_n|v)$ is proportional to $|M(v, G_n)|$. This quantity $|M(v, G_n)|$ denoted by $|M(v, G_n)|$ is the *rumor centrality* in [1] that is crucial to solving the maximum likelihood estimation for degree-regular trees. In particular, the vertex having the maximum rumor centrality is called the *rumor center*. In [8, 11], the authors established its equivalence to the graph-theoretic centroid.

Definition 2 Let G be a tree, for any $v \in G$, define $weight(v) = \max\limits_{c \in child(v)} |T_c^v|$, where T_c^v is the subtree rooted at c by removing the edge (v, c) from G.

Definition 3 Let G_n be an infected subtree of the underlying graph G. The *centroid* v_c of G_n is the vertex v with the minimum $weight(v)$ on G_n.

The *centroid* of G_n is equal to the *rumor center* in the sense of [2] when G_n is a tree [8]. Since we are studying a *generalized rumor centrality* for finite $|V|$ (and thus a *generalized rumor center*) here, we shall call the rumor center in the sense of [2] as the *centroid* for clarity.

3 Trees with a Single End Vertex

Let us consider the case when G is a regular tree that is finite, e.g., there are leaf vertices each with degree one. Now, consider the rumor graph $G_n \subseteq G$, where G_n only has a single *end vertex* that receives the rumor but does not spread the rumor further. In this section, we study how the influence of this single *end vertex* in G_n affects the maximum likelihood estimation performance in finding the rumor culprit.

In particular, we compare this single end vertex special case with a naive prediction that assumes an underlying *infinite graph*. This illustrates that ignoring the boundary effect in the finite graph ultimately leads to a wrong estimate and thus requires an in-depth analysis and new rumor source detection algorithm design for the general case of *finite graphs*.

3.1 Impact of Boundary Effects on $P(G_n|v)$

Example 1 Consider G as a finite 3-regular tree and $G_5 \subseteq G$ as shown in Fig. 1. Consider $P(G_5|v_1)$ and with a spreading order $\sigma : v_1 \to v_2 \to v_5 \to v_3 \to v_4$, we have $P(\sigma|v_1) = (1/3) \cdot (1/4) \cdot (1/3) \cdot (1/4)$. Had v_5 not been the end vertex, then $P(\sigma|v_1) = (1/3) \cdot (1/4) \cdot (1/5) \cdot (1/6)$. This demonstrates that the order at which the rumor spreads to the end vertex v_5 is important when computing $P(\sigma|v_1)$. Table 1 lists down all the spreading orders sorted according to the position of v_5. In particular, $P(G_5|v_1) = 34/720$. We also have $P(G_5|v_4) = P(G_5|v_3) = 7/720$ by symmetry, and $P(G_5|v_2) = 40/720$. Now, observe that v_1 is the *centroid*, but $P(G_5|v_1) < P(G_5|v_2)$, and thus $\hat{v}$ is not v_1.

Example 1 reveals some interesting properties of boundary effects due to even a single end vertex:

- $P(\sigma_i|v)$ increases with how soon the end vertex appears in σ_i (as ordered from left to right of σ_i).

Fig. 1 Example of G as a finite 3-regular tree and G_n as a subtree with a single end vertex $v_e = v_5$. The maximum likelihood estimate $\hat{v}$ is v_2, while a naive application of the rumor centrality in [2], i.e., the centroid v_c of G_n, yields v_1

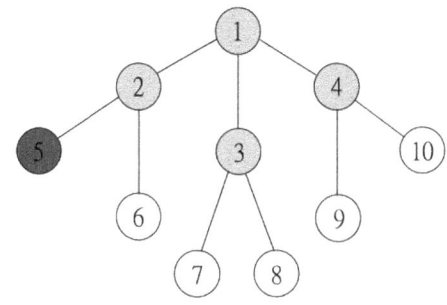

Table 1 Numerical example of $P(\sigma_i|G_5)$ using G_5 in Fig. 1

σ_i	Spreading order	$P(\sigma_i|G_5)$	σ_i	Spreading order	$P(\sigma_i|G_5)$
σ_1	v_1, v_2, v_5, v_3, v_4	$\frac{1}{144}$	σ_7	v_1, v_2, v_3, v_4, v_5	$\frac{1}{360}$
σ_2	v_1, v_2, v_5, v_4, v_3	$\frac{1}{144}$	σ_8	v_1, v_2, v_4, v_3, v_5	$\frac{1}{360}$
σ_3	v_1, v_3, v_2, v_5, v_4	$\frac{1}{240}$	σ_9	v_1, v_3, v_2, v_4, v_5	$\frac{1}{360}$
σ_4	v_1, v_4, v_2, v_5, v_3	$\frac{1}{240}$	σ_{10}	v_1, v_3, v_4, v_2, v_5	$\frac{1}{360}$
σ_5	v_1, v_2, v_3, v_5, v_4	$\frac{1}{240}$	σ_{11}	v_1, v_4, v_2, v_3, v_5	$\frac{1}{360}$
σ_6	v_1, v_2, v_4, v_5, v_3	$\frac{1}{240}$	σ_{12}	v_1, v_4, v_3, v_2, v_5	$\frac{1}{360}$

- When there is at least one end vertex in G_n, then $P(G_n|v)$ is no longer proportional to $|M(v, G_n)|$.

This means that $P(\sigma_i|v)$ is no longer a constant for each i, and is dependent on the position of the *end vertex* in each spreading order. We proceed to compute $P(\sigma_i|v)$ as follows. For brevity of notation, let v_e be the end vertex and define

$$M_v^{v_e}(G_n, k) = \{\sigma \,|\, v_e \text{ is on the } k\text{th position of } \sigma\};$$

$$P_v^{v_e}(G_n, k) = P(\sigma|v), \text{ for } \sigma \in M_v^{v_e}(G_n, k),$$

where $M_v^{v_e}(G_n, k)$ is the set of all the spreading orders starting from v and with v_e at the kth position, and its size is the combinatorial object of interest:

$$m_v^{v_e}(G_n, k) = |M_v^{v_e}(G_n, k)|. \tag{3}$$

Let D be the distance (in terms of number of hops) from v to v_e. Then we have

$$|M(v, G_n)| = \sum_{k=D+1}^{n} m_v^{v_e}(G_n, k). \tag{4}$$

Now, (4) shows that $M(v, G_n)$ can be decomposed into $M_v^{v_e}(G_n, k)$ for $k = D + 1, D + 2, \ldots, n$. This decomposition allows us to handle the boundary effect due to

Fig. 2 G_n as a line graph
with a single end vertex
$v_e = v_{2t+1}$

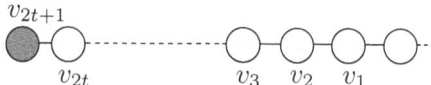

the different position of the end vertex in each spreading order. Let $P_v^{v_e}(G_n, k)$ be the corresponding probability for each k. We can rewrite $P(G_n|v)$ for the finite tree graph as:

$$P(G_n|v) = \sum_{k=D+1}^{n} m_v^{v_e}(G_n, k) \cdot P_v^{v_e}(G_n, k). \tag{5}$$

Thus, the rumor source detection problem is to find the vertex $\hat{v}$ that solves

$$P(G_n|\hat{v}) = \max_{v_i \in G_n} P(G_n|v_i). \tag{6}$$

Since $P(G_n|v)$ is no longer proportional to $|M(v, G_n)|$, we now describe how to compute $P(G_n|v)$ in G_n over an underlying d-regular graph G. First, consider $P_v^{v_e}(G_n, k)$ and let $z_d(i) = (i-1)(d-2)$, then

$$P_v^{v_e}(G_n, k) = \prod_{i=1}^{k-1} \frac{1}{d + z_d(i)} \cdot \prod_{i=k-1}^{n-2} \frac{1}{d + z_d(i) - 1}, \tag{7}$$

where the first factor of $P_v^{v_e}(G_n, k)$ in (7) is the probability that k vertices are infected once the rumor reaches the end vertex, i.e., v_e is the kth vertex infected in G_n, and the second factor is the probability that all remaining $n - k$ vertices are infected thereafter. On the other hand, the value of $m_v^{v_e}(G_n, k)$ in (3) is dependent on the network topology, and thus there is no closed-form expression in general (though when G_n is a line, a closed-form expression for $m_v^{v_e}(G_n, k)$ is given in (8)). We now use this special case to demonstrate how the end vertex affects the probability $P(G_n|v)$.

3.2 Analytical Characterization of Likelihood Function

Suppose G is a finite degree-regular tree and G_n is a line graph with a single end vertex. Without loss of generality, suppose n is odd (to ensure a unique v_c) and $n = 2t + 1$ for some t. Label all the vertices in G_n as shown in Fig. 2. To compute $P(G_n|v_i)$ for $v_i \in G_n$, from (5) and (7), we already have $P_{v_i}^{v_e}(G_n, k)$, so we need to compute $m_{v_i}^{v_e}(G_n, k)$. The enumeration of $m_{v_i}^{v_e}(G_n, k)$ can be accomplished in polynomial-time complexity with a path-counting message-passing algorithm (see, e.g., Chapter 16 in [12]). In particular, we have a closed-form expression for $m_v^{v_e}(G_n, k)$ given by:

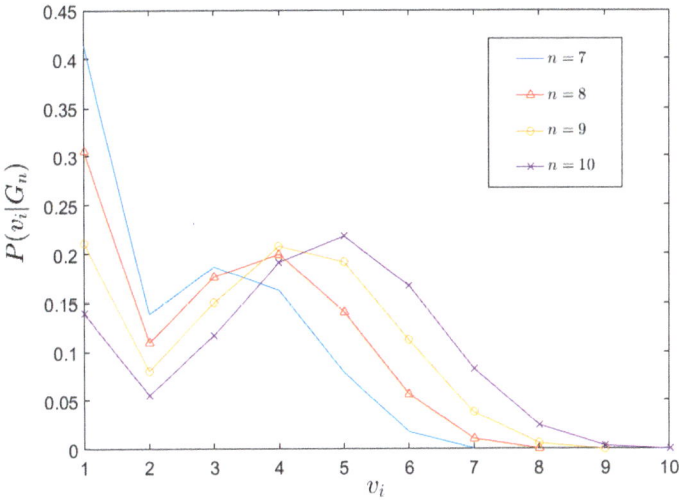

Fig. 3 $P(G_n|v)$, where G_n is a line graph with a single end vertex v_1 over an underlying 4-regular finite graph. Observe that v_1 in this figure is corresponding to v_{2t+1} in Fig. 2

$$m_{v_i}^{v_e}(G_n, k) = \binom{k-2}{k-n+i-1},\tag{8}$$

when $i \neq n$. Thus, we have the following analytical formula for $P(G_n|v_i)$:

$P(G_n|v_i) =$

$$\begin{cases} \prod_{l=1}^{n-1} \dfrac{1}{z_d(l)+1}, & i = n; \\ \sum_{k=n-i+1}^{n} \binom{k-2}{k-n+i-1} \cdot P_{v_i}^{v_e}(G_n, k), & \text{otherwise,} \end{cases}\tag{9}$$

where $P_{v_i}^{v_e}(G_n, k)$ is given in (7).

In (9), we suppose that n is odd. Using (9), let us numerically compute $P(G_n|v_i)$ for all v_i in Fig. 3, where G is a 4-regular tree and G_n is a line graph with a single end vertex $v_e = v_n$ as boundary for different values of $n = 7, 8, 9, 10$. The x-axis is the vertex v_i where $i = 1, 2, \ldots, 10$, and the y-axis plots $P(G_n|v_i = v^\star)$. As shown in Fig. 3, the influence due to the end vertex on $P(G_n|v_i = v^\star)$ dominates that of the centroid when $n = 7, 8, 9$. However, when $n = 10$, the influence due to the centroid v_c on $P(G_n|v_i)$ dominates that of the end vertex v_e.

Theorem 1 *Suppose G is a d-regular graph ($d > 2$) with finite order. If G_n is a line graph with a single end vertex, then $\exists j$ such that $P(G_n|v_c) > P(G_n|v_e)$ when $n > j$.*

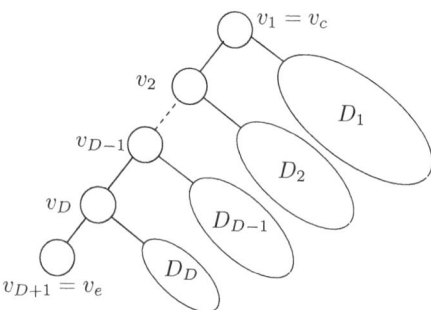

Fig. 4 Theorem 2 illustrates a unique optimality feature that $\hat{v}$ is located on the path from v_c to v_e, i.e., $\hat{v} \in \{v_1, v_2, \ldots, v_{D+1}\}$. Denote the distance (number of hops) from v_c to v_e as D, and let P denote the path from v_c to v_e where $P = (v_1, v_2, lots, v_{D+1})$. We define $D_i = \{ v \in G_n |$ the path from v to v_e containing $v_i \}$, i.e., D_i is a set of subtree vertices as illustrated

Remark When n increases, the location of v_c in G_n converges to a neighborhood as n grows larger.

Example 2 To verify Theorem 1, we plot $P(G_n|v_i)$ for an example of a line G_n with G being a finite 4-regular graph in Fig. 3. Clearly, we have $j = 9$.

Theorem 1 implies that, for any d-regular underlying graph, when G_n is a line with a single end vertex, the influence of the end vertex v_e on $P(v_i|G_n)$ decreases monotonically as n grows. In fact, this reduces to the special case in [2], when n goes to infinity asymptotically, i.e., $\hat{v}$ is the centroid v_c.

3.3 Optimality Characterization of Likelihood Estimate

From (5), we observe that, in addition to the spreading order, the distance (number of hops) between the end vertex and v also affects the likelihood probability $P(G_n|v)$. Let v_c and v_p be two adjacent vertices in G_n with $|M(v_c, G_n)| > |M(v_p, G_n)|$. Suppose G_n has an end vertex v_e and assume that v_c is closer to v_e than v_p. Then, these two assumptions may lead us to $P(G_n|v_c) > P(G_n|v_p)$. We formalize this main optimality result that characterizes the probabilistic inference performance between any two adjacent vertices and the location of $\hat{v}$ in G_n with a single end vertex v_e (Fig. 4).

Theorem 2 *Let G be a tree with finite order and $G_n \subseteq G$ be a subtree of G with a single end vertex $v_e \in G_n$, then the maximum likelihood estimator $\hat{v}$ with maximum probability $P(G_n|v)$ is located on the path from the centroid v_c to v_e.*

3.4 Likelihood Ratio Between Centroid and End Vertex on Different Network Topology

We further elaborate how the network topology affects the search of $\hat{v}$ to either v_c or v_e. Observe that for any two infected subgraph G_n and G'_n with the same underlying graph G, if G_n is not isomorphic to G'_n, then the probability $P(G_n|v)$ for each v is not the same. In other words, the topology of G_n affects the probability $P(G_n|v)$. For G_n and G'_n, if there exists an axis of symmetry of G_n such that G'_n can be obtained by rotating G_n along this axis, then for any $v_i \in G_n$ and its corresponding vertex $v'_i \in G_n$, we have $P(G_n|v_i) = P(G_n|v'_i)$.

In the following, we consider the likelihood ratio between v_c and v_e,

$$
\begin{aligned}
\frac{P(G_n|v_c)}{P(G_n|v_e)} &= \frac{\sum_{k=2}^n m_{v_c}^{v_e}(G_n, k) \cdot P_{v_c}^{v_e}(G_n, k)}{|M(v_e, G_n)| \cdot P_{v_e}^{v_e}(G_n, 1)} \\
&> \frac{P_{v_c}^{v_e}(G_n, n) \cdot \sum_{k=2}^n m_{v_c}^{v_e}(G_n, k)}{|M(v_e, G_n)| \cdot P_{v_e}^{v_e}(G_n, 1)} \\
&= \frac{P_{v_c}^{v_e}(G_n, n) \cdot |M(v_c, G_n)|}{P_{v_e}^{v_e}(G_n, 1) \cdot |M(v_e, G_n)|}.
\end{aligned}
$$

Assume that n and d is fixed, then $P_{v_c}^{v_e}(G_n, n)/P_{v_e}^{v_e}(G_n, 1)$ is a constant, and the lower bound of the likelihood ratio can be written as

$$
\frac{P(G_n|v_c)}{P(G_n|v_e)} > \rho \cdot \frac{|M(v_c, G_n)|}{|M(v_e, G_n)|}, \tag{10}
$$

where ρ is a function of d and n. From (10), we can conclude that $\hat{v} = v_c$ when $|M(v_c, G_n)|/|M(v_e, G_n)| > 1/\rho$. On the other hand, we have

$$
\frac{P(G_n|v_c)}{P(G_n|v_e)} < \tau \cdot \frac{|M(v_c, G_n)|}{|M(v_e, G_n)|}, \tag{11}
$$

where τ is a function of d and n. This implies that $\hat{v} = v_e$ when $|M(v_c, G_n)|/|M(v_e, G_n)| < 1/\tau$. For simplicity, we fix n and d to analyze the affect of the network topology on $|M(v_c, G_n)|/|M(v_e, G_n)|$.

Theorem 3 *Assume that the size n and the degree are fixed. Let $\hat{G}_n$ be the graph with $d(v_c, v_e) = \lfloor (n-1)/2 \rfloor$, and $\hat{g}_n$ be the graph with $d(v_c, v_e) = 1$. Then we have*

$$
\hat{G}_n = \underset{G_n}{\text{argmax}} \frac{|M(v_c, G_n)|}{|M(v_e, G_n)|},
$$

$$
\hat{g}_n = \underset{G_n}{\text{argmin}} \frac{|M(v_c, G_n)|}{|M(v_e, G_n)|},
$$

Fig. 5 An example of a star graph with eight vertices

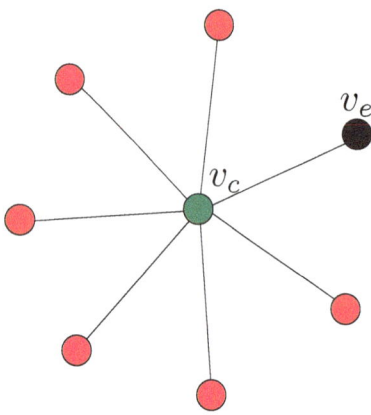

where $\hat{G}_n$ and $\hat{g}_n$ each represents a class of network topology that leads to the extreme value of the ratio

$$|M(v_c, G_n)|/|M(v_e, G_n)|.$$

Theorem 3 reveals that when the distance $d(v_c, v_e)$ reaches its maximum value, then the probability that $\hat{v} = v_c$ is greater than the case when $d(v_c, v_e) < \lfloor (n - 1)/2 \rfloor$. Note that in Theorem 1, we showed that there exists a threshold j such that if $n > j$, then $P(G_n|v_c) > P(G_n|v_e)$. Assume that G_n is a graph with maximum ratio $|M(v_c, G_n)|/|M(v_e, G_n)|$, and G_n' is the graph with

$$|M(v_c', G_n')|/|M(v_e', G_n')| < |M(v_c, G_n)|/|M(v_e, G_n)|.$$

Combining Theorems 1 and 3, we can conclude that the threshold $j' > j$, where j' is the threshold of n such that $\hat{v}$ switches from v_e' to v_c'.

Theorem 4 *Given a fixed d and let G_n be a star graph with a single end vertex v_e and $n < d$, then $\hat{v}$ is always v_e.*

Theorem 4 reveals how the distance $d(v_c, v_e)$ and the ratio $|M(v_c, G_n)|/|M(v_e, G_n)|$ affect the likelihood in an extreme case: a star graph.

Example 3 Let G_n be a star graph as shown in Fig. 5 with the center vertex as the centroid v_c and only one of G_n's leaves as the end vertex v_e. The likelihood ratio $|M(v_c, G_n)|/|M(v_e, G_n)|$ reaches the minimum possible value as compared to the line graph illustrated by Theorem 3. This means that, for a star graph, $P(G_n|v)$ is dominated by v_e, therefore, $\hat{v} = v_e$. However, if we keep adding new vertices to G_n such that $n > d$, then G_n is no longer a star graph, which means that $\hat{v}$ switches from v_e to v_c eventually when n becomes sufficiently large.

4 Trees with Multiple End Vertices

In this section, we consider the case when G_n has more than a single end vertex (naturally, this also means $d > 2$ in G ruling out the trivial case of G being a line). The key insight from the single end vertex analysis still holds: Once the rumor reaches an end vertex in G, $\hat{v}$ can be located near this very first infected end vertex. In addition, the algorithm design approach is to decompose the graph into subtrees to narrow the search for the maximum likelihood estimate solution. To better understand the difficulty of solving the general case, we start with a special case: The entire finite underlying network is infected, i.e., $G_n = G$, then $P(G_n|v) = 1/n$ for each vertex in G_n, as each vertex is equally likely to spread the rumor to all the other vertices in G to yield $G_n = G$. In this case, $P(G_n|\hat{v})$ is exactly the minimum detection probability. For example, consider a 3-regular underlying graph G with 10 vertices. Figure 6 illustrates the detection probability as the number of end vertices in G_n increases with increasing n as the rumor spreads. This means that the problem is harder to solve when the number of end vertices increases.

Note that when there is no end vertex, G_n is composed of four vertices of the inner part of G. We can see that as the number of end vertices increases, $P(G_n|\hat{v})$ decreases to $1/10$. Unlike those previous results, when G is infinitely large, then as G_n growing, the detection probability will converge to some specific number rather than decreasing to $1/n$. So the bound of $P(G_n|\hat{v})$ given in previous study is not suitable for the case with end vertices. Therefore, when simulating the rumor spreading in a network, we will set an upper bound n/k of the number of end vertices where k is some integer greater than 1, once the number of end vertices in G_n reaches to n/k, then we will stop the spreading process.

4.1 Degree-Regular Tree ($d \geq 3$) Special Case: G_n is Broom-Shaped

In Sect. 3, we have shown that, when G_n is sufficiently large, the effect of the single end vertex on $P(v|G_n)$ for each vertex v on the line graph G_n is dominated by the centroid. Now, we study the effect of multiple end vertices on a class of graph whose topology is richer than the line graph in Sect. 3. In particular, as shown in Fig. 7, we add end vertices to v_{2t}, so that when G is d-regular, then there will be at most $d - 1$ end vertices in G_n. We call this the *broom* graph. We can compute $P(v|G_n)$ by extending the result in Sect. 3. Let $P_{v_i}^{\{e_1, e_2, ..., e_k\}}(\{h_1, h_2, \ldots, h_k\}, G_n)$ be the probability of the spreading order starting from v_i with the end vertex set $\{e_1, e_2, \ldots, e_k\}$ and their position set $\{h_1, h_2, \ldots, h_k\}$ in this spreading order. We do not assume that h_i is the position of e_i, as it can be the position of any end vertex in G_n. The probability $P_{v_i}^{\{e_1, e_2, ..., e_k\}}(\{h_1, h_2, \ldots, h_k\}, G_n)$ can be obtained

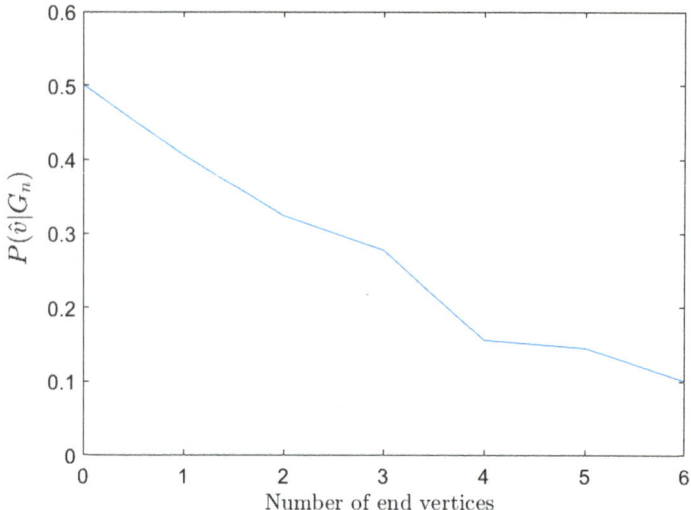

Fig. 6 A numerical plot of $P(\hat{v}|G_n)$ versus the number of end vertices by using the example in Fig. 1

Fig. 7 G_n as a broom graph with k star-like end vertices e_1 to e_k

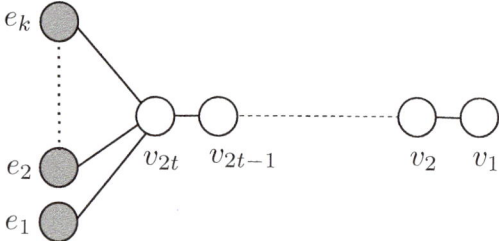

by the same analysis in (7). To compute $m_{v_c}^{\{e_1,e_2,\ldots,e_k\}}(\{h_1, h_2, \ldots, h_k\}, G_n)$, we first consider the line-shaped part of G_n, i.e., the part $\{v_1, v_2, \ldots, v_{2t}\}$, say G_n'. From the previous discussion, we have

$$m_{v_i}^{v_{2t}}(G_n', j) = \binom{j + (2t + i - 1)}{j},$$

and for each spreading order that v_{2t} lies on the jth position, the end vertices $e_1, e_2, \ldots, e_k$ can be placed on any position after the jth position. So for each spreading order in $m_{v_i}^{v_{2t}}(G_n', j)$, there are $k! \cdot \binom{n-k-j+1}{k}$ corresponding spreading orders in G_n. Thus, we have

$$m_{v_i}^{\{e_1,\ldots,e_k\}}(G_n, \{h_1, \ldots, h_k\}) = k! \sum_{j=2t-i+1}^{h_1-1} \binom{j-2}{2t-i-1}. \qquad (12)$$

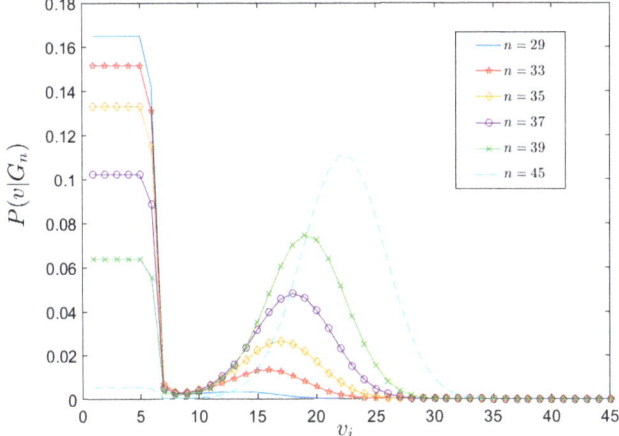

Fig. 8 Probability distribution of each vertex on G_n with five end vertices when G is 6-regular. The y-axis plots the probability $P(v_i|G_n)$ and the x-axis plots the vertex v_i's number i. In particular, $v_1, \ldots, v_5$ are the leaves (end vertices) corresponding to $e_1, \ldots, e_k$ in Fig. 7, where $k = 5$. Observe that the transition phenomenon happens when n grows from 37 to 39

With $P_{v_i}^{\{e_1, e_2, \ldots, e_k\}}$ and $m_{v_i}^{\{e_1, e_2, \ldots, e_k\}}$, we can now compute the probability $P(v_i|G_n)$ by going through all possible $\{h_1, h_2, \ldots, h_k\}$. Figure 8 shows that even though there are five end vertices, the effect of the centroid on $P(v|G_n)$ eventually dominates that of the end vertices as n grows from 37 to 39. These results imply that: When there are more end vertices in G_n, n needs to be sufficiently large to offset the effect of end vertices, i.e., for the transition phenomenon to take place. For other d and n in the *broom* graph, as shown in the proof of Theorem 1, we can prove this in the same way to conclude that, if we fix the number of end vertex, the probability $P(v_c|G_n)$ will be greater than $P(v_e|G_n)$ when n is large enough.

4.2 Message-Passing Algorithm

We propose a message-passing algorithm to find $\hat{v}$ on the finite regular tree G by leveraging the key insights derived in the previous sections. We summarize these features as follows:

1. If there is only a single end vertex v_e in G_n, then $\hat{v}$ is located on the path from v_c to v_e.
2. If $G_n = G$, then for all $v_i \in G_n$, $P(G_n|v_i) = 1/n$.
3. A larger ratio $|M(v_c, G_n)|/|M(v_e, G_n)|$ implies a smaller likelihood of the event that $\hat{v}$ equals to v_e. The ratio is maximum when $d(v_c, v_e) = \lfloor (n-1)/2 \rfloor$, and the minimum happens when $d(v_c, v_e) = 1$.

Fig. 9 An illustration of how
Algorithm 1 works on a tree
graph rooted at v_c with six
end vertices (more shaded).
Observed that v_c branches out
to three subtrees. Here, t_{ML} is
the subtree containing the five
vertices within the dotted line.
The numerical value on the
edge indicates the message
containing the number of end
vertices being counted

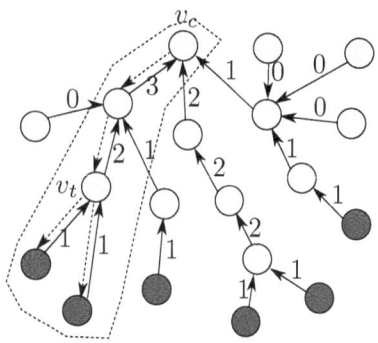

4. If G_n has q end vertices, then there exists an n' such that, if $n > n'$, then
   $P(G_n|v_c) > \max_{1 \le i \le k} \{P(G_n|v_{e_i})\}$. Furthermore, n' increases as q increases.
5. If two vertices v_1 and v_2 are on the symmetric position of G_n, then $P(G_n|v_1) = P(G_n|v_2)$. For example, v_3 and v_4 are topologically symmetric in Fig. 1.

In particular, Feature 1 is the optimality result pertaining to the decomposition of G_n into subtrees to narrow the search for $\hat{v}$. The subtree t_{ML} in G_n corresponds to first finding the decomposed subtree containing the centroid and the likelihood estimate needed for Theorem 2 to apply. Then, Features 3 and 4 identify $\hat{v}$ on a subtree t_{ML} of G_n as Theorem 2 only pinpoints the relative position of $\hat{v}$.

Algorithm 1 first finds the centroid v_c of G_n, and then determines the number of end vertices corresponding to each branch of the centroid v_c. The final step is to collect vertices on the subtree where $\hat{v}$ is, and this leads to a subtree of G_n denoted as t_{ML}. Observe that each step requires $O(n)$ computational time complexity. Observe that t_{ML} in a graph with multiple end vertices is akin to the *path* from the centroid to the end vertex in a rumor graph with a single end vertex in Sect. 3. Finally, we obtain a set κ containing the parent vertices of the leaves of t_{ML} and v_c.

Now, let us use the example in Fig. 9 to illustrate how Algorithm 1 runs. Let G_{19} be the network in Fig. 9 with the six end vertices depicted as more shaded. Suppose v_c is determined by the end of Step 1. Then, Step 2 enumerates the number of end vertices at each branch of the subtrees connected to v_c, and these numbers

---

Algorithm 1 Message-passing algorithm to compute $\hat{v}$ for G_n with multiple end vertices

---

Input: $G_n, \kappa = \{\}$

Step 1: Compute the centroid v_c of G_n.

Step 2: Choose v_c as the root of a tree and use a message-passing algorithm to count the number of end vertices on each branch of this rooted tree.

Step 3: Starting from v_c, and at each hop choose the child with the maximum number of end vertices (if there were more children with the same maximal number of end vertices, then choose all of them). This tree traversal yields a subtree t_{ML} rooted at v_c.

Output: $\kappa = \{$parent vertices of leaves of $t_{ML}, v_c\}$

---

are then passed iteratively from the leaves to v_c. These messages correspond to the numerical value on the edges in Fig. 9. The message in Step 2 is an *upward* (leaf-to-root) message. Step 3 is a message-passing procedure from v_c back to the leaves, which is a *downward* message, and the message is the maximum of number of end vertices in each branch. For example, the message from v_c to $child(v_c)$ is max$\{1, 2, 3\}$ which is 3. Lastly, the second part of Step 3 collects those vertices whose *upward message = downward message*. For example, the left-hand side child of v_c is first added to t_{ML}, and then v_t is added to t_{ML}, and finally, the two leaves on the left-hand side are added to t_{ML}. Observe that t_{ML} must be connected.

4.3   Simulation Results for Finite d-Regular Tree Networks

In our simulation, we set κ to be the set of v_c and parent vertices of the end vertices corresponding to t_{ML}. For example, $\kappa = \{v_t, v_c\}$ is used in the example in Fig. 9. Since as d becomes larger, $|\kappa|$ will grow bigger, for example, the average value of $|\kappa|$ is 6.34 when $d = 3$, and the average value of $|\kappa|$ exceeds 10 if we pick the leaves of t_{ML}.

We simulate the rumor spreading in the degree-regular tree network G for $d = 3, 4, 5, 6$ with $|G| = 1000$ and $|G_n| = 100$. For each d, we simulate a thousand times the spread of a rumor on G by picking $v^\star$ uniformly on G, and compare the average performance of Algorithm 1 and a naive heuristic that simply uses the rumor centrality approach in [8]. To fairly compare these two algorithms, say let $k = |\kappa|$ when Algorithm 1 yields a set with k vertices, then the naive heuristic finds a set of k vertices having the top k maximum $|M(v, G_n)|$ for all v of G_n. Obviously, k depends on the topology of G_n for each run of the simulation, and thus is not a constant in general over than thousand times. To quantify the performance of these two algorithms, let us define the error function of a set S:

$$error(S) = \min\{distance(v, v^\star)|\forall v \in S\}.$$

This is simply the smallest number of hops between $v^\star$ and the nearest vertex in S. Figure 10 shows the distribution of these error hops for both algorithms when the underlying graph G is 4-regular. This illustrates that Algorithm 1 can make a good guess for $P(error(\kappa) \leq 1 \text{ hop}) > 0.70$ in most cases, but there are occasions when the error is large. Table 2 shows the average of the error (number of hops) between the estimate and $v^\star$ for a thousand simulation runs. We can observe that the average error decreases as d grows. The reason is that the number of infected vertices is fixed, and so as d becomes larger, the diameter of the graph becomes smaller, and moreover, the Top-k heuristic always chooses the set of vertex in the "center" of G_n. Hence, the average error decreases.

Fig. 10 Comparing the error distribution (in the number of hops) between Algorithm 1 and the top-k algorithm when G is a 4-regular finite tree

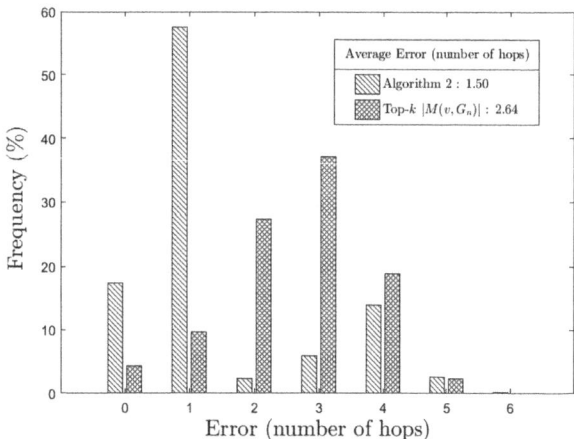

Table 2 Average error (in terms of number of hops) comparing Algorithm 1 and top-k algorithm when G is a d-regular graph, for $d = 3, 4, 5, 6$

d	$|\kappa|$	Algorithm 1	Top-k algorithm
3	6.34	1.44	3.26
4	5.65	1.50	2.64
5	4.05	1.48	2.36
6	3.72	1.40	2.32

4.4 Simulation Results for Finite General Tree Networks

In this section, we evaluate the performance of Algorithm 1 for a finite general tree graph. In particular, the underlying graph G is a tree satisfying the condition, that the degree of each vertex is less than or equal to d_m, where d_m is a fixed positive integer. The construction of G starts with a single vertex v_1, and we then randomly pick an integer, say i, from 0 to d_m to be the degree of v_1, and then assign v_2 to v_{i+1} to be the neighborhood of v_1. Recursively applying these steps, the finite tree graph G is generated with a size of one thousand vertices. The maximum degree in G will be less than or equal to $d_m + 1$. The spreading model used is the same as in the previous simulation. We simulate the rumor spreading for hundreds of times, particularly noting that G is randomly generated and thus in each simulation G is different. Note that, in the d-regular graph simulation, G is however always the same. From Fig. 11, we can observe that the error distribution is similar to the regular tree case in Fig. 10, but with a smaller 1-hop error. The average error is roughly 1-hop larger than the regular case. The number of vertices in κ is surprisingly small as compared to the regular case. Moreover, $|\kappa|$ is decreasing as d_m increases (Table 3).

Fig. 11 Comparing the error distribution (in the number of hops) between Algorithm 1 and the top-k algorithm when G is a general tree with $d_m = 4$

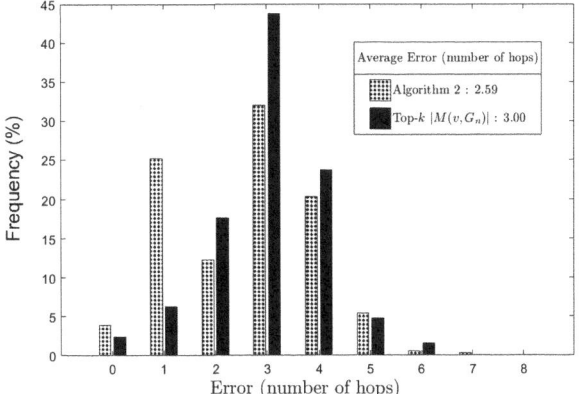

Table 3 Average error (in terms of number of hops) comparing Algorithm 1 and top-k algorithm when G is a general tree with degree of each vertex less or equal to $d_m + 1$, for $d_m = 3, 4, 5, 6, 10$

d_m	$|\kappa|$	Algorithm 1	Top-k algorithm
3	2.82	3.07	3.34
4	2.6	2.59	3.00
5	2.46	2.46	2.85
6	2.45	2.33	2.61
10	2.32	2.00	2.09

5 Conclusion

We proposed a generalized rumor centrality to solve the rumor source detection problem for degree-regular tree graphs with boundary effects. The boundary effect models finite underlying graphs or more complex spreading, and non-trivially affects the likelihood $P(G_n|v)$. For the special case of a single end vertex, we proved a unique optimality characterization that the *most probable source* lies on the path from the centroid to the end vertex. To tackle the general case with multiple end vertices, we proposed a message-passing algorithm to narrow down the search to a set of vertices containing the maximum likelihood estimate. We evaluated our algorithm to be near-optimal that can outperform the heuristic that naively ignores the boundary effects.

References

1. D. Shah, T. Zaman, Rumors in a network: who's the culprit? IEEE Trans. Inf. Theory **57**, 5163–5181 (2011)
2. D. Shah, T. Zaman, Rumor centrality: a universal source detector, in *Proceedings of ACM SIGMETRICS* (2012)

3. L. Vassio, F. Fagnani, P. Frasca, A. Ozdaglar, Message passing optimization of harmonic influence centrality. IEEE Trans. Control Netw. Syst. **1**(1), 109–120 (2014)
4. N. Karamchandani, M. Franceschetti, Rumor source detection under probabilistic sampling, in *Proceedings of IEEE ISIT* (2013)
5. W. Dong, W. Zhang, C.W. Tan, Rooting out the rumor culprit from suspects, in *Proceedings of IEEE ISIT* (2013)
6. W. Luo, W.P. Tay, M. Leng, Identifying infection sources and regions in large networks. IEEE Trans. Signal Process. **61**(11), 2850–2865 (2013)
7. Z. Wang, W. Dong, W. Zhang, C.W. Tan, Rumor source detection with multiple observations: fundamental limits and algorithms, in *Proceedings of ACM SIGMETRICS* (2014)
8. C.W. Tan, P.D. Yu, C.K. Lai, W. Zhang, H.L. Fu, Optimal detection of influential spreaders in online social networks, in *Proceedings of CISS* (2016), pp. 145–150
9. J. Khim, P. Loh, Confidence sets for the source of a diffusion in regular trees. IEEE Trans. Netw. Sci. Eng. **4**(1), 27–40 (2017)
10. N.T.J. Bailey, *The Mathematical Theory of Infectious Diseases and its Applications*, 2nd edn. (Griffin, New York, 1975)
11. B. Zelinka, Medians and peripherians of trees. Arch. Math. **4**(2), 87–95 (1968)
12. D.J.C. Mackay, *Information Theory, Inference and Learning Algorithms*, 1st edn. (Cambridge University Press, Cambridge, 2003)

Robustness of Influence Maximization Against Non-adversarial Perturbations

Sho Tsugawa and Hiroyuki Ohsaki

1 Introduction

The influence maximization problem in social networks has been intensively studied [3, 8, 11, 17, 21, 25, 26, 28, 31]. Influence maximization is a combinatorial optimization problem on a graph that aims to identify a small set of influential nodes (i.e., seed nodes) such that the expected size of the influence cascade triggered by the seed nodes is maximized [17]. More specifically, given a social network G, an influence cascade model, and a small integer k, the influence maximization problem aims to identify a set of k seed nodes in graph G such that the expected number of nodes influenced under the given cascade model initiated by those k seed nodes is maximized. Graph G represents social relationships among individuals, and an influence cascade in the graph represents information diffusion among those individuals. Thus, studying the influence maximization problem is expected to be useful for finding influencers who can disseminate information to many other individuals in viral marketing [17, 29] or who can stop the spreading of misinformation [2].

Several algorithms for the influence maximization problem have been proposed [3, 4, 6, 12, 16, 17, 28, 31, 32]. Since the influence maximization problem is NP-hard [17], both of approximation algorithms and heuristic algorithms have been proposed. Approximation algorithms identify seed nodes based on Monte Carlo simulations of influence spreading on the social network [17]. Since the

S. Tsugawa (✉)
University of Tsukuba, Tsukuba, Ibaraki, Japan
e-mail: s-tugawa@cs.tsukuba.ac.jp

H. Ohsaki
Kwansei Gakuin University, Sanda, Hyogo, Japan
e-mail: ohsaki@kwansei.ac.jp

© Springer Nature Switzerland AG 2019
M. Kaya, R. Alhajj (eds.), *Influence and Behavior Analysis in Social Networks and Social Media*, Lecture Notes in Social Networks,
https://doi.org/10.1007/978-3-030-02592-2_10

Monte Carlo simulation of influence spreading is computationally expensive, the approximation algorithms typically require high computational costs. However, they work effectively for finding influential seed nodes with a theoretical guarantee. Moreover, thanks to the recent efforts of many researchers, the state-of-the-art algorithms can be applied to large-scale networks with millions of nodes [31, 32]. In contrast, heuristic algorithms identify seed nodes without performing simulations by utilizing the topological structure of the social network and by estimating the size of the influence spread among nodes [3, 4, 16]. Although the heuristic algorithms have no theoretical guarantee on their effectiveness, the state-of-the-art heuristic algorithms find influential seed nodes comparable to those found by approximation algorithms with relatively low computational cost [16].

Most influence maximization algorithms proposed in the literature assume complete knowledge of the social network, but, in reality, there is uncertainty about the social networks [13, 14, 25]. Most influence maximization algorithms utilize the complete structure of a social network together with the social tie strength (i.e., influence spread probability) for every pair of individuals. However, such information is difficult to obtain, and, in particular, social ties between individuals are fundamentally difficult to observe [13, 14, 35]. Even if complete data about the structure of Twitter and Facebook were available, we cannot know the social tie strength that must be significantly affected by unobservable factors [14]. Moreover, since human behavior is influenced by many factors, social tie strengths are difficult to estimate even if we can observe many interactions between individuals [14].

Recently, aiming at dealing with social networks with uncertainty, influence maximization for incomplete social networks has been studied [13, 14, 25, 26]. He and Kempe study the stability of the influence maximization approximation algorithm against adversarial perturbations to influence spread probability [13]. He and Kempe have also proposed a new framework called Robust Influence Maximization for identifying influential seed nodes under uncertainty [14]. Mihara et al. study the influence maximization problem when the network is only partially observed [25, 26]. These studies investigate the effectiveness of influence maximization when complete knowledge on social network is not available.

This paper follows these trends and examines the robustness of influence maximization algorithms against non-adversarial perturbations of influence spread probability. He and Kempe focus on the worst-case effectiveness of influence maximization algorithms for finding influential nodes by considering adversarial perturbations of influence spread probability [13]. In contrast, this paper examines the robustness of the algorithms under non-extreme conditions for the algorithms by simulations of random perturbations to influence spread probability. Goyal et al. study the robustness of the algorithms against random uniform noise [11]. We extend their work and examine the effects of three types of random perturbation. Moreover, while existing works focus on the robustness of the approximation algorithms for influence maximization, we examine the robustness of heuristic algorithms as well. Figure 1 illustrates the overview of this work.

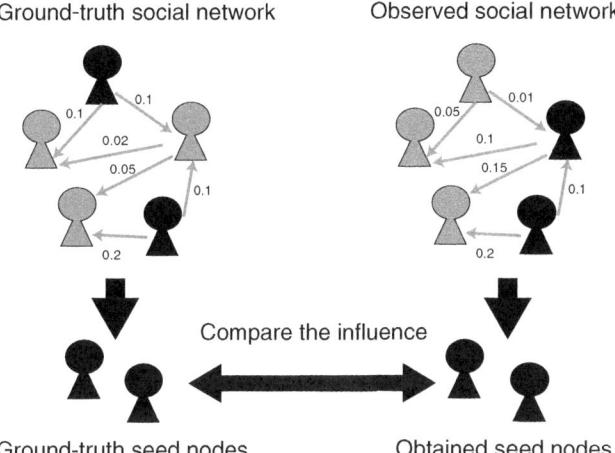

Fig. 1 Overview of this work. An observed social network used for influence maximization algorithms is different from the ground-truth one. Therefore, seed nodes obtained from the observed network may be different from the seed nodes obtained from the ground-truth social network. This paper examines the difference between these seed nodes and the difference between their influence

Our contributions are summarized as follows:

- We show that, even against non-adversarial perturbations, the effectiveness of the state-of-the-art influence maximization algorithms may be significantly degraded. We show that lightweight heuristic algorithms can outperform the state-of-the-art algorithms under large perturbations.
- We study the robustness of heuristic influence maximization algorithms as well as approximation algorithms and show that the effectiveness of the efficient heuristic algorithm IRIE (influence ranking and influence estimation) [16] can also be significantly degraded. To the best of our knowledge, this is the first study to investigate the robustness of heuristic algorithms of influence maximization.
- We study three different types of perturbation and find that the effects of the perturbations on the effectiveness of influence maximization algorithms are very similar. We find that the effectiveness of influence maximization algorithms using influence spread probabilities gradually decreases as the amount of error introduced by the perturbations increases.

This paper is an extended version of our conference short paper [34]. We added extensive analyses (Sects. 5.1 and 5.3) and discussions on the results (Sect. 6).

This paper is organized as follows. Section 2 introduces related works on influence maximization. Section 3 formulates the problem studied in this paper. In Sect. 4, we explain the research methodology. In Sect. 5, we present the results and examine the robustness of influence maximization algorithms against non-adversarial perturbations. Section 6 discusses the implications and the limitations of this work. Finally, Sect. 7 concludes this paper.

2 Related Work

The problem of detecting a set of influential individuals, which is called as the influence maximization problem, was first proposed by Domingos et al. [8, 29] and formulated as an optimization problem by Kempe et al. [17]. Although the influence maximization problem has been studied under several influence cascade models [5, 9, 11, 32], the independent cascade (IC) model [17] is the most popular one. As discussed in Sect. 1, the influence maximization problem under the IC model is NP-hard [17]. However, the objective function of the problem is nonnegative, monotone, and submodular, which gives us the greedy $(1 - 1/e)$-approximation algorithm [17]. Kempe et al. [17] have proposed a simple greedy algorithm for influence maximization. Since the Kempe's algorithm requires high computational costs [3, 4], studies for faster approximation algorithms have been performed until now [12, 28, 31, 32]. Another line of research aims to develop effective heuristic algorithms [4, 16]. Heuristic algorithms avoid accurate estimation of influence spread and aim to find seed nodes with low computational costs. Thanks to these studies, influence maximization algorithms have been shown to be applicable to huge networks with millions of nodes [16, 31, 32]. Recent surveys on influence maximization algorithms can be found in [21, 24, 33].

Most influence maximization algorithms use social tie strengths (i.e., influence spread probabilities) between individuals, and estimating these influence spread probabilities is also an active research topic [7, 10, 30]. These studies propose models for estimating influence spread probabilities from past traces of influence cascades. When sufficient past traces of influence cascades are available, these models are effective, and the estimated influence spread probabilities can be used for influence maximization. However, as discussed in Sect. 1, to obtain correct influence spread probabilities for all pairs of individuals is a fundamentally difficult task, and, therefore, estimation errors are unavoidable. In this paper, we investigate the effects of this estimation error on influence maximization algorithms.

The robustness of influence maximization under uncertainty is a relatively new research topic, but there are some works on this topic in the literature. He and Kempe study the stability of influence maximization against adversarial perturbations of influence spread probability [13]. They show that adversarial perturbations can cause instability of the approximation algorithms for influence maximization, and the effectiveness of the algorithms is significantly degraded. While they focus on the worst-case effectiveness of the algorithms, we consider on more relaxed situations. Goyal et al. [11] and Adiga et al. [1] studied the effects of random noise. We extend their work in the following ways: we examine three types of perturbation, and we investigate the robustness of heuristic algorithms as well as approximation algorithms.

New frameworks of influence maximization under uncertainty have also been proposed. He and Kempe [14] proposed robust influence maximization. They study influence maximization problem when the diffusion model is uncertain. Mihara et al. [25, 26] and Wilder et al. [36] study influence maximization for unknown social networks. The problem is to find influential seed nodes from partially observed social network structure. Zhuang et al. [37] proposed influence maximization for dynamically changing social networks. As we will discuss in Sects. 5 and 6, the results of this work suggest the importance of studying robust influence maximization under uncertainty.

3 Preliminaries and Problem Formulation

We first introduce the notation used in this paper. Let $G = (V, E, P)$ be a weighted directed graph, where V is a set of nodes, E is a set of links, and P is a set of link weights representing influence spread probability. Let $S \subseteq V$ be a subset of nodes in graph G and $\sigma(S)$ be the expected number of active nodes at the end of the process of an influence cascade model when S is the initial set of active nodes (i.e., seed nodes). Table 1 summarizes this notation used in this paper.

Among several influence cascade models, this paper uses the IC model, which is the most popular one [17]. In the IC model, each node is either active or inactive. When node u becomes active at time step t, node u will influence inactive neighbor node v $((u, v) \in E)$ with probability $p_{u,v}$ at the next time step $t + 1$. Namely, node v becomes active with a probability $p_{u,v}$. The probability $p_{u,v}$ is the influence spread probability between node u and v, which is a parameter in the IC model. Note that each node has a single chance to influence each of its neighbors. At time step 0, the nodes selected as seed nodes ($S \subseteq V$) become active, and other nodes are inactive. Then the stochastic process explained above is repeated until no new active nodes are created, at which time the process ends. This paper particularly focuses on the influence maximization with the IC model. The influence maximization problem with the IC model is defined as follows [17].

Problem 1 (Influence Maximization Problem) *Given a social network G, an integer k, the aim is to find a set of seed nodes S (S $\subseteq$ V with |S| = k) such that $\sigma(S)$, which we call the* influence spread, *is maximized under the IC model.*

This paper investigates the robustness of influence maximization algorithms against perturbations of influence spread probability. Let $P = \{p_{u,v}|(u, v) \in E\}$ be the set of the ground-truth probabilities and $P' = \{p'_{u,v}|(u, v) \in E\}$ be the set of estimated or observed (i.e., perturbed) influence spread probabilities. Since

Table 1 Notation used in this paper

G	Ground-truth social network
G'	Observed social network
P	Set of ground-truth influence spread probabilities
P'	Set of estimated influence spread probabilities
S	Set of seed nodes
$\sigma(S)$	Size of influence cascades triggered by seed nodes S

the ground-truth influence spread probability P is generally unknown or difficult to observe, influence maximization algorithms use the estimated probability, P', instead of P. Namely, influence maximization algorithms find seed nodes S' using graph $G' = (V, E, P')$. Let S be the ground-truth set of seed nodes obtained by using the ground-truth graph $G = (V, E, P)$. Then, our research questions are as follows:

(RQ1)   How do seed set S obtained from the ground-truth graph G and the seed set S' obtained from graph G' differ for each algorithm?

(RQ2)   How do influence spread $\sigma(S)$ and $\sigma(S')$ differ for each algorithm?

Note that both $\sigma(S)$ and $\sigma(S')$ are calculated by simulations on graph $G = (V, E, P)$ starting with seed nodes S and S', respectively. We empirically investigate the difference between $\sigma(S)$ and $\sigma(S')$ while changing the strength of perturbations of influence spread probabilities (i.e., the differences between P and P').

4   Methodology

4.1   Networks

We performed experiments on four real social networks: NetHEPT [3], NetPHY [3], Facebook [20], and Wikipedia [19]. In NetHEPT and NetPHY, link (u, v) represents that researcher u and researcher v are co-authors. In Facebook, link (u, v) represents that user u and user v are friends. In Wikipedia, link (u, v) represents that editor u votes for editor v. These networks are widely used for evaluating influence maximization algorithms [3, 4, 12, 15, 17, 18, 22, 23, 31]. Multiple links are simply converted to a single link [13, 25, 37]. Figure 2 shows degree distributions of the four networks.

4.2   Influence Spread Probability and Types of Perturbations

Since the actual influence spread probabilities for the networks are not available, the ground-truth influence spread probabilities $P = \{p_{u,v}|(u, v) \in E\}$ are synthetically generated using the weighted cascade (WC) model [3] on each network. Specifically, on each link (u, v), we use $p_{u,v} = 1/d_v$, where d_v is the in-degree of node v. The WC model is widely used for generating influence spread probabilities for the evaluation of influence maximization algorithms [3, 12, 16, 31].

The estimated probability P' is obtained by introducing perturbations to the ground-truth influence spread probability P. We assume that the estimated influence spread probabilities contain error, and there exist differences between P and P'. However, it is difficult or impossible to know the actual type of error contained in influence spread probabilities used for influence maximization. We therefore adopt

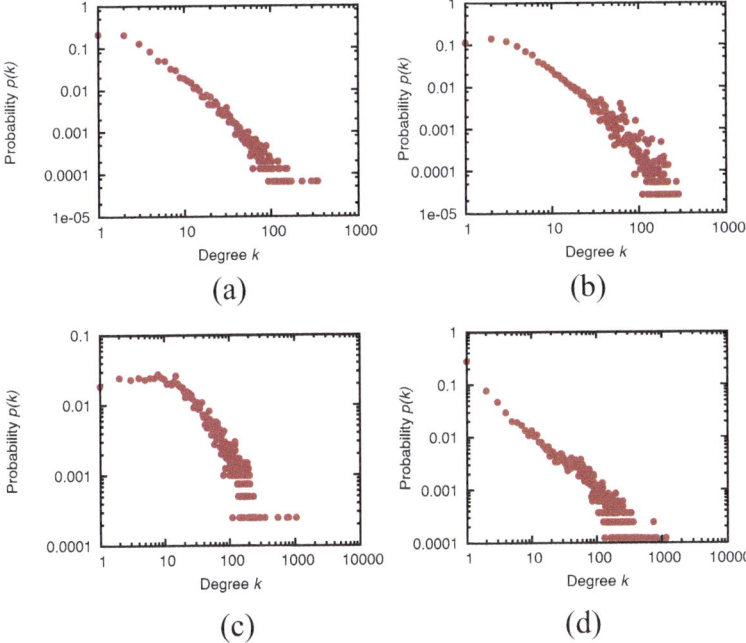

Fig. 2 Degree distributions of the four social networks. (**a**) NetHEPT. (**b**) NetPHY. (**c**) Facebook. (**d**) Wikipedia

three types of simple error patterns rather than try to correctly model the errors. To introduce errors to influence spread probabilities, we used the following three types of non-adversarial perturbation.

Shuffle Perturbation type *Shuffle* assumes the situation where the influence spread probability of some of the links cannot be observed due to incompleteness of data. For randomly selected $1 - \alpha$ of links in graph G, we assign $p'_{u,v} = p_{u,v}$ (i.e., the estimated probability is exactly same as the ground-truth). For the remaining α links, we determine $p'_{u,v}$ by randomly shuffling the influence spread probabilities on them. This procedure is intended to keep the distribution of influence spread probabilities unchanged.

Gaussian Perturbation type *Gaussian* assumes the situation where the influence spread probabilities contain Gaussian noise due to incompleteness of data or modeling error. We assign $p'_{u,v} = \max(0, \min(1, p_{u,v} + x))$, where x is a random variable generated from the Gaussian distribution with mean 0 and standard deviation $\beta\mu$, where μ is the average of $p_{u,v}$.

Uniform Perturbation type *Uniform* assumes the situation where influence spread probabilities are uniformly perturbed within a certain interval due to incompleteness of data or modeling error. We assign $p'_{u,v} = x$, where x is a random variable generated from the uniform distribution over the interval of $[\max(0, (p_{u,v} - \mu\gamma)),$ $\min(1, (p_{u,v} + \mu\gamma))]$, where μ is the average of $p_{u,v}$. Following the previous study [11], we used this type of perturbation.

In the above three types of perturbations, α, β, and γ are parameters controlling the strength of the perturbations, and they are referred to as perturbation strengths in what follows.

4.3 Influence Maximization Algorithms

We use two influence maximization algorithms that are affected by perturbations. One is TIM+ (two-phase influence maximization+) [31], which is a state-of-the-art approximation algorithm for influence maximization that is applicable to huge networks, and the other is IRIE [16], which is an efficient heuristic algorithm. These algorithms have been shown to be effective for several real social networks when complete knowledge of the influence spread probabilities is available.

We also use two lightweight heuristic algorithms that are not affected by perturbations: collective influence (CI) [27] and single discount (Discount) [3]. These two algorithms select seed nodes solely using the topological structure of a social network without using influence spread probability. Discount runs fast, but its effectiveness is not high when compared with TIM+ and IRIE. CI is a recently proposed algorithm that also runs fast, but its effectiveness for influence maximization under the IC model has not yet been explored.

In the following experiments, we generated 100 different sets P', and for each P', seed nodes S' are selected by each algorithm using $G' = (V, E, P')$. We calculated $\sigma(S')$, which is obtained from simulations on the ground-truth graph $G = (V, E, P)$, for each algorithm. The number of simulation runs is 1000, and the number of seed nodes is $k = 50$, which is the default value in [31, 32]. We used $\epsilon = 0.1$ as the parameter of TIM+, which is recommended in [31]. We used $l = 3$ for NetHEPT, NetPHY, and Facebook as the parameter of CI, which is recommended in [27]. We used $l = 2$ for Wikipedia since CI with $l = 3$ could not find influential nodes in this network due to its small shortest path length. For the parameters of IRIE, we used the ones recommended by Jung et al. [16]. Table 2 summarizes characteristics of the networks used in the experiment.

Table 2 Characteristics of networks

	NetHEPT	NetPHY	Facebook	Wikipedia
Number of nodes	15,233	37,149	4039	7115
Number of links	64,470	361,652	176,468	103,689
Average degree	4.232	9.735	43.691	14.5733
Clustering coefficient	0.313	0.744	0.519	0.125
Average shortest path length	5.840	6.259	3.693	3.341
Average of influence spread probability	0.236	0.103	0.023	0.023

5   Results

5.1   Overlap of Seed Nodes

We first address **RQ1**: How do the seed nodes S' obtained from a perturbed graph $G' = (V, E, P')$ and the seed nodes S obtained from the ground-truth graph $G = (V, E, P)$ differ? We obtained seed nodes S' with each algorithm using perturbed graph G' while changing the perturbation strength, α, β, or γ. We also obtained seed nodes S with TIM+ using the ground-truth graph G. We then calculate overlap between S' and S as

$$\text{Overlap} = \frac{|S \cap S'|}{k}. \tag{1}$$

Figures 3, 4, 5, and 6 show the relation between the perturbation strength and Overlap for NetHEPT, NetPHY, Facebook, and Wikipedia, respectively. Note that Discount and CI are not affected by perturbations because these algorithms do not use influence spread probability.

These results show that seed node selections by TIM+ and IRIE become unstable as the perturbation strength increases. Seed node selections of algorithms using

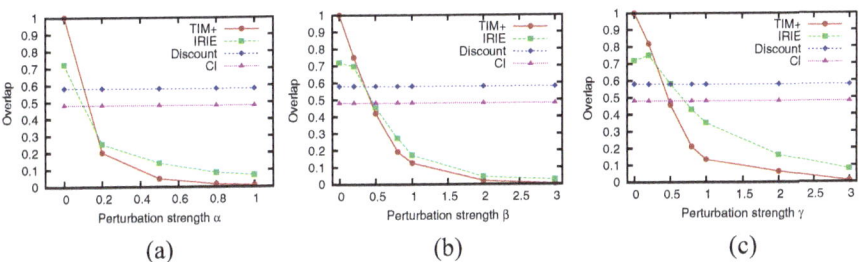

Fig. 3 Overlap between seed nodes obtained from a perturbed graph and those obtained from the ground-truth graph in NetHEPT vs. perturbation strength. (**a**) Shuffle. (**b**) Gaussian. (**c**) Uniform

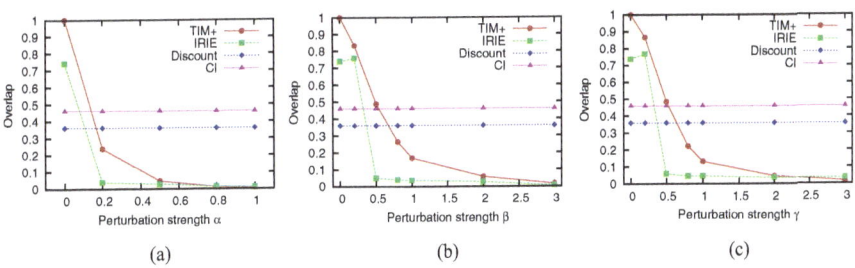

Fig. 4 Overlap between seed nodes obtained from a perturbed graph and those obtained from the ground-truth graph in NetPHY vs. perturbation strength. (**a**) Shuffle. (**b**) Gaussian. (**c**) Uniform

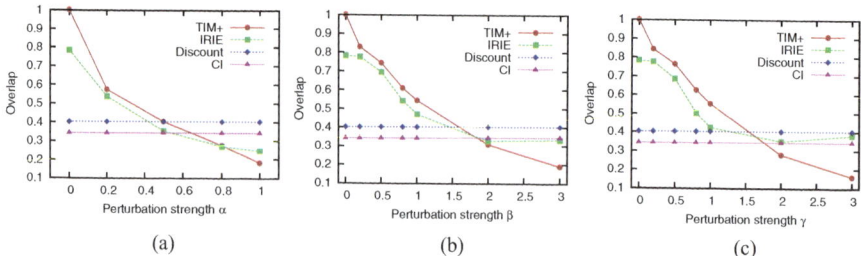

Fig. 5 Overlap between seed nodes obtained from a perturbed graph and those obtained from the ground-truth graph in Facebook vs. perturbation strength. (**a**) Shuffle. (**b**) Gaussian. (**c**) Uniform

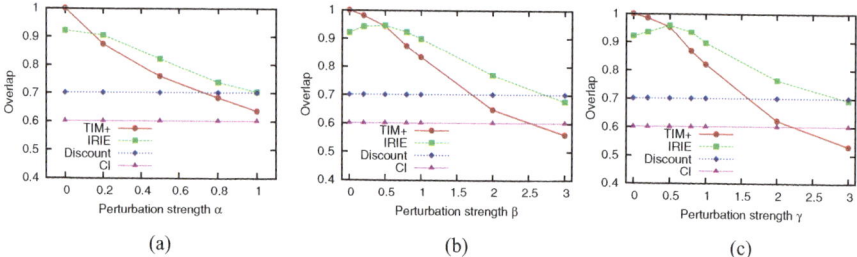

Fig. 6 Overlap between seed nodes obtained from a perturbed graph and those obtained from the ground-truth graph in Wikipedia vs. perturbation strength. (**a**) Shuffle. (**b**) Gaussian. (**c**) Uniform

perturbed probabilities are significantly different from those of TIM+ using ground-truth probabilities, which suggests that TIM+ and IRIE cannot select influential seed nodes when the perturbation strength is large. Particularly in NetHEPT and NetPHY, overlap between ground-truth seed nodes and obtained seed nodes is low even under small perturbations. For instance, when $\alpha = 0.2$, *Overlap* of TIM+ is only approximately 0.2 in NetHEPT and NetPHY.

These results also show that seed nodes selected via TIM+ with ground-truth probabilities and those selected via lightweight heuristic algorithms (i.e., Discount and CI) are also different. But when the perturbation strength is large, the overlaps of TIM+ and IRIE are lower than those of Discount and CI. This suggests that the lightweight heuristic algorithms Discount and CI may outperform TIM+ and IRIE when the perturbation strength is large.

5.2 Influence Spread

We now tackle **RQ2**: How do influence spread $\sigma(S)$ and $\sigma(S')$ differ for each algorithm? We investigate how the effectiveness of the various influence maximization algorithms, as measured by influence spread, is affected by perturbations. We obtain the influence spread achieved by each algorithm while changing the perturbation strength α, β, or γ.

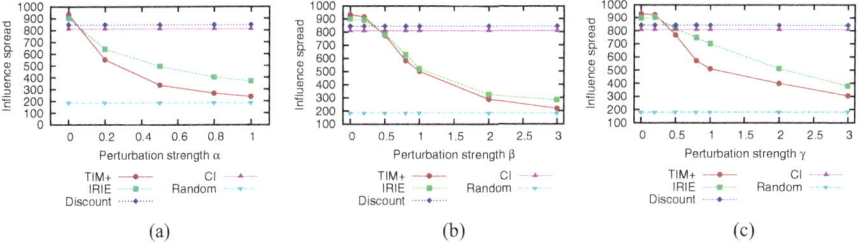

Fig. 7 Influence spread on NetHEPT vs. perturbation strength. (**a**) Shuffle. (**b**) Gaussian. (**c**) Uniform

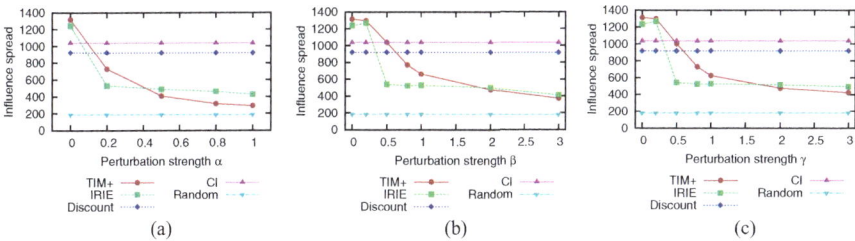

Fig. 8 Influence spread on NetPHY vs. perturbation strength. (**a**) Shuffle. (**b**) Gaussian. (**c**) Uniform

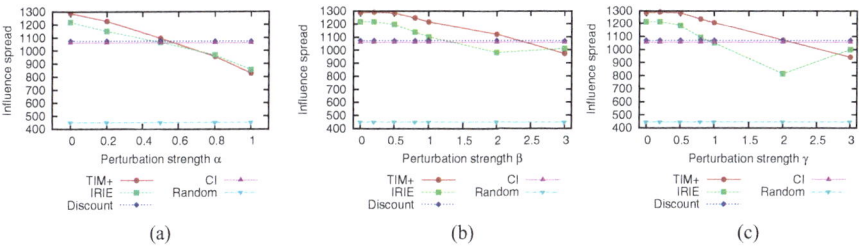

Fig. 9 Influence spread on Facebook vs. perturbation strength. (**a**) Shuffle. (**b**) Gaussian. (**c**) Uniform

Figures 7, 8, 9, and 10 show influence spread achieved by each algorithm when changing the perturbation strength in NetHEPT, NetPHY, Facebook, and Wikipedia, respectively. Note again that influence spreads achieved by Discount and CI are not affected by perturbations. For comparison purposes, results when seed nodes are randomly selected (Random) are included in the figures.

As suggested by the results in the previous subsection, these results indicate that the effectiveness of TIM+ and IRIE degrades as the perturbation strength increases. The influence spreads achieved by TIM+ and IRIE are comparable with those by the lightweight heuristic algorithms (Discount and CI), and, in some cases, they are significantly lower than the spreads achieved by lightweight heuristic algorithms. Particularly in NetHEPT and NetPHY, the effectiveness of TIM+ and

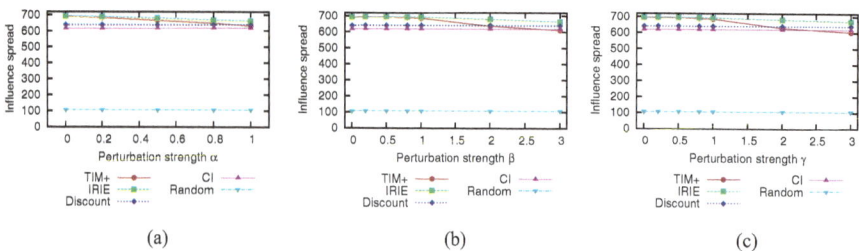

Fig. 10 Influence spread on Wikipedia vs. perturbation strength. (**a**) Shuffle. (**b**) Gaussian. (**c**) Uniform

IRIE is significantly affected by small perturbations. For instance, focusing on the perturbation type Shuffle, TIM+ achieves only approximately 80% by the influence spread of the simple heuristic algorithm (Discount) in NetHEPT and NetPHY even when the perturbation strength is only $\alpha = 0.2$ (i.e., the influence spread probability on 80% of links is correctly observed and the remaining 20% are shuffled). As discussed in Sect. 1, estimating influence spread probability is a fundamentally challenging task, and we expect that this level of perturbations is not uncommon in real situations.

Focusing on the difference among different types of perturbations, we can see that the effects of the three types of perturbations on the influence maximization algorithms are similar. We will conduct detailed investigations on the effects of three types of perturbations in the next subsection.

5.3 Relation Between Amount of Error and Effectiveness of Algorithm

We finally investigate how the amount of error contained in the influence spread probabilities affects the effectiveness of the influence maximization algorithms. We use root-mean-square error (RMSE) between the ground-truth influence spread probability P and the perturbed probability P' for quantifying the amount of error. RMSE of influence spread probabilities is defined as

$$\text{RMSE} = \sqrt{\frac{\sum_{(u,v)\in E}(p_{u,v} - p'_{u,v})^2}{|E|}}. \tag{2}$$

By using RMSE, the effects of different types of perturbations on the influence maximization algorithms can be compared.

Figure 11 shows the relation between RMSE of influence spread probabilities and the influence spread of TIM+ for each network. Figure 12 shows the same results for IRIE. In these figures, three types of perturbations are compared. Figure 11

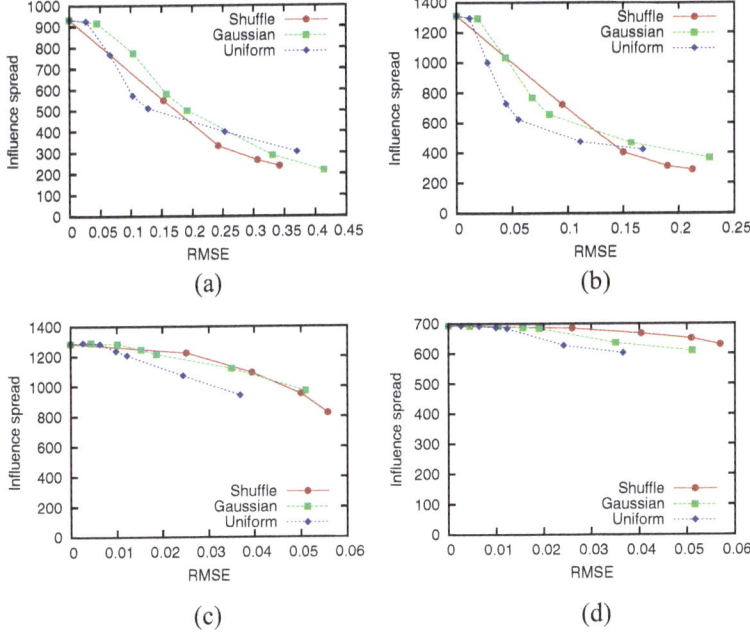

Fig. 11 Influence spread of TIM+ vs. RMSE of influence spread probabilities. (**a**) NetHEPT. (**b**) NetPHY. (**c**) Facebook. (**d**) Wikipedia

indicates that the influence spread of TIM+ gradually decreases as RMSE of influence spread probabilities increases. Moreover, we can find that this tendency is similar for three types of perturbations. This suggests that, for non-adversarial perturbations, we can roughly estimate the influence spread of each algorithm under perturbations only from the amount of error contained in the influence spread probabilities even if the type of error is unknown. Moreover, this also suggests that the reducing RMSE of influence spread probabilities contributes to increase the influence spread almost linearly. Figure 12 also indicates that the influence spread of IRIE decreases as RMSE of influence spread probabilities increases. We can also find from Fig. 12b that the effectiveness of IRIE in NetPHY with the small amount of error is significantly lower compared with that in other networks and that of TIM+ in NetPHY. This result suggests that IRIE is less robust than TIM+ in some networks.

We next compare the effects of perturbations on influence spread of the algorithms among different networks. Figures 13 and 14 show the relation between RMSE and the normalized influence spread of TIM+ and IRIE for each type of perturbation. The normalized influence spread is defined as $\sigma(S')/\sigma(S)$ where S is a set of seed nodes obtained using the ground-truth influence spread probabilities and S' is a set of seed nodes obtained using the perturbed influence spread probabilities. Different networks are compared in the figures. This result suggests that TIM+ and

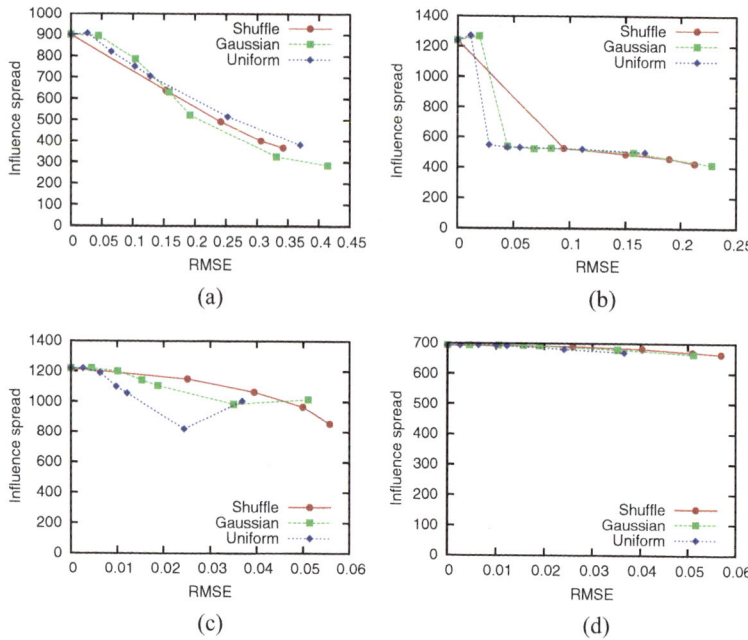

Fig. 12 Influence spread of IRIE vs. RMSE of influence spread probabilities. (**a**) NetHEPT. (**b**) NetPHY. (**c**) Facebook. (**d**) Wikipedia

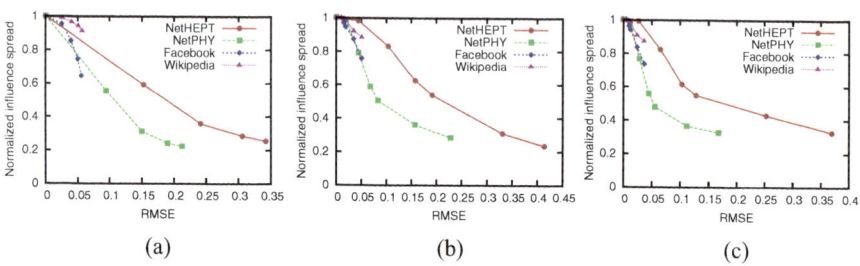

Fig. 13 Normalized influence spread of TIM+ vs. RMSE of influence spread probabilities. (**a**) Shuffle. (**b**) Gaussian. (**c**) Uniform

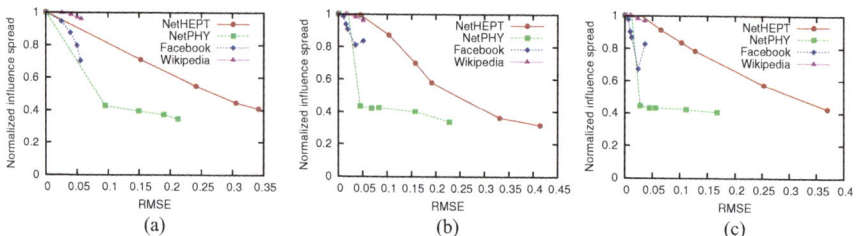

Fig. 14 Normalized influence spread of IRIE vs. RMSE of influence spread probabilities. (**a**) Shuffle. (**b**) Gaussian. (**c**) Uniform

IRIE are relatively more robust against perturbations in NetHEPT and less robust in NetPHY. While Fig. 10 suggests that TIM+ and IRIE are robust in Wikipedia, Fig. 13 reveals that the effectiveness of the algorithms in Wikipedia and other networks are similar when RMSE of influence spread probabilities are similar.

6   Discussion

6.1   Implication

Our results show the instability of the state-of-the-art influence maximization algorithms. Although our experiments used non-adversarial perturbations, the effectiveness of the algorithms was significantly degraded. As discussed in Sect. 1, uncertainty is unavoidable for real social networks. Therefore, our results suggest that influence maximization algorithms may fail to correctly identify influencers in real viral marketing scenarios.

Moreover, our results show that using lightweight heuristic algorithms, such as CI and Discount, is a reasonable approach when the influence spread probability is not accurately known. From the overlap results, we see that the seed nodes selected by the lightweight algorithms are far from the optimal ones (i.e., those selected by TIM+). However, in terms of influence spread, lightweight algorithms are not so bad and achieve over 80% of the influence spread of TIM+ regardless of the perturbation strength. Our past findings have also shown that lightweight heuristics are reasonable for influence maximization on unknown graphs [25, 26]. Therefore, in uncertain situations, one possible approach is using such simple heuristic algorithms that are based on only topological structure.

One direction of future research suggested by the results is the development of methods for estimating influence spread probabilities. If the probability is correctly known, approximation algorithms perform well; but, if they are not known, the algorithm may fail. Fast and scalable algorithms have been developed recently [31, 32], and the scalability issues of influence maximization algorithms are almost solved. Therefore, in future research, it will be more important to study the methods of estimating influence spread probabilities [7, 10, 30].

Another direction suggested by the results is the development of influence maximization algorithms that are robust against uncertainty. While the influence maximization problem when the network structure is uncertain has been studied [25, 26, 36], the influence maximization when the influence diffusion process is uncertain has just begun to be studied [14]. Our results show the importance of such research.

6.2 Limitations

One limitation of this paper is that we defined ground-truth influence spread probabilities using only the WC model. Because the actual ground-truth influence spread probabilities are not available, we chose to synthetically generate them using the WC model. However, the definition of the ground-truth probability may affect the results.

Another limitation is that we only use the IC model as an influence cascade model. Although the IC model is widely used [3, 13, 16, 17, 31, 32] and expected to be a suitable model for influence cascade, investigating the robustness of influence maximization based on other cascade models such as linear threshold model [17] is an important future work.

Moreover, we need to investigate the relation between the robustness of algorithms and the characteristics of the network topology. Although we used four real social networks, their topological characteristics may differ from those of other networks. Results in Sect. 5.3 show that TIM+ is more robust against perturbations in NetHEPT and less robust in NetPHY. Investigating the cause of such difference is an important future work.

7 Conclusion

In this paper, we have investigated the robustness of influence maximization against non-adversarial perturbations in influence spread probabilities. We introduced three types of non-adversarial perturbation to the influence spread probabilities between individuals in four real social networks. Then, we investigated the effectiveness of influence maximization algorithms in the networks through simulation experiments. Our experimental results have shown that the effectiveness of the state-of-the-art influence maximization algorithms is significantly degraded under large perturbations. Moreover, the results suggest that lightweight heuristic algorithms are better than the state-of-the-art algorithms under situations of great uncertainty. Overall, our study indicates the importance of developing influence maximization algorithms that are robust against uncertainty in social networks.

Acknowledgment This work was partly supported by JSPS KAKENHI Grant Number 16H02815 and 16K20931.

References

1. A. Adiga, C. Kuhlman, H. Mortveit, A.K.S. Vullikanti, Sensitivity of diffusion dynamics to network uncertainty, in *Proceedings of the 27th AAAI Conference on Artificial Intelligence (AAAI'13)* (2013), pp. 2–8

2. C. Budak, D. Agrawal, A. El Abbadi, Limiting the spread of misinformation in social networks, in *Proceedings of the 20th International Conference on World Wide Web (WWW'11)*, March 2011, pp. 665–674
3. W. Chen, Y. Wang, S. Yang, Efficient influence maximization in social networks, in *Proceedings of the 15th ACM SIGKDD International Conference on Knowledge Discovery and Data Mining (KDD'09)*, June 2009, pp. 199–208
4. W. Chen, C. Wang, Y. Wang, Scalable influence maximization for prevalent viral marketing in large scale social networks, in *Proceedings of the 16th ACM SIGKDD International Conference on Knowledge Discovery and Data Mining (KDD'10)* July, 2010, pp. 1029–1038
5. W. Chen, W. Lu, N. Zhang, Time-critical influence maximization in social networks with time-delayed diffusion process, in *Proceedings of the Twenty-Sixth AAAI Conference on Artificial Intelligence (AAAI'12)*, July 2012, pp. 592–598
6. E. Cohen, D. Delling, T. Pajor, R.F. Werneck, Sketch-based influence maximization and computation: scaling up with guarantees, in *Proceedings of the 23rd ACM International Conference on Information and Knowledge Management (CIKM'14)*, July 2014, pp. 629–638
7. H. Daneshmand, M. Gomez-Rodriguez, L. Song, B. Schoelkopf, Estimating diffusion network structures: recovery conditions, sample complexity & soft-thresholding algorithm, in *Proceedings of the 31st International Conference on Machine Learning (ICML'14)* (2014), pp. 793–801
8. Domingos, P., Richardson, M.: Mining the network value of customers, in *Proceedings of the 7th ACM SIGKDD International Conference on Knowledge Discovery and Data Mining (KDD'01)*, August 2001, pp. 57–66
9. M. Gomez-Rodriguez, L. Song, N. Du, H. Zha, B. Schölkopf, Influence estimation and maximization in continuous-time diffusion networks. ACM Trans. Inf. Syst. (TOIS) **34**(2), 9:1–9:33 (2016)
10. A. Goyal, F. Bonchi, L.V. Lakshmanan, Learning influence probabilities in social networks, in *Proceedings of the 3rd ACM International Conference on Web Search and Data Mining (WSDM'10)*, February 2010, pp. 241–250
11. A. Goyal, F. Bonchi, L.V. Lakshmanan, A data-based approach to social influence maximization. Proc. VLDB Endowment **5**(1), 73–84 (2011)
12. A. Goyal, W. Lu, L.V. Lakshmanan, CELF++: optimizing the greedy algorithm for influence maximization in social networks, in *Proceedings of the 20th International Conference Companion on World Wide Web (WWW'11)*, March 2011, pp. 47–48
13. X. He, D. Kempe, Stability of influence maximization (April 2015). http://arxiv.org/pdf/1501. 04579v2.pdf
14. X. He, D. Kempe, Robust influence maximization, in *Proceedings of the 22nd ACM SIGKDD International Conference on Knowledge Discovery and Data Mining (KDD'16)*, August 2016 (ACM, New York, 2016), pp. 885–894
15. Z. Huiyuan, T.N. Dinh, M.T. Thai, Maximizing the spread of positive influence in online social networks, in *Proceedings of the 33rd IEEE International Conference on Distributed Computing Systems (ICDCS'13)*, July 2013, pp. 317–326
16. K. Jung, W. Heo, W. Chen, IRIE: scalable and robust influence maximization in social networks, in *Proceedings of the 12th IEEE International Conference on Data Mining (ICDM'12)*, December 2012, pp. 918–923
17. D. Kempe, J.M. Kleinberg, E. Tardos, Maximizing the spread of influence through a social network, in *Proceedings of the 9th ACM SIGKDD International Conference on Knowledge Discovery and Data Mining (KDD'03)*, August 2003, pp. 137–146
18. H. Lamba, R. Narayanam, A novel and model independent approach for efficient influence maximization in social networks, in *Proceedings of the 14th International Conference on Web Information Systems Engineering (WISE'13)*, October 2013, pp. 73–87
19. J. Leskovec, D. Huttenlocher, J. Kleinberg, Signed networks in social media, in *Proceedings of the SIGCHI Conference on Human Factors in Computing Systems (CHI'10)*, April 2010, pp. 1361–1370

20. J. Leskovec, J.J. Mcauley, Learning to discover social circles in ego networks, in *Proceedings of the Neural Information Processing Systems (NIPS'12)*, December 2012, pp. 539–547
21. Y. Li, J. Fan, Y. Wang, K.L. Tan, Influence maximization on social graphs: a survey. IEEE Trans. Knowl. Data Eng. **30**(10), 1852–1872 (2018)
22. Q. Liu, B. Xiang, E. Chen, H. Xiong, F. Tang, Y.X. Jeffrey, Influence maximization over large-scale social networks: a bounded linear approach, in *Proceedings of the 23rd ACM International Conference on Information and Knowledge Management (CIKM'14)*, November 2014, pp. 171–180
23. X. Liu, M. Li, S. Li, S. Peng, X. Liao, X. Lu, IMGPU: GPU-accelerated influence maximization in large-scale social networks. IEEE Trans. Parall. Distrib. Syst. **25**(1), 136–145 (2014)
24. L. Lü, D. Chen, X.L. Ren, Q.M. Zhang, Y.C. Zhang, T. Zhou, Vital nodes identification in complex networks. Phys. Rep. **650**, 1–63 (2016)
25. S. Mihara, S. Tsugawa, H. Ohsaki, Influence maximization problem for unknown social networks, in *Proceedings of the 2015 IEEE/ACM International Conference on Advances in Social Networks Analysis and Mining (ASONAM'15)*, August 2015, pp. 1539–1546
26. S. Mihara, S. Tsugawa, H. Ohsaki, On the effectiveness of random jumps in an influence maximization algorithm for unknown graphs, in *Proceedings of the 31st International Conference on Information Networking (ICOIN'17)*, January 2017
27. F. Morone, H.A. Makse, Influence maximization in complex networks through optimal percolation. Nature **524**(7563), 65–68 (2015)
28. N. Ohsaka, T. Akiba, Y. Yoshida, K. Kawarabayashi, Fast and accurate influence maximization on large networks with pruned Monte-Carlo simulations, in *Proceedings of the 28th AAAI Conference on Artificial Intelligence (AAAI'14)*, July 2014, pp. 138–144
29. M. Richardson, P. Domingos, Mining knowledge-sharing sites for viral marketing, in *Proceedings of the 8th ACM SIGKDD International Conference on Knowledge Discovery and Data Mining (KDD'02)* (2002), pp. 61–70
30. K. Saito, R. Nakano, M. Kimura, Prediction of information diffusion probabilities for independent cascade model, in *Proceedings of International Conference on Knowledge-Based and Intelligent Information and Engineering Systems* (2008), pp. 67–75
31. Y. Tang, X. Xiao, Y. Shi, Influence maximization: near-optimal time complexity meets practical efficiency, in *Proceedings of the 2014 ACM SIGMOD International Conference on Management of Data (SIGMOD'14)*, June 2014, pp. 75–86
32. Y. Tang, Y. Shi, X. Xiao, Influence maximization in near-linear time: a martingale approach, in *Proceedings of the 2015 ACM SIGMOD International Conference on Management of Data (SIGMOD'15)*, May 2015, pp. 1539–1554
33. S. Tsugawa, A survey of social network analysis techniques and their applications to socially aware networking. IEICE Trans. Commun. **E102-B**(1) (2018)
34. S. Tsugawa, H. Ohsaki, On the robustness of influence maximization algorithms against non-adversarial perturbations, in *Proceedings of the 2017 IEEE/ACM International Conference on Advances in Social Networks Analysis and Mining (ASONAM'17)* (2017), pp. 91–94
35. S. Tsugawa, Y. Matsumoto, H. Ohsaki, On the robustness of centrality measures against link weight quantization in social networks. Comput. Math. Organ. Theory **21**(3), 318–339 (2015)
36. B. Wilder, N. Immorlica, E. Rice, M. Tambe, Maximizing influence in an unknown social network, in *Proceedings of the AAAI Conference on Artificial Intelligence (AAAI'18)* (2018)
37. H. Zhuang, Y. Sun, J. Tang, J. Zhang, X. Sun, Influence maximization in dynamic social networks, in *Proceedings of the 13th IEEE International Conference on Data Mining (ICDM'13)*, December 2013, pp. 1313–1318

Analyzing Social Book Reading Behavior on Goodreads and How It Predicts Amazon Best Sellers

Suman Kalyan Maity, Abhishek Panigrahi, and Animesh Mukherjee

1 Introduction

"If one cannot enjoy reading a book over and over again, there is no use in reading it at all."
—Oscar Wilde

Analysis of reading habits has been an active area of research for quite long time [1–5]. While most of these research investigate blog reading behavior [1, 2, 4], there have been some work that also discuss about interactive and connected book reading behavior [3, 5]. Despite such active research, very little investigation has been done so far to understand the characteristics of social book reading sites and how the collective reading phenomena can even influence the online sales of books. In this work, we attempt to bridge this gap and analyze the various factors related to book reading on a popular platform—Goodreads and apply this knowledge to distinguish Amazon best seller books from the rest.

This research had been performed when all the researchers were at IIT Kharagpur, India.

S. K. Maity (✉)
Kellogg School of Management and Northwestern Institute on Complex Systems, Northwestern University, Evanston, IL, USA
e-mail: suman.maity@kellogg.northwestern.edu

A. Panigrahi
Microsoft Research India, Bengaluru, Karnataka, India

A. Mukherjee
Department of Computer Science and Engineering, Indian Institute of Technology Kharagpur, Kharagpur, West Bengal, India
e-mail: animeshm@cse.iitkgp.ernet.in

© Springer Nature Switzerland AG 2019
M. Kaya, R. Alhajj (eds.), *Influence and Behavior Analysis in Social Networks and Social Media*, Lecture Notes in Social Networks,
https://doi.org/10.1007/978-3-030-02592-2_11

Goodreads is a popular social book-reading platform that allows book lovers to rate books, post and share reviews, and connect with other readers. On Goodreads website, users can add books to their personal bookshelves[1] for reading, track the status of their readings and post a reading status, find which books their friends are reading and what their favorite authors are reading and writing, and get personalized book recommendations. Goodreads also promotes social interactions among users; users can participate in discussions and take part in group activities on various topics and allow users to view his/her friends' shelves, read reviews, and comment on friends' pages.

Popularity of a book depends on various factors. They can be broadly classified into two groups: intrinsic or innate content factors and external factors. Intrinsic content factors mostly concern quality of books that include its interestingness, the novelty factor, the writing style, the engaging story line, etc. in general. However, these content and quality factors of books are very different for different genres. For example, a successful thriller requires a credible, big story line, strong narrative thrust, different viewpoints, complex twists and plots, escalating stakes and tensions, and breakneck speed with occasional lulls,[2] whereas a popular romantic novel does not require complex twists and plots, tension, or shock effect; what it requires are variety, demonstration of strong and healthy relationship, once-in-a-lifetime love,[3] conflicts, sexual tension, etc. [6]. It is, therefore, difficult to find common grounds for books belonging to various genres and to quantify those aspects. External factors driving books' popularity include the readers' reading behavior, social contexts, book critics' reviews, etc. In this work, we try to quantify the external factors of books' popularity by analyzing the characteristics of the entities and the book-reading behavior as reflected on the Goodreads platform. Particularly, we are interested to understand whether the collective reading behavior on Goodreads can distinguish the Amazon best sellers from the rest of the books.

Research Objectives and Contributions We analyze a large dataset from Goodreads to understand various characteristic differences existing between the Amazon best-selling books and the rest and make the following contributions:

---

[1]In Goodreads, a book shelf is a list where one can add or remove books to facilitate reading similar to real-life book shelf where one keep books.

[2]https://hunterswritings.com/2012/10/12/elements-of-the-psychological-thriller-mystery-suspense-andor-crime-fiction-genres/.

[3]http://www.writersdigest.com/wp-content/uploads/Essential_Elements.pdf.

- We study the characteristics of Amazon best sellers in terms of various Goodreads entities—books, authors, shelves, genres, and user status posts. We observe that across various features extracted from these entities, the best sellers are significantly different from an equal-sized sample of books selected uniformly at random.
- We leverage upon the characteristic properties of these best sellers and propose a framework to predict whether a book will become a best seller in the long run or not, considering review and reading behaviors of the books for various time periods of observation $t = 15$ days, 1 month post-publication. For 1 month, we achieve average accuracy **88.87%** with average precision and recall of **0.887** for tenfold cross-validation on a balanced set. The results are very similar for the other observation window. One of the most nontrivial results is that our user status and genre-based prediction framework yield much better performance than traditional popularity indicators of books like ratings and reviews ($\sim$ 16.4% improvement). We would like to stress here that this result has a very important implication—*the Amazon best seller books might not necessarily be qualified by high-quality reviews or a high volume of ratings; however, a large majority of them have user status post patterns that strongly distinguish them from the rest of the books.*
- Since the number of ABS books should, in reality, be far lower than the other set of randomly chosen Goodreads books, we also evaluate our model under class imbalance in the test data set and achieve good result as the balanced one. In specific, even for as small observation period as 15 days, we achieve a weighted average accuracy of $\sim$ **86.67%** with weighted average precision of 0.901 and recall of 0.867 and a very high area under the ROC curve.
- We further show that the proposed features can also discriminate between the best sellers and two competing sets of books that are (a) highly rated, have a large volume of reviews but are not best sellers (HRHR), and (b) Goodreads Choice Awards Nominated (GCAN) but not best sellers. The average accuracy of prediction for ABS vs GCAN is as high as **87.1%**, while for ABS vs HRHR, the average accuracy is **86.22%**.

We believe that this work[4] is an important contribution to the current literature as it not only unfolds the collective reading behavior of a social book-reading platform through a rigorous measurement study but also establishes a strong link between two orthogonal channels—Goodreads and Amazon. Such a linkage might be extremely beneficial in fostering business for both the organizations through novel cross-platform policy designs.

---

[4]This research is an extension of our earlier published work [7] at ASONAM '2017 and reporting a much more detailed analysis emphasizing various aspects of social book reading in more detail and perform detailed comparison of the best sellers with other kind of competitors

Organization of the Paper The remainder of the paper is organized as follows: in the next section, we discuss the state of the art. In Sect. 3, we describe the method for dataset preparation. Section 4 is devoted to the analysis of various characteristic properties of the Goodreads entities for the Amazon best sellers. In Sect. 5, we discuss the prediction framework built for predicting whether a book will be an Amazon best seller or not and evaluate our proposed model. In Sect. 6, we provide a discussion concerning the Amazon best sellers and the set of books with high ratings and reviews. In Sect. 7, we draw conclusions pointing to the key contributions of our work and discuss potential future directions.

2 Related Works

There are some research works on the success of novels/books. Some of the early works [8–10] provide quantitative insights to stylistic aspects in successful literature relying on the knowledge and insights of human experts on literature. Harvey [9] and Hall [6] focus mainly on the content of the best-selling novels and try to prepare the secret recipes of the successful novels/books. Yun [11] study the success of motion pictures based mainly on external, non-textual characteristics. Ashok et al. [12] focus on writing styles of the novels and establish the connection between stylistic elements and the literary success of novels providing quantitative insights to them.

One of the related domains of understanding success of books is that of text readability. Some of the early works propose various readability metrics based on simple characteristics of text documents like sentence length, number of syllables per word, etc., for example, FOG [13], SMOG [14], and Flesh-Kincaid [15] metrics. More advanced readability measures based on the list of predetermined words are the Lexile measure [16], the Fry Short Passage measure [17], and the Revised Dale-Chall formula [18]. Recently, there have been several works [19–24] that focus on predicting and measuring readability of texts based on linguistic features. Collins-Thompson and Callan [23] adopt simple language modeling approach using a modified Naïve Bayes classifier to estimate reading difficulty of texts. Heilman et al. [22] and Schwarm and Ostendorf [21] use syntactic features apart from language model features to estimate grade level of texts. Pitler and Nenkova [24] predict readability of texts from The Wall Street Journal using lexical, syntactic, and discourse features. Kate et al. [20] propose a model using syntactic and language model features to predict readability of natural language documents irrespective of genres, whereas Louis [19] proposes a novel text quality metric for readability that considers unique properties of different genres.

Apart from understanding the success of books and readability of documents, there have been studies to identify author styles [25–30]. Peng et al. [27] build a character-level n-gram language model for authorship identification. Stamatatos et al. [29] use a combination of word-level statistics and part-of-speech counts or n-grams for author attribution. Baayen et al. [30] suggest that the frequencies with which syntactic rewrite rules are put to use provide a better clue to authorship than word usage and thus can improve accuracy of authorship attribution.

Another spectrum of works have been done in pursuit of understanding social blog and book reading behavior. Rideout et al. [31] study shared book reading behavior and show that reading (or being read to) remains a constant in most young children's lives. Nardi et al. [4] examine the social nature of blogging activity and demonstrate that blogs are quite unlike a personal diary. Baumer et al. [1] perform a qualitative study focusing on blog readers, their reading practices, their perceptions of blogs and bloggers. The blogging activity is found to be far more heterogeneous and multifaceted than previously suggested. In a subsequent paper, Baumer et al. [2] study blog readers, their interactions with bloggers, and their impact on blogging focusing on political blogs. Follmer et al. [3] introduce an interactive book-reading platform "People in Books" using FlashCAM technology. The system supports children and their long-distance family members to interact via a play where the children and their family members can assume various characters/roles in children's story books over distance. Raffle et al. [5] design "Family Story Play," a book-reading system which supports book reading among grandparents and their grandchildren over distance. Family Story Play establishes the hypothesis that there is a synergy between young children's education (a rich shared reading experience) and communication with long-distance family.

There have been several works on book recommendations and author ranking. Huang and Chen [32] analyze user-item interactions as graphs and employ link prediction method for making collaborative filtering-based recommendation for books on a book sale dataset. Kamps [33] investigates the effectiveness of author rankings in a library catalog to improve book retrieval. Vaz et al. [34] propose a hybrid recommendation system combining two item-based collaborative filtering algorithms to predict books and authors that the user will like. Zhu and Wang [35] apply improved algorithm through filtering basic item set or ignoring the transaction records that are useless for frequent items generated to mine association rules from circulation records in a university library. Vaz et al. [36] explore the use of stylometric features in the book recommendation task. Yang et al. [37] present framework of clustering and pattern extraction by using supervised ARTMAP neural network by formation of reference vectors to classify user profile patterns into classes of similar profiles forming the basis of recommendation of new books. Givon and Lavrenko [38] try to solve the "cold-start" problem (books with no tags) in book recommendations by proposing a probabilistic model for inferring the most probable tags from the text of the book. Zhou [39] analyzes the problem of trust in social network and proposes a recommender system model based on social network trust. Pera and Ng [40] propose a recommender system tailored to K-12 (Kindergarten to 12th grade) readers, which makes personalized suggestions on books that satisfy both the preferences and reading abilities of its users. In a subsequent work, Pera and Ng [41] propose a personalized book recommender system that emulates the readers' advisory process offered at public/school libraries to recommend books that are similar in contents, topics, and literary elements of other books appealing to a reader, with the latter based on extracted appeal-term descriptions. In another work, Pera and Ng [42] propose unsupervised book recommendation framework for very young children especially K-3 (Kindergarten to 3rd grade) readers.

On Goodreads platform, there has been very little research till date. Dimitrov et al. [43] study the behavioral differences of reviews in Amazon and Goodreads. Adam Worrall [44] have done an analysis on message posted by users in Library-Thing and Goodreads. Thelwall and Kousha [45] provide insights in Goodreads users' reading characteristics. Thelwal [46] shows the existence of gender differences in authorship within genres for English language books. Our work differs from the above in the following ways. We study the characteristics of various entities on Goodreads and try to establish whether these factors can discriminate between Amazon best sellers from other books. We use both the external characteristics of a book and the content of the reviews in our study. To the best of our knowledge, we are the first who try to explicitly provide quantitative insights, based on collective reading habits, on the unstudied connection between the entities of a book-reading platform (Goodreads), and on the success of a book (best sellers on Amazon).

3 Dataset Preparation

We obtain our Goodreads dataset through APIs and web-based crawls over a period of 9 months. This crawling exercise has resulted in the accumulation of a massive dataset spanning a period of around 9 years. We first identify the unique genres from https://www.goodreads.com/genres/list. Note that genres in the Goodreads community are user defined. Next, we collect unique books from the above list of genres and different information regarding these books are crawled via Goodreads APIs. Each book has information like the name of the author, the published year, the number of ratings it received, the average rating, the number of reviews, etc. In total, we could retrieve information of 558,563 books. We then find out the authors of these books and their information like number of distinct works, average rating, number of ratings, number of fans, etc. In total, we have information of 332,253 authors. We separately collect the yearly Amazon best sellers[5] from 1995 to 2016 and their ISBNs and then re-crawl Goodreads if relevant information about some of them is not already present in the crawled dataset. For these books, we separately crawl up to 2000 reviews and ratings in chronological order. We also crawl relevant shelves information of those books.

---

[5]http://www.amazon.com/gp/bestsellers/1995/books.

4 Characteristic Behavior

In this section, we shall study the characteristic properties of various Goodreads entities for the Amazon best sellers and compare them with the rest of the books. We have 1468 Amazon best sellers in our dataset. To compare with the rest of the books, we choose random samples of books from the entire set of books minus the Amazon best sellers. We obtain ten such random samples and report averaged results for them. Goodreads has three primary entities: books, authors, and users. Here, we attempt to discriminate the Amazon best sellers from the others by analyzing these Goodreads entities.

4.1 Book Ratings and Reviews

Ratings and reviews received by a book are common factors that reflect aspects of collective reading and, in turn, govern the popularity of a book. We study the average rating distribution of the books in Fig. 1a. On average scale, there does not exist any significant difference in the ratings a best seller receives compared to the other books. In Fig. 1b, we compare the total number of ratings received—Amazon best sellers receive more ratings than the other books; however, they receive both high and low ratings in larger proportions compared to the other books. We then calculate the rating entropy of the books which is a measure of diversity of ratings. Rating entropy ($\text{rating}_{\text{entropy}}$) of a book is formally defined as follows:

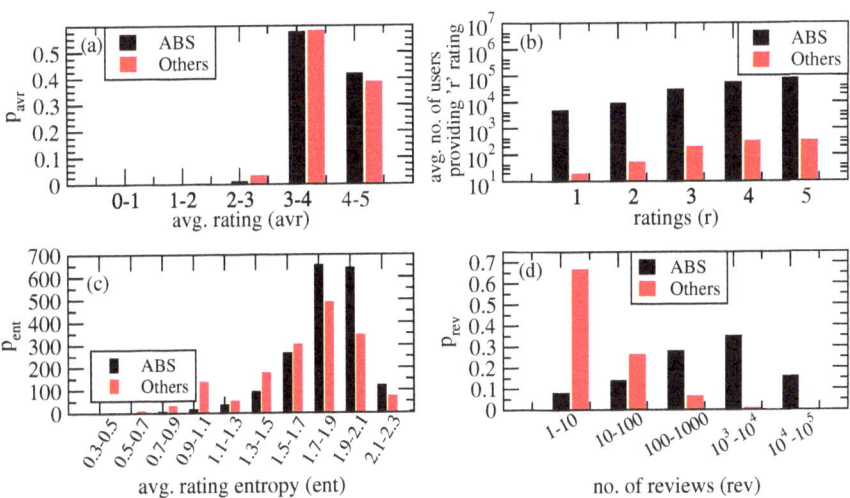

Fig. 1 Book rating and reviews: distribution of (**a**) average rating, (**b**) number of ratings, (**c**) average rating entropy, (**d**) number of reviews for Amazon best sellers (ABS) vs other books

$$\text{rating}_{\text{entropy}}(b) = -\sum_{j \in 1..5} p_j \times \log(p_j)$$

where p_j is the probability of the book receiving a rating value j. Figure 1c shows the distribution of the rating entropy of the books. The Amazon best sellers receive more diverse ratings compared to the other books. In Fig. 1d, we show the distribution of a number of reviews. Amazon best-selling books tend to get more reviews, whereas majority of other books receive 10–100 reviews.

4.2 Book Genres and Book Shelves

Genres Genres of books could be an important determinant of popularity. Not all of the genres attract equal number of readers. Some are very popular, whereas some require very specific taste. In Table 1, we observe the differences in various genres. $\sim$ 57% of the Amazon best sellers belong to the "Nonfiction" category, followed by the "Fiction" category constituting $\sim$ 35% of the books. Since one book can belong to multiple genres, the sum of all these fractions denoting the fraction of books belonging to that genre does not sum up to 1. For books that are not best sellers (i.e., others), the rank order for fiction and nonfiction gets reversed. Another striking difference in genres is that "Self-Help," "Reference," "Adult," "Business," etc. have higher contribution of books to the Amazon best-selling books compared

Table 1 Top 15 genres corresponding to each category of books

Categories			
Amazon best sellers	Fraction of books	Others	Fraction of books
Nonfiction	0.577	Fiction	0.221
Fiction	0.349	Nonfiction	0.202
Self Help	0.219	Romance	0.119
Adult	0.219	Fantasy	0.103
Reference	0.19	Literature	0.103
Business	0.185	History	0.091
History	0.179	Cultural	0.084
Biography	0.151	Historical	0.063
Science	0.143	Children	0.063
Novels	0.143	Historical fiction	0.06
Psychology	0.141	Mystery	0.06
Literature	0.137	Contemporary	0.058
Fantasy	0.131	Sequential art	0.054
Contemporary	0.128	Science fiction	0.051
Adult fiction	0.117	Young adult	0.051

to the set of other books. As we shall see, the genre characteristics turn out to be one of the most distinguishing factors between the Amazon best sellers and the other books.

Shelves To facilitate ease of book reading, Goodreads provides a unique feature of organizing books into various shelves. It provides three default self-explanatory bookshelves, "read," "currently-reading," and "to-read," and also provides opportunity to the user to create customized shelves to categorize his/her books. We shall analyze these book shelves to identify if they are relevant for popularity/success of a book. Figure 2a shows the distribution of number of bookshelves a book is kept in. We observe that the Amazon best sellers are placed in a much larger number of book shelves (as large as $> 10^5$) by the users compared to the rest of the books. We then concentrate on the content of four specific shelves and their variants: "read," "to-read," "currently reading," and "rereads" shelves. We observe that for the Amazon best sellers, all these shelves are more dense compared to the other books (see Fig. 2b).

Shelf Diversity Similar to rating entropy defined earlier, we calculate shelf diversity which quantifies the idea of how users put their books in various shelves. Formally, shelf diversity (ShelfDiv) can be defined as follows:

$$\text{ShelfDiv}(b) = - \sum_{j \in \text{shelf}_{\text{set}}} s_j \times \log(s_j)$$

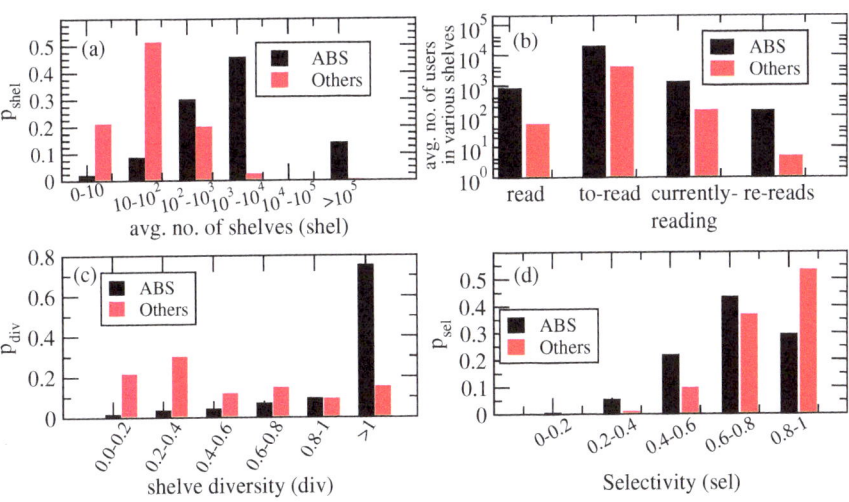

Fig. 2 Characteristic properties of bookshelves: distribution of (**a**) number of shelves, (**b**) average number of users tagging their books to "read," "to-read," "currently-reading," and "rereads" shelves, (**c**) Shelf diversity, (**d**) selectivity for ABS vs other books

where s_j is the probability that the book belongs to the jth shelf in the set of book shelves. Figure 2c shows that the Amazon best sellers have higher shelf diversity. ~75% of the best sellers have diversity score of >1.

Selectivity We define a selectivity metric which tells us how users are selective in putting the books in their shelves. More formally, k-shelf selectivity of a book is defined as the fraction of users being covered if one selects only top k shelves used for keeping the book. In Fig. 2d, we show the distribution of *selectivity*. Here, we show 3-shelf selectivity of the books. It is observed that the readers of the Amazon best sellers are less selective compared to the readers of the other Goodreads books.

4.3   Goodreads Users' Status Posts

While reading, a Goodreads user can post status updates about reading the book. For example, one can post how much of the book has been read, which page he/she is in, also can comment about the book so far read, etc. (see Fig. 3). We separately crawl the first 2000 user status posts for each book in our dataset. These book reading

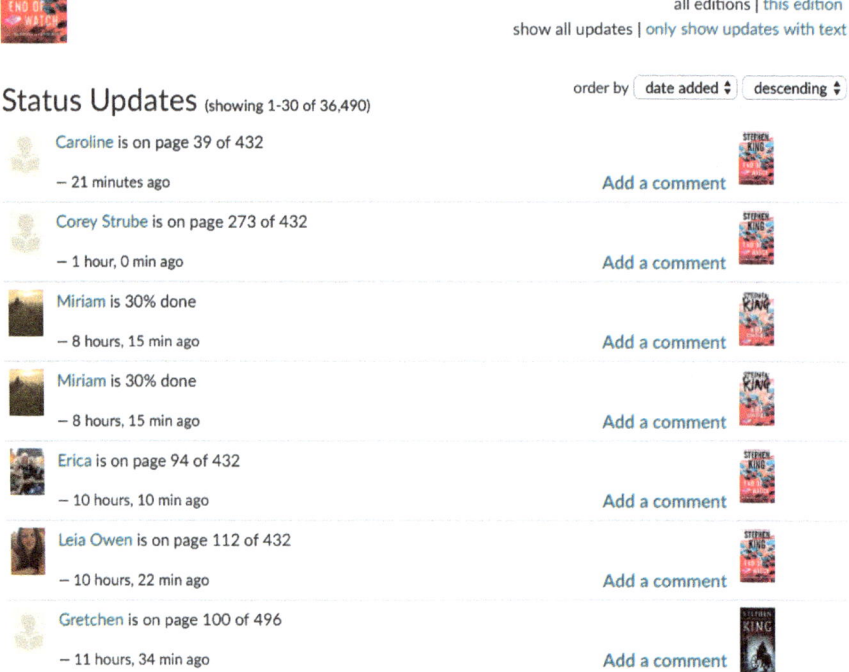

Fig. 3   Status page for "End of Watch (Bill Hodges Trilogy, #3) by Stephen King"

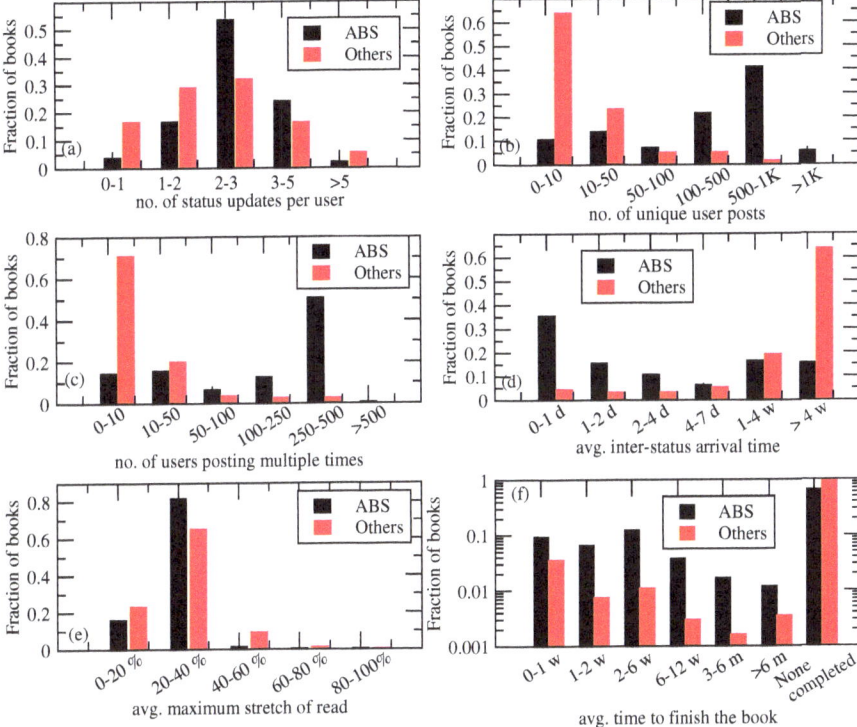

Fig. 4 Characteristic properties of Goodreads users' status posts: distribution of (**a**) number of status updates per user, (**b**) number of unique users updating status, (**c**) number of users updating multiple times, (**d**) inter-status arrival time, (**e**) average maximum stretch of reading, (**f**) average time to finish reading for ABS vs other books

status postings for a book also drive its popularity. We attempt to differentiate the Amazon best sellers with the other Goodreads books through the reading status postings.

In Fig. 4a, we show the distribution of the number of status update posts per user. The results show that while reading the Amazon best seller books, readers tend to post status updates more often as compared to the readers of other books. Figure 4b presents the distribution of unique readers posting status updates. The Amazon best sellers engage more readers in posting status updates compared to other Goodreads books. Also, the Amazon best sellers engage better the same readers in posting multiple status updates compared to other Goodreads books (see Fig. 4c). We also study the distribution of average inter-status arrival time (see Fig. 4d) which shows that readers of Amazon best sellers post status updates more frequently (for more than 35% books, average inter-status arrival time is less than a day) than the readers of other Goodreads books. Figure 4e shows the distribution of average maximum concentrated reading efforts at a stretch (in terms of percentage read). Readers of ~80% of the Amazon best-selling books show maximum percentage stretch of read

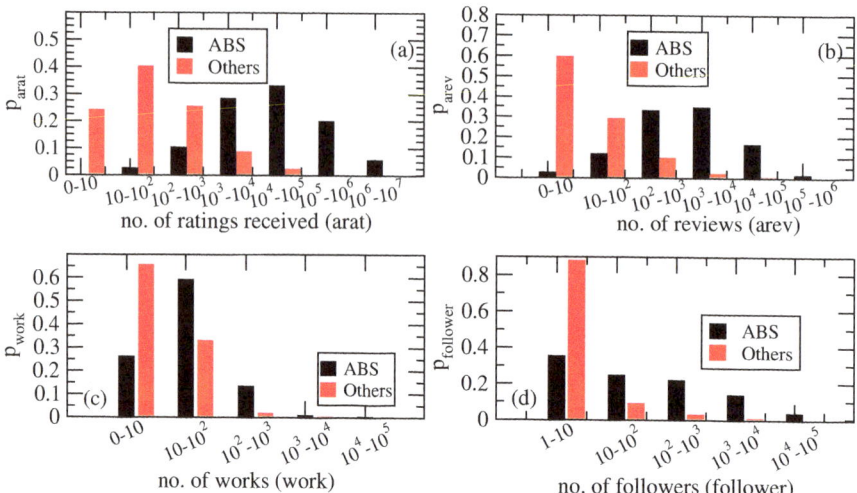

Fig. 5 Characteristic properties of the authors of the book: distribution of (**a**) number of ratings received by the author, (**b**) number of reviews received, (**c**) number of literary works, and (**d**) number of followers for ABS vs other books

as 20–40%. Though, for other Goodreads books also, the fraction is largest for the same zone; the relative number of books in this stretch is lesser than that of the best sellers. In Fig. 4f, we show the distribution of average time to finish book reading. We observe that for ∼63% of the Amazon best sellers, there are no readers who have completed reading the whole book, whereas for the other books, this number is quite high (∼94%). Among the books where one of the readers have at least finished reading the book, the fraction of books for Amazon best sellers are higher compared to the other books in all the time buckets. Note that features extracted from the status posts of users strongly discriminate the Amazon best sellers from the rest of the books (see Sect. 5).

4.4 Author Characteristics

Authors play an important role in driving the popularity of a book. Already successful or highly reputed authors have higher chance of having their books more popular than a novice writer. In Fig. 5, we show the distribution of various author features of the Amazon best sellers and compare them with that of the other set of Goodreads books selected uniformly at random. In Fig. 5a, we show the distribution of number of ratings received by the authors. We observe that the authors of Amazon best sellers receive more ratings (more than 30% of the authors of the best-selling books receive 10^4–10^5 ratings from the book readers; also a significant number of authors receive more than million ratings) compared to the authors of the other books (~40% of these authors receive 10–100 ratings from the book readers). Figure 5b presents the reviews that the books of the authors receive. Likewise, ratings and the number of reviews received also follow a similar distribution. The authors of the Amazon best sellers tend to receive higher number of reviews with ~51% of them receiving more than 1000 reviews, whereas the authors of the other Goodreads books receive less number of reviews (more than 60% of these authors receive less than ten reviews).

In Fig. 5c, the distribution of the number of works is shown. ~60% of the authors of the Amazon best sellers pen around 10–100 literary works, whereas more than 60% of the authors of the other Goodreads books on average pen less than ten books. There are also some authors (mostly publishing houses) who publish more than 10^4 works, and this number is much higher in case of the Amazon best sellers. Figure 5d demonstrates the characteristic differences in follower/fans distribution of the authors of various categories of books. The authors of the Amazon best sellers receive large number of fan following on Goodreads, whereas 88% of the authors of the other books on Goodreads have less than 10 fans; a large fraction of the Amazon best sellers' authors have more than 10,000 fans/followers.

5   Will a Book Become an Amazon Best Seller?

From the discussions in the previous sections, it is evident that there exist differences among various Goodreads entities for Amazon best sellers and the other Goodreads books. In this section, we attempt to build a prediction framework that can early predict whether a book will be an Amazon best sellers or not. We shall try to leverage upon the various characteristic properties of the Goodreads entities that we have studied earlier. Note that many of these features, for example, the number of followers of an author, the behavior of shelves, etc., are temporal in nature; however, due to the limitations on data crawl imposed by Goodreads, we do not possess the temporal profile of all these features. Therefore, we shall attempt to build the predictors using minimal external and content features and will evaluate our framework against standard evaluation metrics like accuracy, precision, recall, etc. Our goal is to predict whether a book will be an Amazon best seller or not just by observing the data up to various time periods from Goodreads starting from the date of publication of the book ($t = 15$ days, 1 month). As Goodreads was launched in 2007, we consider only those Amazon best sellers that are published on or after 2007. To compare against these sets of books, we consider a same-sized random sample of books from Goodreads, none of which ever became an Amazon best seller, and all of which have been published after 2007. In total, we have ~ 380 books in each class. For the task of prediction, we consider the following set of minimal features:

– **Novelty of the book:** Novelty of a book is a key for its acceptability/success in the readers' circle. For each book in Goodreads, a short summary about the book is provided. We separately crawl this "About" information of the book (say, the document containing the summary of the book be A) and of all the other books that are published before this book in question (say, the concatenated summary of all those books be B). We then extract keywords[6] [47] from documents A and B, respectively, (Keywords$_A$ and Keywords$_B$) and design a metric of keyword overlap as follows:

$$\text{Overlap}(A, B) = \frac{|\text{Keywords}_A \cap \text{Keywords}_B|}{\min(|\text{Keywords}_A|, |\text{Keywords}_B|)}$$

The higher the keyword overlap, the lower is the novelty score. We use this as a feature for our model.

We also define another novelty feature which is measured as the Kullback-Leibler (KL) divergence between the unigram language model inferred from the document A containing all the words except the stop words from the book's summary for the ith book and the background language model from document B and formally defined this as follows:

$$\text{KLDiv}(i) = -\sum_{w \in A} p(w|A) \times \log \frac{p(w|A)}{p(w|B)}$$

The higher the divergence value, the higher is the novelty of the book. Once again, this is used as a feature in the prediction model.

– **Genres**—As mentioned earlier, genres of a book are an important feature in deciding the destiny of it. In this prediction model, we consider top 15 genres for Amazon best sellers and other books as shown in Table 1. In total, we have 24 genres—fantasy, fiction, nonfiction, children, romance, etc. We use each of them as a binary feature.

Goodreads book reading status posts: We compute several features out these book reading posts. The list is as follows:

– number of status updates of the readers (mean, min, max, and variance),
– number of unique readers posting status updates,
– number of readers posting status updates more than once (twice/thrice/five times),
– inter-status arrival time (mean, min, max, and variance),
– maximum percentage stretch of read (mean, min, max, and variance). We also use the maximum stretch of read in terms of time.
– rate of reading of the readers (mean, min, max, and variance),
– fastest rate of reading (mean, min, max, and variance),
– time taken to finish reading the book (mean, min, max, and variance),
– average positive and negative sentiments from the status posts.

---

[6]https://github.com/aneesha/RAKE

Baseline Features The ratings and reviews of book are the most common indicators of popularity, and in this paper, we shall consider features extracted from them as baselines and compare them with the more nontrivial features related to reading behavior of users for the task of prediction. The rating- and review- related features are described below:

- average number of rating
- number of 1-star ratings, 2-star ratings, 3-star ratings, 4-star ratings, 5-star ratings
- rating entropy
- number of reviews received
- **Sentiment of the reviews:** For each book, we concatenate all the reviews in 1 month and find out the fraction of positive sentiment words (positive sentiment score) and the fraction of negative sentiment words (negative sentiment score) by using MPQA sentiment lexicon [48]. We use these two sentiment scores as two separate features.
- **Cognitive dimension of the reviews:** There could be differences in the cognitive dimension (linguistic and psychological) for the two categories of books. To quantify this, we consider Linguistic Inquiry and Word Count (LIWC) software [49]. LIWC takes a text document as input and outputs a score for the input over all the categories based on the writing style and psychometric properties of the document.

5.1 Performance of the Prediction Model

In this subsection, we shall discuss the performance of our prediction model. We use tenfold cross-validation technique and use SVM and logistic regression classifier [50]. For the prediction task, we consider t time periods (t)—15 days, 1 month from the publication date. We compute all the feature values from the data available only within the time period t from the publication date. We ensure that all the books that we select in both the classes are published after 2007 since Goodreads was launched in 2007. Table 2 shows the various classification techniques we employ and the evaluation results. The classifiers yield very similar classification performance with logistic regression performing a little better; with logistic regression classifier, we obtain average accuracy of 88.72% with average precision and recall of 0.887 each and the average area under the ROC curve as 0.925 for $t = 1$ month on a balanced dataset with tenfold cross-validation method. Note that the classification results for other time periods also give very similar results. The user status and genre-based features are the most prominent ones and significantly outperform the ratings- and review feature-based baselines. For $t = 1$ month, our method yields 16.4% improvement over the best performing baseline (for $t = 15$ days, we also yield similar improvement) suggesting that user's status on Goodreads are very important indicators of popularity and are, in fact, much better indicators than reviews or ratings. In other words, this shows that all Amazon

Table 2 Evaluation results in comparison with baselines (baseline1—ratings, baseline2—reviews)

t	Method	Accuracy	Precision	Recall	F-Score	ROC area
15 days	LR	**85.66%**	0.857	0.857	0.857	**0.917**
	SVM	85.3%	0.853	0.853	0.853	0.853
	Baseline1—LR	76.7%	0.774	0.767	0.766	0.826
	Baseline2—LR	75.98%	0.76	0.76	0.76	0.829
1 month	LR	**88.72%**	0.888	0.887	0.887	**0.925**
	SVM	88.71%	0.888	0.887	0.887	0.887
	Baseline1—LR	76.22%	0.766	0.762	0.762	0.808
	Baseline2—LR	75.91%	0.76	0.759	0.759	0.812
Unbalanced testset ($t = 15$ d)	LR	**86.67%**	0.901	0.867	0.876	**0.963**
	SVM	86.67%	0.924	0.867	0.879	0.919
	Baseline1—LR	75.56%	0.897	0.756	0.784	0.851
	Baseline2—LR	75.5%	0.839	0.756	0.78	0.78

Bold values suggest the best performance result among various methods

best seller books might not necessarily have high-quality reviews or a high volume of ratings; however, a large majority of them have user status post patterns very different from the other set of books.

Since in real life, the proportion of the Amazon best sellers is far lower than the other types of books, we also consider testing our model on an unbalanced test set. Here, the training and test sample sets are taken in 3:1 ratio. In training set, both the class samples are taken in equal proportion (to guarantee fair learning), whereas in test sample, the Amazon best sellers and the other books are taken in 1:9 ratio. We then train our classifiers on the balanced training set and test on the unbalanced one. We report the weighted average values for all the metrics in Table 2. For an observation period of even as small as 15 days, we achieve weighted average accuracy of ~86.67% with weighted average precision of 0.901 and recall of 0.876. Note that compared to the balanced set, the performance is slightly better. The weighted average ROC area under the curve is quite high (0.963 on weighted averaging—but same value is found for the individual classes also).

5.2 Discriminative Power of the Features

Here, we shall discuss about the importance of the individual features (i.e., the discriminative power of the individual features). In order to determine the discriminative power of each feature, we compute the chi-square (χ^2) value and the information gain. Table 3 shows the order of all features based on the χ^2 value, where the larger the value, the higher is the discriminative power. The ranks of the features are very similar when ranked by information gain (Kullback-Leibler divergence). The most prominent features on individual level are the user status

Table 3 Features and their discriminative power

χ^2 value	Rank	Feature
194.0324	1	Mean reading rate
121.7847	2	Number of readers posting status
109.8861	3	Fastest rate of reading (min)
96.0871	4	Inter-status post time (min)
92.1124	5	Min. reading rate
88.2171	6	Number of readers posting status updates twice
82.5114	7	Variance of reading rate
75.9434	8	Maximum percentage stretch of read (min)
75.0442	9	Number of readers posting status updates thrice
74.0946	10	Inter-status post time (mean)
71.7962	11	Time taken to finish the book (max)
71.7024	12	Maximum percentage stretch of read w.r.t time (max)
69.5682	13	Number of readers posting status updates five times
63.3696	14	Genre (Romance)
56.759	15	Time taken to finish the book (variance)

features. There are several user status features that come in the list of the top 15. Among those status features, the most discriminative ones are mean reading rate, number of status posts, fastest rate of reading, inter-status post time, etc.

6   Close Competitors

In this section, we shall study the characteristic behavior of the Amazon best sellers, contrasting them with two sets of close competitors described below.

HRHR We have observed in the earlier section that Amazon best sellers tend to have high ratings and reviews. Therefore, we retrieve a set of books from the Goodreads dataset that are published on or after 1995 and have received average rating of 4 or more and received at least 900 reviews. Note that the parameters of ratings and reviews are chosen in such a way so that we get a comparable number of books as that of the Amazon best sellers. We have termed these highly rated and reviewed non-best-selling competitor books as "HRHR." HRHR actually constitutes a weaker contrast class compared to the random set of books.

Goodreads Choice Awards Nominee Goodreads Readers' Choice Award[7] is an annual event. This was first launched in 2009. From then on, Goodreads users can take part in this award to nominate as well as to vote their nominations. There are 20 categories of awards, and in each category, 20 nominations are made. We

---

[7]https://www.goodreads.com/choiceawards/.

Table 4 Top 15 genres corresponding to each category of books

Categories					
Amazon Best Sellers	Fraction	HRHR	Fraction	GCAN	Fraction
Nonfiction	0.577	Fiction	0.737	Fiction	0.875
Fiction	0.349	Fantasy	0.464	Adult	0.75
Self-Help	0.219	Romance	0.388	Contemporary	0.625
Adult	0.219	Young adult	0.332	Historical fiction	0.625
Reference	0.190	Adult	0.298	Mystery	0.625
Business	0.185	Mystery	0.212	Adult fiction	0.625
History	0.179	Contemporary	0.207	Young adult	0.5
Biography	0.151	Adventure	0.186	Fantasy	0.5
Science	0.143	Historical fiction	0.159	Autobiography	0.375
Novels	0.143	Literature	0.159	Nonfiction	0.375
Psychology	0.141	Historical	0.156	Biography	0.375
Literature	0.137	Science fiction	0.155	Biography memoir	0.375
Fantasy	0.131	Paranormal	0.145	Historical	0.375
Contemporary	0.128	Classics	0.144	Thriller	0.375
Adult Fiction	0.117	Children	0.137	Science fiction	0.375

have considered the non-best-selling Goodreads Choice Awards' nominees (GCAN) from 2009 to 2015 as another competitive set to compare with the Amazon best sellers.

6.1 Comparisons

Genre Characteristics First, we study the competitors from the point of view of genres. In Table 4, we show top ten genres from each of these categories. We observe that there exist significant differences in genre distribution. Amazon best seller books appear most in "Nonfiction" category, whereas ~74% of the HRHR books as well as ~87% of the GCAN books appear in the "Fiction" category. Also, these competitor books belong to "Adult," "Fantasy," "Contemporary," "Romance," and other "Fiction" category in large proportions. Another interesting observation is that quite a large proportion of these competitor books (~30% for HRHR books and ~ 75% for GCAN books) belong to the "Adult" category compared to a much smaller proportion (~22%) for the Amazon best sellers. Similarly, a large proportion of competitor books (~33% for HRHR books and ~50% for GCAN books) belong to "Young Adult" category.

Book Shelves Characteristics We then attempt to differentiate the Amazon best sellers from the competitor books in terms of their book shelf properties. In Fig. 6, we show the distribution of various shelf properties for Amazon best sellers vis-a-vis the competitor books. An interesting observation is that most of the competitor

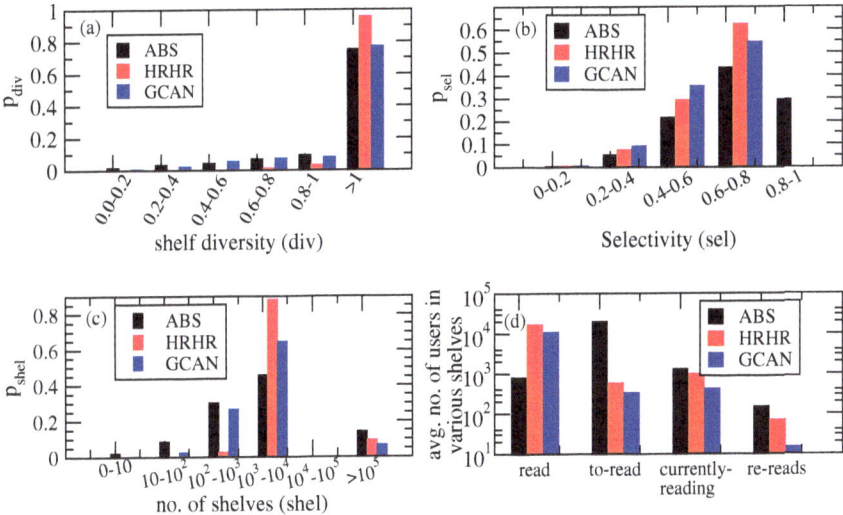

Fig. 6 Characteristic properties of bookshelves: (**a**) distribution of number of shelves; (**b**) average number of users tagging their books to "read," "to-read," "currently-reading" and "rereads" shelves; (**c**) shelf diversity; and (**d**) selectivity for ABS vs HRHR and GCAN books

books (∼88% for HRHR and ∼65% for GCAN) are parts of a large number of shelves (10^3–10^4), while this proportion is significantly smaller for Amazon best sellers (∼40%) (see Fig. 6a). Also these close competitor books have been "read" by more than ten times more readers than the Amazon best sellers; on the other hand, for the Amazon best sellers, more users (more than ten times) have put them into "to-read" shelf compared to these competitors. Therefore, the competitor books are already read by a significant number of users on average, whereas the Amazon best sellers are successful in engaging more users to still read them (see Fig. 6b). In terms of rereading behavior, more readers reread the Amazon best sellers than the competitor books. The competitor books are put in a higher variety of different shelves by the users leading to higher shelf diversity compared to the Amazon best sellers (see Fig. 6c), whereas the Amazon best seller readers are more selective in placing the books in the shelves compared to the competitor books (see Fig. 6d).

Goodreads Users' Status Posts As shown earlier, Goodreads users' reading status posting behavior is a key discriminator between the Amazon best sellers and other Goodreads books. Here, we repeat the analysis in the context of the competitor books. In case of the number of status posts, we observe that the readers of the competitor books post more status updates than that of the Amazon best sellers (see Fig. 7a). The number of unique users posting status updates as well the users posting multiple updates is higher for the competitor books in comparison with the Amazon best sellers (see Fig. 7b and c, respectively). Figure 7d shows that the average inter-status arrival time is lesser (larger fraction of books garner status posts within a day on average) for the competitor books in comparison with the Amazon best sellers.

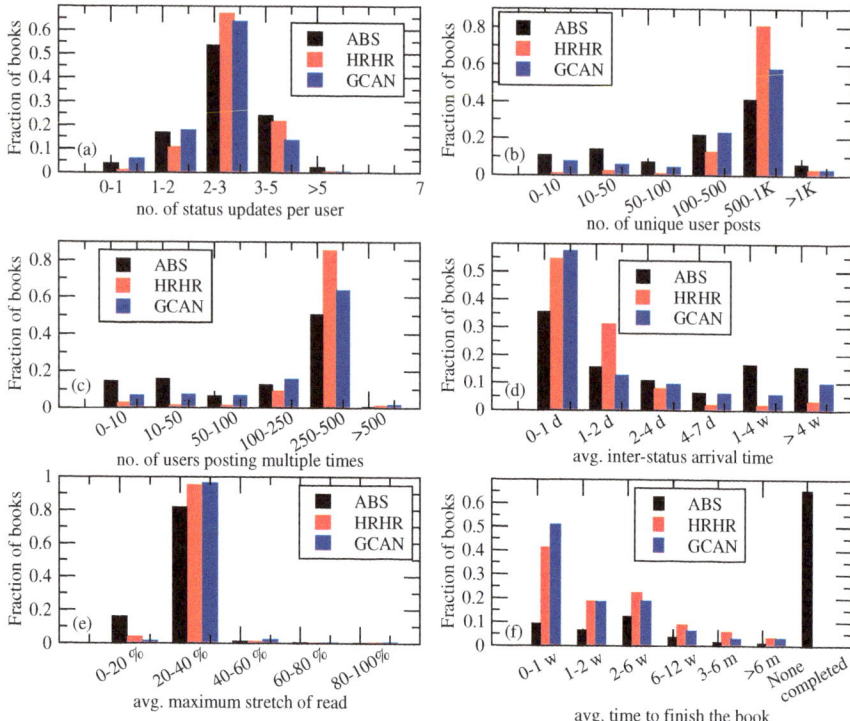

Fig. 7 Characteristic properties of Goodreads users' status posts: distribution of (**a**) number of status updates per user, (**b**) number of unique users updating status, (**c**) number of users updating multiple times, (**d**) inter-status arrival time, (**e**) average maximum stretch of reading, (**f**) average time to finish reading for ABS vs HRHR and GCAN books

The maximum reading effort also shows distinct characteristic with the competitor book readers lying in more proportion in the 20–40% reading zone compared to the Amazon best sellers (Fig. 7e). Figure 7f shows the distribution of average time taken by the readers to finish reading the books. One notable observation is that for all the competitor books, there is at least one reader who has finished reading the book. Also the fraction of books in various time buckets are higher for the competitor books compared to the Amazon best sellers.

Author Characteristics Here, we study the author characteristics of the competitor books. In terms of number of ratings received, the authors of the competitor books receive larger fraction of ratings in the high-rating zone (10^4–10^6) compared to the authors of the Amazon best sellers (see Fig. 8a). The number of review distribution also follows similar trend with authors of competitor books receiving higher fraction of reviews in the high zone (10^3–10^5); however, for the highest zone (10^5–10^6 reviews), the fraction is a little higher for the Amazon best sellers compared to that of the competitor books (see Fig. 8b). In terms of the number of literary works (see

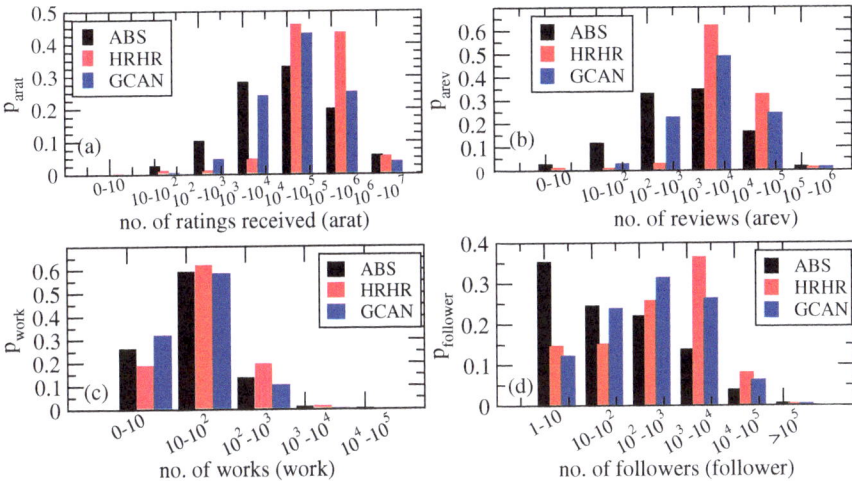

Fig. 8 Characteristic properties of the authors of the book: distribution of (**a**) number of ratings received by the author, (**b**) number of reviews received, (**c**) number of literary works, (**d**) number of followers for ABS vs HRHR and GCAN books

Fig. 8c), we observe that authors of HRHR books tend to write more than the authors of the Amazon best sellers and the GCAN books. The fan/follower distribution also shows that the authors of the competitor books have larger number of followers compared to the authors of the Amazon best sellers (see Fig. 8d). This analysis reveals an interesting fact that success of a book (in terms of financial profit/best seller) does not always necessary mean best-quality books. There are also books which are qualitatively better than an Amazon best seller but have not been the most successful.

We then attempt to evaluate our prediction model with these two sets of books— (a) the Amazon best sellers and the HRHR books and (b) the Amazon best sellers and the GCAN books. For the prediction task, we consider the HRHR and GCAN books published after 2007 and take the data for $t = 15$ days, 1 month post publication to predict. Once again, we compute all the features from the data available only within this time period t only. We observe that the classifiers are yielding best results for ABS vs GCAN with average accuracy $\sim$88% (see Table 5 for details). Even the prediction performance for the classifiers when ABS books are taken into competition with the HRHR books yields average accuracy of $\sim$80% though the discriminating power of the classifiers is better for ABS vs GCAN classification.

Table 5 Evaluation results for (a) ABS vs GCAN (top four lines) and (b) ABS vs HRHR (bottom four lines)

Time period	Classifier	Accuracy	Precision	Recall	F-Score	ROC Area
15 days	LR	**87.1%**	0.884	0.871	0.871	**0.898**
	SVM	83.27%	0.833	0.833	0.833	0.833
1 month	LR	**86.39%**	0.864	0.864	0.864	**0.909**
	SVM	86.1%	0.866	0.861	0.861	0.861
15 days	LR	**80.72%**	0.808	0.807	0.807	**0.849**
	SVM	79.64%	0.796	0.796	0.796	0.796
1 month	LR	**86.22%**	0.862	0.862	0.862	**0.919**
	SVM	84.89%	0.849	0.849	0.849	0.849

Bold values suggest the best performance result among various methods

7 Conclusions and Future Works

In this paper, we study the characteristic properties of Amazon best sellers in terms of various Goodreads entities—books, authors, shelves, and genres—by analyzing a large Goodreads dataset. We observe that there exist characteristic differences between the Amazon best sellers and the other books. We then use these characteristic properties as features for a prediction model that attempts to predict whether a book will be an Amazon best seller or not.

Our proposed prediction framework achieves a very high average accuracy of **88.72%** with high average precision and recall (**0.887**) for observation time period t = 1 month. Our results also hold true for an unbalanced test data set. We observe that the user status post features are the most discriminative ones. We also evaluate our model with two different and more competitive sets of books—HRHR and GCAN and obtain very good results (even better than the above result for ABS vs GCAN).

There are quite a few other interesting directions that can be explored in the future. One such direction could be to understand the detailed user reading dynamics focusing on various inter-dependent entities like shelves and user status posts. We are also interested in performing other cross-platform study to understand this unique dynamics between the platforms in more detail.

References

1. E. Baumer, M. Sueyoshi, B. Tomlinson, Exploring the role of the reader in the activity of blogging, in *CHI* (2008), pp. 1111–1120
2. E.P. Baumer, M. Sueyoshi, B. Tomlinson, Bloggers and readers blogging together: collaborative co-creation of political blogs. Comput. Supported Coop. Work **20**(1–2), 1–36 (2011)
3. S. Follmer, R.T. Ballagas, H. Raffle, M. Spasojevic, H. Ishii, People in books: Using a flashcam to become part of an interactive book for connected reading, in *CSCW*, 685–694 (2012)
4. B.A. Nardi, D.J. Schiano, M. Gumbrecht, Blogging as social activity, or, would you let 900 million people read your diary? in *CSCW*, 222–231 (2004)

5. H. Raffle, R. Ballagas, G. Revelle, H. Horii, S. Follmer, J. Go, E. Reardon, K. Mori, J. Kaye, M. Spasojevic, Family story play: Reading with young children (and elmo) over a distance, in *CHI*, pp. 1583–1592 (2010)

6. J.W. Hall, *Hit Lit: Cracking the Code of the Twentieth Century's Biggest Bestsellers* (Random House, New York, 2012)

7. S.K. Maity, A. Panigrahi, A. Mukherjee, Book reading behavior on goodreads can predict the amazon best sellers, in *Proceedings of the 2017 IEEE/ACM International Conference on Advances in Social Networks Analysis and Mining 2017. ASONAM '17* (2017), pp. 451–454

8. A. Ellegård, *A Statistical Method for Determining Authorship: The Junius Letters*, vol. 13 (Acta Universitatis Gothoburgensis, Göteborg, 1962), pp. 1769–1772

9. J. Harvey, The content characteristics of best-selling novels. Public Opin. Q. **17**(1), 91–114 (1953)

10. J.J. McGann, *The Poetics of Sensibility: A Revolution in Literary Style* (Oxford University Press, Oxford, 1998)

11. C.J. Yun, Performance evaluation of intelligent prediction models on the popularity of motion pictures, in *2011 4th International Conference on Interaction Sciences (ICIS)* (IEEE, New York, 2011), pp. 118–123

12. V.G. Ashok, S. Feng, Y. Choi, Success with style: using writing style to predict the success of novels, in *Proceedings of EMNLP* (2013), pp. 1753–1764

13. R. Gunning, *The Technique of Clear Writing* (McGraw-Hill, New York, 1952)

14. G.H. Mc Laughlin, Smog grading-a new readability formula. J. Read. **12**(8), 639–646 (1969)

15. J.P. Kincaid, R.P. Fishburne Jr, R.L. Rogers, B.S. Chissom, Derivation of new readability formulas (automated readability index, fog count and flesch reading ease formula) for navy enlisted personnel. Technical report, DTIC Document (1975)

16. A. Stenner, I. Horabin, D.R. Smith, M. Smith, *The Lexile Framework* (MetaMetrics, Durham, 1988)

17. E. Fry, A readability formula for short passages. J. Read. **33**(8), 594–597 (1990)

18. J.S. Chall, E. Dale, *Readability Revisited: The New Dale-Chall Readability Formula* (Brookline Books, Brookline, 1995)

19. A. Louis, Automatic metrics for genre-specific text quality, in *Proceedings of the 2012 Conference of the North American Chapter of the Association for Computational Linguistics: Human Language Technologies: Student Research Workshop, Association for Computational Linguistics* (2012), pp. 54–59

20. R.J. Kate, X. Luo, S. Patwardhan, M. Franz, R. Florian, R.J. Mooney, S. Roukos, C. Welty, Learning to predict readability using diverse linguistic features, in *Proceedings of the 23rd International Conference on Computational Linguistics, Association for Computational Linguistics* (2010), pp. 546–554

21. S.E. Schwarm, M. Ostendorf, Reading level assessment using support vector machines and statistical language models, in *Proceedings of the 43rd Annual Meeting on Association for Computational Linguistics, Association for Computational Linguistics* (2005), pp. 523–530

22. M. Heilman, M. Eskenazi, Language learning: challenges for intelligent tutoring systems, in *Proceedings of the Workshop of Intelligent Tutoring Systems for Ill-Defined Tutoring Systems. Eight International Conference on Intelligent Tutoring Systems* (2006), pp. 20–28

23. K. Collins-Thompson, J.P. Callan, A language modeling approach to predicting reading difficulty, in *HLT-NAACL* (2004), pp. 193–200

24. E. Pitler, A. Nenkova, Revisiting readability: a unified framework for predicting text quality, in *Proceedings of the Conference on Empirical Methods in Natural Language Processing, Association for Computational Linguistics* (2008), pp. 186–195

25. S. Raghavan, A. Kovashka, R. Mooney, Authorship attribution using probabilistic context-free grammars, in *Proceedings of the ACL 2010 Conference Short Papers, Association for Computational Linguistics* (2010), pp. 38–42

26. S. Feng, R. Banerjee, Y. Choi, Characterizing stylistic elements in syntactic structure, in *Proceedings of the 2012 Joint Conference on Empirical Methods in Natural Language Processing and Computational Natural Language Learning, Association for Computational Linguistics* (2012), pp. 1522–1533
27. F. Peng, D. Schuurmans, S. Wang, V. Keselj, Language independent authorship attribution using character level language models, in *Proceedings of the tenth conference on European chapter of the Association for Computational Linguistics-Volume 1, Association for Computational Linguistics* (2003), pp. 267–274
28. H.J. Escalante, T. Solorio, M. Montes-y Gómez, Local histograms of character n-grams for authorship attribution, in *Proceedings of the 49th Annual Meeting of the Association for Computational Linguistics: Human Language Technologies-Volume 1, Association for Computational Linguistics* (2011), pp. 288–298
29. E. Stamatatos, N. Fakotakis, G. Kokkinakis, Automatic authorship attribution, in *Proceedings of the ninth conference on European chapter of the Association for Computational Linguistics, Association for Computational Linguistics* (1999), pp. 158–164
30. H. Baayen, H. Van Halteren, F. Tweedie, Outside the cave of shadows: using syntactic annotation to enhance authorship attribution. Lit. Linguist. Comput. **11**(3), 121–132 (1996)
31. V.J. Rideout, E.A. Vandewater, E.A. Wartella, Zero to six: electronic media in the lives of infants, toddlers and preschoolers (2003)
32. H. Chen, X. Li, Z. Huang, Link prediction approach to collaborative filtering, in *Proceedings of the 5th ACM/IEEE-CS Joint Conference on Digital Libraries, 2005, JCDL'05* (IEEE, New York, 2005), pp. 141–142
33. J. Kamps, The impact of author ranking in a library catalogue, in *Proceedings of the 4th ACM Workshop on Online Books, Complementary Social Media and Crowdsourcing* (ACM, New York, 2011), pp. 35–40
34. P.C. Vaz, D. Martins de Matos, B. Martins, P. Calado, Improving a hybrid literary book recommendation system through author ranking, in *Proceedings of the 12th ACM/IEEE-CS joint conference on Digital Libraries* (ACM, New York, 2012), pp. 387–388
35. Z. Zhu, J.Y. Wang, Book recommendation service by improved association rule mining algorithm, in *2007 International Conference on Machine Learning and Cybernetics*, vol. 7 (IEEE, New York, 2007), pp. 3864–3869
36. P.C. Vaz, D. Martins de Matos, B. Martins, Stylometric relevance-feedback towards a hybrid book recommendation algorithm, in *Proceedings of the fifth ACM Workshop on Research Advances in Large Digital Book Repositories and Complementary Media* (ACM, New York, 2012), pp. 13–16
37. X. Yang, H. Zeng, Y. Huang, Artmap-based data mining approach and its application to library book recommendation, in *2009 International Symposium on Intelligent Ubiquitous Computing and Education* (IEEE, New York, 2009), pp. 26–29
38. S. Givon, V. Lavrenko, Predicting social-tags for cold start book recommendations, in *Proceedings of the Third ACM Conference on Recommender Systems* (ACM, New York, 2009), pp. 333–336
39. M. Zhou, Book recommendation based on web social network, in *International Conference on Artificial Intelligence and Education (ICAIE)* (IEEE, New York, 2010), pp. 136–139
40. M.S. Pera, Y.K. Ng, What to read next?: making personalized book recommendations for k-12 users, in *Proceedings of the 7th ACM Conference on Recommender Systems* (ACM, New York, 2013), pp. 113–120
41. M.S. Pera, Y.K. Ng, Automating readers' advisory to make book recommendations for k-12 readers, in *Proceedings of the 8th ACM Conference on Recommender Systems* (ACM, New York, 2014), pp. 9–16
42. M.S. Pera, Y.K. Ng, Analyzing book-related features to recommend books for emergent readers, in *Proceedings of the 26th ACM Conference on Hypertext & Social Media* (ACM, New York, 2015), pp. 221–230
43. S. Dimitrov, F. Zamal, A. Piper, D. Ruths, Goodreads vs amazon: the effect of decoupling book reviewing and book selling, in *Proceedings of ICWSM '15* (2015)

44. A. Worrall, "Back onto the tracks": convergent community boundaries in librarything and goodreads, in *9th Annual Social Informatics Research Symposium* (2013)
45. M. Thelwal, K. Kousha, Goodreads: a social network site for book readers. J. Assoc. Inf. Sci. Technol. **68**(4), 972–983 (2017)
46. M. Thelwall, Book genre and author gender: Romance > paranormal-romance to autobiography > memoir. J. Assoc. Inf. Sci. Technol. **68**(5), 1212–1223 (2017)
47. S. Rose, D. Engel, N. Cramer, W. Cowley, Automatic keyword extraction from individual documents, in *Text Mining* (2010), pp. 1–20
48. L. Deng, J. Wiebe, Mpqa 3.0: an entity/event-level sentiment corpus, in *Conference of the North American Chapter of the Association of Computational Linguistics: Human Language Technologies* (2015)
49. J.W. Pennebaker, M.E. Francis, R.J. Booth, *Linguistic Inquiry and Word Count* (Lawerence Erlbaum Associates, Mahwah, 2001)
50. M. Hall, E. Frank, G. Holmes, B. Pfahringer, P. Reutemann, I.H. Witten, The weka data mining software: An update. SIGKDD Explor. Newsl. **11**(1), 10–18 (2009)

Printed by Printforce, the Netherlands